PROFILING HACKERS

The Science of Criminal Profiling as
Applied to the World of Hacking

PROFILING HACKERS

The Science of Criminal Profiling as Applied to the World of Hacking

Raoul Chiesa • Stefania Ducci

Silvio Ciappi

CRC Press
Taylor & Francis Group
Boca Raton   London   New York

CRC Press is an imprint of the
Taylor & Francis Group, an **informa** business

AN AUERBACH BOOK

Original edition: Profilo Hacker - La scienza del Criminal Profiling applicata al mondo dell'hacking by Raoul Chiesa and Silvio Ciappi, Milan, Italy. Copyright (c) 2007 by Apogeo s.r.l. - Socio Unico Giangiacomo Feltrinelli Editore s.r.l. All Rights Reserved.

The views expressed are those of the authors and do not necessarily reflect the views of UNICRI. Contents of this report may be quoted or reproduced, provided that the source of information is acknowledged.

UNICRI would like to receive a copy of the document in which this study is used or quoted.

Auerbach Publications
Taylor & Francis Group
6000 Broken Sound Parkway NW, Suite 300
Boca Raton, FL 33487-2742

© 2009 by Taylor & Francis Group, LLC
Auerbach is an imprint of Taylor & Francis Group, an Informa business

No claim to original U.S. Government works
Printed in the United States of America on acid-free paper
10 9 8 7 6 5 4 3 2 1

International Standard Book Number-13: 978-1-4200-8693-5 (Softcover)

Library of Congress Cataloging-in-Publication Data

Chiesa, Raoul, 1973-
[Profilo hacker. English]
Profiling hackers : the science of criminal profiling as applied to the world of hacking / authors: Raoul Chiesa, Stefania Ducci, Silvio Ciappi.
p. cm.
Includes bibliographical references and index.
ISBN 978-1-4200-8693-5 (alk. paper)
1. Computer crimes. 2. Computer security. 3. Computer hackers. 4. Criminal behavior, Prediction of. I. Ducci, Stefania. II. Ciappi, Silvio, 1965- III. Title.

HV6773.C477 2009
363.25'968--dc22   2008024603

Visit the Taylor & Francis Web site at
http://www.taylorandfrancis.com

and the Auerbach Web site at
http://www.auerbach-publications.com

Contents

Acknowledgments

Profiling Hackers is dedicated to our dearest friends, our families, and especially to all the people who made this book possible: all the black-, grey-, and white-hats who have helped us to carry out these fascinating behavioral and social investigations by giving us their time and telling us their stories.

As authors, we were extraordinarily lucky to work with a publisher like Apogeo. Fabio Brivio was responsible for this publication, and we'll never be able to thank him enough for his commitment, care, and attention in reviewing the texts; the brainstorming sessions; his unstinting advice; and the ideas that were bandied about at the oddest times via the many e-mails that followed us around during the many months spent writing the Italian edition of the book. We must also thank Virginio Sala and Marco Ghezzi for having believed in our project for a book, and Aurelio Costa, absolutely irreplaceable, for the work he put in every day.

Many thanks go also to Taylor & Francis, the publisher who believed in the project immediately and without whose support this book would never have been published in English.

The authors would also like to thank UNICRI (United Nations Interregional Crime and Justice Research Institute), which supported the project right from the start, making the project and the book its own, and covering the translation costs from Italian into English. Regarding the translation, the authors wish to thank Theresa

Tomasetti for the extraordinary work done, as well as Liliana Wuffli for the proofreading.

Special thanks goes also to Prof. Dr. Emilio C. Viano, who wrote the Afterword.

Raoul Chiesa would also like to thank Daniele Poma, Marco "Raptor" Ivaldi, Maurizio Agazzini, Luca Borgis, and all the staff at @Mediaservice.net Srl, who have been spurring us on since 1996, never permitting us to surrender in the face of what appeared to be "impossible" odds and, most importantly, always believing in what we are doing.

There are some people we feel indebted to, including Alessio L.R. "Mayhem" Pennasilico, for having believed in HPP from the first day and giving us his help and support to build the technological infrastructure, taking time away from his company, and spending night after night working for us. There is also Elisa Bortolani, for her charm, intelligence, and beauty, as well as for her input and the many corrections she has made over the years. Finally, there is Enrico Pasqualotto, author of the Web site hpp.recursiva.org and designer of the database for the questionnaires.

We also thank all the staff at Alba S.T., a wonderful company in the northeast area of Italy, and Pete Herzog, ISECOM managing director, and Marta Barcelò, director of operations, for trusting us blindly and believing in our crazy idea.

Also, in no particular order: Pavel Maximov, for the HPP logo; Francesco "Ascii" Ongaro and Luca "Lamerone" Legato, for the security audit and site defacement part of the HPP project, both principal and mirror sites; all the translators of the questionnaire into French, English, Greek, Romanian, German, Spanish, Arabic, Bulgarian, Slovakian and Albanian; our mirror partners Hack in the Box (Dhillon Andrew Kannabhiran and Belinda Choong), Web-hack.ru (Alissa "Nerd"), Phenoelit.de (FX); CLUSIT; and especially the president, Gigi Tagliapietra, general secretary, Paólo Giudice, and the irreplaceable Giorgio Giudice.

Phase 2 of HPP would certainly not have been able to reach the high quality standards it has today without the personal contacts that were possible with members from associations and institutions and during the following events and hacker meetings: Chaos Communication Congress, CanSecWest, Hack In The Box (HITB), Italian Hack-meeting, SysCan, ConFidence, Hack.lu, MOCA,

OpenExp, BlackHat, RuxCon, EUROSEC, CCC chapters, CLUSIS, CLUSIF, ISECOM, ISACA (Italian chapter), OWASP (Italian chapter), ISO 27001 IUG (Italian chapter), BellUA, X4all.nl, Blackhats.it, Digital Equipment Corporation (DEC), Telecom Security Task Force (TSTF), NoConName, Infosecurity Italia, IT Underground, Phrack, 2600 Magazine, Xcon/Xfocus Team, S0ftPJ, Antifork Research, Ticino Communications Forum, Transcrime, Recursiva.org, and Italian LUG.

Finally, a multitude of people helped us during these two years, all giving their own, unique contribution. We would like to say something special to each and every one of them, but this is really impossible—there were really many of you. To make it easier, we have split you into two different categories ;-)

Gurus, Mentors, and Muses

Raist, Inode, Synack, Cla'75, Lorenzo "Dialtone" Migliardi, Stefano Chiccarelli, Gabriele Faggioli, Emmanuel Gadaix, Pengo, Wau Holland, Trek/3K, Philippe Langlois, Elsa, Gabriella Mainardi, Prof. Ernesto Savona, Andrea Di Nicola, De10rean, Kevin David Mitnick, Igor "Koba" Falcomatà, Alessandro Scartezzini, Antonis Anagnostopoulos, Fabio "Naif" Pietrosanti, Marco Tracinà, Vittorio Pasteris, Pietro Gentile, Salvatore Aranzulla, Dario "Zeus" Meoli, Massimo Picozzi, Fabrizio Ciraolo, Alessandra Vitagliozzi, Laura Aduso, Scusi and Lisa from CCC of Berlin, Enno Ray's interns, Piotr Oleszkiewicz, Thomas B. Rücker, Silvia Scaglia, Indianz.ch, Caterina Kertesz, Silvia "Silvietta," Jim Geovedi and Anthony Zboralski of BellUA, the Grugq, Fabrice Marie, Valentina Colombani, Dino C, Paul-Loup Sulitzer, Job De Haas, Annaliza Savage, Roelef9, Dhillon Kannabhiran of HITB, FX di Phenoelit, Col. Umberto Rapetto, Antonella "Shalom" Beccaria, Prof. Francesco Bricolo, Manuela "Psaico," Carlo Massarini, Gabriella Dal Farra, Suelette Dreyfus, Manu-Manu, Ivan "Kaos" Scalise, Beppe Grillo, Moreno Guiotto, Maria Cristina Ascenzi.

Key People

Sentinel, Otto Sync, Andrea "Pila" Ghirardini, Andrea Barisani, Fabrizio Matta, Angelo Zappalà, Anna Masera, Sandro Calvani and Angela Patrignani from UNICRI, Patrizia Bertini, Mario Prati, Raffaella D'Alessandro, Ettore e Federico Altea, Vincenzo Voci, Massimiliano Graziani, Mimmo Cortese, Lapo Masiero, Simona Macellari, Amodiovalerio "Hypo" Verde, Salvatore Romagnolo, Annarita Gili, Raffaela Farina, Enrico Novari, Nicoletta Bressan, Laura Casanova De Marco, Fabrizio Cirilli, Eleonora Cristina Gandini, Alessandro Scartezzini, Stavroula Ventouri, Rosanna and Francesca D'Antona, Alberto Pietro Contaretti, Matteo G.P. Flora, Alicia Burke, Andrey Buikis, Flaminia Zanieri and "il nano," Giovanni Lo Faro, Carla Fortin, Martin Bruckmanns, Stefano Buzzelli, Mirko "Mitch" Arcese, Lidia Galeazzo, Freddy "Seabone" Awad, Margherita Bo and Chantal, Matteo Curtoni and Maura Parolini, Veronica Galbiati, Maya and Barbara "Wolf," Loren Goldig, Alessandro "Cyberfox" Fossato, Laura Di Rauso, Silvia Luzi and Heather Robitaille.

Raoul Chiesa
Stefania Ducci
Silvio Ciappi

Foreword

**Phishing, Pharming, Viruses, Worms…New Definitions for
Cybercrime Risks, or New Expressions for Hackers' Behaviors?**

At the dawn of the information technology (IT) era, computers were huge and heavy machines, barely fitting in a room, used for processing complex calculations. After the creation of ARPANET, a military purpose–only network, and its evolution into the Internet, computers were no longer standalone machines. For the first time, personal computers were connected to a web of other systems.

The Internet breakthrough represented the technical factor that allowed for the emergence of cybercrime. Phenomena such as phishing, pharming, credit card fraud, identity theft, computer espionage, hacking, elaboration and diffusion of viruses and worms, to mention but a few, were completely nonexistent before the arrival of the Internet.

Today, computers manage and control every aspect of our life. They are often part of a network of other computers, such as the ones belonging to industries or hospitals, which greatly rely on computerized equipment for diagnostics or treating diseases. For example, both CAT scans and robots for remote surgical operations rely on the Internet.

Computers are not self-programmed, neither do they represent a hidden threat to communities; hackers are the real risk in a wired society. Hackers can be aggressive and destructive, but computers are not.

What would happen if a hacker were to violate these computer systems and take possession and control of the machine?

National stability and security can only be guaranteed by an accurate and safe computerized management of these critical sectors. An attack carried out against these targets through the Internet could be catastrophic, given that critical infrastructures represent a probable target for computer attacks, both in the daily lives of citizens and in situations of information warfare.

UNICRI will continue to work on the Hackers Profiling Project (HPP), which represents a first step in understanding an extensive and underground phenomenon such as hacking, including the distinction between the various categories of hackers vs. malicious—or criminal—attackers.

Sandro Calvani
Director, UNICRI

Foreword to the Italian Edition

Scientific literature today just shows us results, and the process involved is limited to showing evidence supporting these results; technical handbooks are aimed at displaying the tools of the trade neglecting the creative process necessary to find solutions. No one has time anymore. The attitude is rather to cut straight to the bone, and the sooner the better. However, in this way a lot of the allure of research is lost, and the meaning of what has been going on is understood only in part. Once the dust has settled, the upshot seems to be very little (much ado about nothing?) and all the work and effort put in seem to be unjustified.

For those involved in the process itself, the view is quite different. All results count, no matter how small, because what really counts is the process itself. A lot can be learned from the way in which ideas are formulated, from the difficulties overcome, and from the mistakes made along the tortuous path followed to reach a solution. "Popularization" books often try to tell the story, but the voices of the main characters are usually missing.

When someone from the world of research is willing to tell us about how a project was born and involves us in the whole process of discovery, we again feel the fascination of the quest itself.

This is the reason why, when Raoul Chiesa, Stefania Ducci, and Silvio Ciappi submitted their proposal, it wasn't just left to gather dust in a desk drawer. It was an opportunity to observe "men at work" on a research project that was still ongoing. We could closely watch an excellent research team at work, and this seemed far more interesting than the project itself.

Furthermore, the subject matter fits well in the editor's list; the editor remembers with satisfaction books like the Italian *Spaghetti Hacker* by Stefano Chiccarelli and Andrea Monti, published around ten years ago, and smiles a little at the idea of placing a book on *Profiling Hackers* written by Italian authors—dealing with a unique research project, Italian but with international appeal, too—side by side with the many literary fictions and books on all kinds of criminal investigations, crime scene investigations, forensic analysis, and criminal science. This proves yet again that fact is stranger than fiction and that reading the story of a scientific process can be as absorbing and thrilling as reading (or watching) fiction.

The fact that both the project and the text deal with a subject close to our heart, from exploring virtual space to the concept of freedom on the Web, the ethics of Internet users, property rights, and copyrights, all this at the start just made it easier to publish the book and today increases the pleasure of seeing it in print.

We are sure that the readers we are offering it to will find much in it of their interest.

With our best wishes to the research team for the completion of the remaining steps of their work.

Virginio Sala
Publisher, Apogeo Publishing House

Book Presentation

I Am a Hacker, Enter My World...

This book serves to bear witness to the first three years of the ISECOM project named HPP, the Hacker's Profiling Project. What you are about to read are the results obtained to date. We do not claim they are the ultimate truth but rather the first steps on a far from simple path toward the formulation of a profiling method applicable to the world of hacking.

The first period of investigation maps the first three steps of the eight that make up the entire project. As this period has reached its conclusion, and we thought it would be useful and interesting to set down the situation as it stands, comparing the attempts made in the past to study the "hacker phenomenon" with what has emerged from our studies.

We also believe that it is extremely important to do away with preconceived ideas if we want to fully understand this fascinating world.

The HPP Core Research Team—Hacker's Profiling Project
UNICRI–ISECOM
Raoul "Nobody" Chiesa, UNICRI Consultant for Cybercrime Projects
Stefania Ducci, UNICRI HPP Project Manager

Alessio L.R. "Mayhem" Pennasilico HPP Co-manager, recursiva.org
Elisa Bortolani, University of Verona, Department of Psychology and
Cultural Anthropology, HPP Co-manager
Enrico Pasqualotto, Technical Implementation, recursiva.org

Introduction

Another One Got Caught Today, It's All Over the Papers. "Teenager Arrested in Computer Crime Scandal," "Hacker Arrested After Bank Tampering..." Damn Kids. They're All Alike

Even though the subject we are about to address can be labeled "hacker profiling," it needs to be said that each hacker is different from another; they each have their own history, their own cultural and family background, and their own real-life stories. All these elements made them what they are, unique and unrepeatable, as for all human beings.

It is, however, possible to identify certain constants—common traits that link all these individuals. One must be careful, though, not to generalize, because this would be the gravest mistake ever.

It would be scientifically improper to attribute to hackers in general characteristics that belong to only a few, just as it is inadmissible to extend the distinctive traits common to most hackers to all members of the underground world, as there could always be that one individual who represents the so-called *exception to the rule*. So, if you can't make horizontal generalizations, as has just been explained, this is just as true if not more so on a vertical-chronological level.

To clarify, if certain traits are typical of hackers of the 1980s and 1990s, they might not necessarily still be true for the hackers of this century. As will become clear from the following chapters, there are different generations of hackers, each one with characteristics, motivations, and targets different from another's. When trying to define a criminal profile of hackers, it becomes necessary to avoid common platitudes, which often have no scientific basis but are rather constructed *ad hoc* by the media, while trying to identify the various existing profiles.

In order to do this, it becomes necessary to identify the points in common that hackers of the same type share, without neglecting, however, the distinctive traits of each individual.

Basically one can say that most hackers show the following fundamental traits:

- They usually have an above average IQ and great technical and problem-solving skills.
- They are brilliant adolescents, suffocated by an inadequate school system and by ill-prepared or poorly equipped teachers.
- They generally come from problem families.
- They rebel against all symbols or expressions of authority.

We must also point out that there are hackers of all ages, social classes, professions, and geographic and ethnic origins.

As to the constants we analyzed during the first two years of the Hacker's Profiling Project, we must bear in mind that they have been formulated positively here, but they can also be considered negatively, as, for example, the evolving of more in-depth technical know-how vs. stabilization, or the presence or absence of specific, precise qualities and traits.

Before analyzing the data collected, another premise is necessary, basically stressing the need to avoid terms such as "real-world" and "virtual reality," which have been and still are abused, apart from being evidently wrong. In fact, those who commit electronic attacks not only don't consider there to be any difference between the two, but indeed the second category does not exist, as whatever takes place on a network, Web, or "behind the scenes" of telephone exchanges or lines is not at all virtual but is real.

We believe it to be more precise and less misleading to talk about *electronic world* and *physical world*. There are also hackers who are quite capable of living between these two worlds, by means of hacking on the one hand and *social engineering** on the other.

Throughout their career as hackers (whereby "career" we are referring to both personal development and evolution of technical capabilities), they seek answers to the following questions:

- Why am I interested in hacking?
- What are my objectives?
- What am I trying to obtain through hacking?
- What do I want to become?
- What do I want people to think of me?
- How do I want to be remembered, and what for?

These are the very same questions we try to answer in the chapters that follow, but we believed that this premise was at the very least mandatory.

---

* "Social engineering" is a hacker technique used to obtain information either for future attacks or simply as an end in itself. It uses persuasion techniques to convince and influence the other party.

Introduction to Criminal Profiling

Mine is a world that begins with school...I'm smarter than most of the
other kids, this crap they teach us bores me...
Damn kid. Probably copied it. They're all alike.

When *criminal profiling* is mentioned, we often think of scenes from
famous films, such as "The Silence of the Lambs" or "The Bone
Collector," where investigators and criminologists hunt dangerous
serial killers who are sowing panic in a spiral of death and suspense.
But what is exactly criminal profiling? What does it consist of, and,
more importantly, to what type of crime can it be applied?

Before looking for answers to all these confusing questions, a brief
historical overview of profiling can help us identify the information
needed to fill out our knowledge of this science.

Brief History of Criminal Profiling

London, 1888

The first example of criminal profiling is supplied by Dr. Thomas
Bond, professor of forensic medicine, who carried out the autopsy on
Mary Jane Kelly, the last of Jack the Ripper's victims.

Dr. Bond was called upon to carry out an assessment of the surgical
skills of the aggressor. Basing his deductions on the *modus operandi,* he
also presented his own interpretation of the behavior of the murderer.

Quantico, Virginia, 1970

The modern concept of a criminal profile arises in 1970, when FBI special agents Howard Teten and Patrick Mullany started up a criminal
profile program called *Applied Criminology,* which led to the creation of

the *Behavioural Sciences Unit* (BSU), founded by Jack Kirsch at the FBI (Federal Bureau of Investigation) Academy in Quantico, Virginia.

The program received an added boost when, in 1976, Robert Ressler, followed by John Douglas, started to interview convicted serial killers to find a possible connection between the crime scene and the personality of the criminal. They were later joined by Ann Burgess, a psychiatrist who participated in the interviews and helped to process the data obtained. Her contribution was invaluable for the development of the fundamental concepts of criminal profiling, including the organized/disorganized model, which is still largely in use today (Table 1.1).

The model developed by the FBI consists of analyzing the behavior and the characteristics of selected groups in the prison population during the commission of a crime and applying them by analogy to a single unidentified criminal, thereby predicting future behavior. This model, based on statistical analysis is called *Criminal Scene Analysis* (*CSA*).

The great success of criminal profiling then led to the development of the *Crime Classification Manual* (*CCM*), a handbook classifying violent crimes, which was published in 2006 by Robert Ressler, Ann and Allen Burgess, and John Douglas. Douglas is already known

Table 1.1   Organized/Disorganized Model

ORGANIZED OFFENDER	DISORGANIZED OFFENDER
Normal-to-superior intelligence	Below-average intelligence
Socially adequate	Socially inadequate
Prefers skilled employment	Prefers simple unskilled work
Sexually adequate	Sexually inadequate
High social standing	Low social standing
Father in stable employment	Father in temporary employment
Inconsistent discipline in childhood	Strict discipline in childhood
Emotional control during crime	Anxiety during commission of crime
Use of alcohol during crime	Limited use of alcohol
Precipitating situational stress	Minimal situational stress
Lives with partner	Lives alone
Uses a car in good condition	Lives/works near to crime scene
Follows crimes in the media	Minimal interest in news in media
May change jobs or leave city	Will undergo significant behavioral changes (Drug/alcohol abuse, excessive religiousness, etc.)

to the public for having written successful and thought-provoking books such as *Mindhunter* and *Journey into Darkness*,* which describe in detail how his team of BSU investigators tracked down the most famous serial killers of the last few years.

Various programs, databases, and specialized profiling units started appearing on the international investigation scene, from FBI VICAP (Violent Criminal Apprehension Program), a research and investigation program and database for serial crimes, to the Canadian Police VICLAS (Violent Crime Linkage Analysis System), a VICAP analogue. As to Italy, the Unit for the Analysis of Violent Crime (UACV—*Unita' di Analisi del Crimine Violento*) was founded in 1995 within the state police, making use of the system for crime scene analysis (SASC—*Sistema per l'Analisi della Scena del Crimine*).

Liverpool, 1993

Meanwhile, in the 1990s, the English researcher David Canter developed IP (*investigative psychology*), and *geographical profiling*. Canter's method was mainly based on a statistical-inductive approach, similar to the FBI's. Canter based his theories of investigative psychology on a constantly updated database of the criminal population. Specifically, he studied the population of criminals known to the police, defined types and groups, and compared the offenses of a still unidentified criminal with those of known offenders in order to identify possible analogies or identical traits.

Canter deduced the traits that could be presumed typical of a group and of its members. In order to do this, Canter took various principles from psychology and adapted them to profiling for criminal investigations, hence the term *investigative psychology*.

Geographical profiling, as evinced by the name of the theory, is based on two behavioral models that deal with the range of action of the *offender* and the distance between the criminal range and the home range. Canter identified two behavioral models, which he defined as *marauder* and *commuter*.

---

* *Journey into Darkness*, by Douglas, J.E. and Olshaker, M., New York, Simon & Schuster, 1997.

The first term identifies offenders who act inside a hypothetical range that extends around their area of residence (Figure 1.1). The second covers offenders who act outside their area of residence (Figure 1.2).

The so-called Canter model, developed on the basis of the geographic behavior of 45 serial rapists operating in London, is based on the *Offender Circle Concept,** an area defined by a circle whose radius is obtained by connecting the farthest points from the offender's home where the offenses were perpetrated.

This model has been widely criticized, as it cannot predict the area of residence of the perpetrator, but it works in retrospect; in other words, it is based on solved cases, where both the residence and the area where

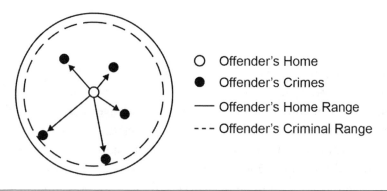

○	Offender's Home
●	Offender's Crimes
—	Offender's Home Range
---	Offender's Criminal Range

Figure 1.1   Marauder model.

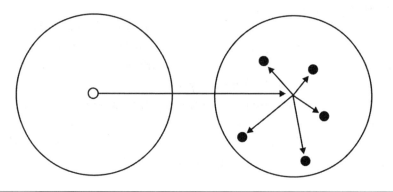

Figure 1.2   Commuter model.

---

* The Offender Circle Concept analyzes four points of reference: offender's home, offender's crimes, offender's home range, and offender's criminal range.

the crime was committed are known. The model, however, does have statistical value, as it gives us two fundamental assumptions:

- Most criminals, especially if they are just embarking on their criminal career, usually commit their crimes within their area of residence.
- The distance between the offender's residence and the crime scene increases in direct proportion to the number of crimes committed.

California, 1997

In 1997, Brent Turvey developed *Behavioural Evidence Analysis (BEA)*, which draws on Teten and Mullany's *Applied Criminology* method.

BEA is based principally on four levels of analysis:

- *Equivocal forensic analysis,* aimed at finding the most probable interpretation of a series of documents relating to the crime scene (photos, videos, police and forensic medical reports, witness declarations, etc).
- *Victimology,* aimed at defining the psychological profile of the victim.
- *Crime scene characteristics,* an analysis of the crime scene to try and deduce elements defining the behavior of the offender.
- *Offender characteristics,* final phase, defining the personality of the perpetrator of the crime but also identifying elements that can lead to the criminal's identification, such as age, gender, physical build, ethnic group, residence, marital status, degree of education, type of job, prior convictions, lifestyle, etc.

The difference from other methods, such as the FBI's Crime Scene Analysis and Canter's Investigative Psychology, is that BEA does not rely on statistical data relating to a group of offenders, but rather employs a mix of forensic science, psychology, and psychiatry to reconstruct the crime and define the profile of the offender.

Furthermore, Turvey's approach is *deductive*, while CSA and IP are *inductive*.

The deductive method is based on the assumption that the criminal profile is obtained from an analysis of the crime scene *modus operandi,* while the inductive method starts from the statistical data available on the characteristics of groups of known offenders, checking whether elements pertaining to an as yet unidentified offender can be matched with those of one of the groups, and then assuming the same distinguishing traits.

Serial Crimes and Criminal Profiling: How to Interpret Them

Given this brief overview of criminal profiling, we can now make certain assumptions and simplify the effort necessary to apply it to the hacking world. This step is not all that straightforward; what is normal procedure for criminal profiling in the real world might not be correct in the electronic world. In order to avoid losing our way during the transition, it is worthwhile to spend a few pages looking at keys to understanding these crimes and at systems for analyzing them.

The concept of serial crime derived from a simple idea that arose in the course of investigations: a series of crimes with apparently incomprehensible motives can be connected to each other.

When faced with a homicide, investigators traditionally tend to make an assumption common in most criminological literature: the presumed perpetrator of the crime is a member of the family or someone known to the victim. For this reason, in the early 1980s, the FBI developed a system *linking* inexplicable homicides presumably committed by someone from outside the family environment or circle of acquaintances of the victim.

Linking is the result of an operation that stores specific data obtained following crime scene investigation and observation, plus an analysis of the victim's characteristics.

FBI researchers explain that the crime scene often holds the real motives for the crime, and also helps to identify the type of perpetrator; therefore, the investigation must pay attention to each single detail, with the help of visual and photographic aids.

Often the opinion that a serial killer is involved might arise when, following the crime scene investigations and victim analysis of a series of homicides, characteristics in common appear, leading to the possibility of a single *modus operandi:* all serial killers leave their signature on the crime scene, their distinctive trait.

One of the most widespread investigative techniques used to identify potential suspects in cases involving serial killers is the so-called *psychological profile*. The profile can be defined as the analysis of the main behavioral characteristics and personality traits of an individual inferred from an analysis of the crimes committed by that person, which leads to the premise that a correct interpretation of the crime scene can reveal the type of personality of the perpetrator.

Profiling technique is based on comparing similar cases with the help of sophisticated statistical analysis methods resulting in an "if-then" probable solution. Put in a very simple way, the profile answers the following questions:

- What happened during the crime?
- What type of person could have committed this type of crime?
- What are the characteristics usually associated with this type of person?

Given its probabilistic nature, the profile must take into consideration a series of characteristics common to perpetrators of various crimes of a similar type. The variables considered can be *physical* such as age, gender, or race; *social,* such as socioeconomic status, residence of the perpetrator, level of education, marital status, type of job, sexual preferences (heterosexual, homosexual, pedophilic, etc.), or level of social skills; *historical-judiciary,* covering past crimes and psychiatric events; *investigative,* such as behavior following the crime, means of transporting the victim, and the possible presence of accomplices.

The technique of profiling is therefore based on the following assumptions:

The Crime Scene Reflects the Personality of the Perpetrator   The method with which the victim was killed is crucial even though other evidence found at the crime scene must not be underestimated, as other clues that may lead back to the perpetrator (the weapon used was left at the crime scene, the body was not hidden, etc.), for example pointing the investigators toward a disorganized type of personality.

The Crime Method Tends to Remain the Same over Time   This is the so-called crime signature, which we referred to earlier in the text.

We can add as a corollary that *the personality of the perpetrator tends to remain fundamentally the same over time.*

David Canter makes an important contribution to criminal profiling when he reminds us that, in delinquent behavior, just as in any other kind of human behavior, there are repetitive patterns, leading to the establishment of significant links between specific models of behavior and personality traits.

According to Canter, the main issue underlying profiling techniques can be illustrated by the so-called *canonical correlations,* basically a statistical procedure used to analyze the relation between two groups of variables:

$$(F_1A_1 + \ldots + F_nA_n = K_1C_1 + \ldots + K_mC_m)$$

On one side we have the information on the characteristics of the crime (F_nA_n), on the other the characteristics of the criminal (K_mC_m).

The aim of the profile is to prove that significant correlations exist between the criminal behavior and the personality traits of the perpetrator, both in the real world and on the level of specific relations between variables.

The picture of the investigation starts filling out when we add environmental criminology analysis to explain what can be defined as "the fourth dimension of the crime"* to the traditional biological, psychological, and social analysis and interpretation of the criminal phenomenon.

Environmental analysis uses the so-called *routine activity approach,* according to which crime is the result of three minimal but necessary elements: a motivated aggressor, feasible criminal objectives, and the absence of efficient surveillance of the area.

At this point, the spatial analysis of the crime must fulfill the following conditions:

- The range of potential aggressors—in other words, an analysis of the city and of its demographic, economic, and social components. In order to assess this type of spatial distribution, the urban territory is mapped according to certain economic indicators, such as income brackets (*census trait*) and criminological indicators, such as the incidence of violent crimes.

---

* Brantingham, P.J. and Brantingham, P.L., *Patterns in Crime,* Macmillan, 1984, New York.

- The spatial distribution of risk zones (*potential target*), which are the locations of public and private residences, commercial venues, and amenities within the urban area.
- Identification of possible safe areas in order to establish where criminal targets are to be found within this area.
- Analysis of escape routes, which considers the main roads connecting the various areas of the city.

In conclusion, the spatial model for crime analysis takes into consideration the urban structure of the city and the degree of motivation and opportunity that leads the aggressor to commit the crime within a certain area, added to degree of mobility and risk perception.

It is therefore possible to state that if we follow an environmental criminology approach, criminal activity (C) varies depending on the offender's degree of motivation (M), opportunity (O), degree of mobility (Lm), and risk perception (R):

$$C = f(M, O, Lm, R)$$

But more about this later in the text, when we will go into the details of hacker profile analysis. Now we must move our attention to the possible convergence between criminal profiling techniques and the hacker world.

Criminal Profiling: Applying It to Study Hackers

This brief historical overview, with an illustration of some of the main theories involved, is certainly not exhaustive, but some analysis patterns have been established, and by now it should be becoming clear that criminal profiling is a tool that can help crime scene investigators get to know the perpetrator. By supplying elements such as personality, lifestyle, social status, etc, the number of suspects can be reduced on the basis of the information obtained, and a speedier resolution of the case can be reached.

Profiling in effect is based on the assumption that the perpetrator's decisions and behavior at the crime scene reflect personality traits (deductive method). Comparing the data gathered at the crime scene with similar elements among a group of known offenders, the characteristics of the group can be applied to the individual by analogy (inductive method) to obtain further information about the characteristics of the perpetrator.

It becomes important to bear in mind that criminal profiling on its own cannot solve the case; rather, is an investigative tool to:

- Reduce the number of potential suspects
- Connect correlated crimes to the same author (*crime linkage system*)
- Supply clues
- Supply interview and interrogation strategies
- Suggest trial strategies

Hacking isn't the preferred field of application for criminal profiling techniques, which are usually used to define the psychological profile of the criminal in cases of violent crimes—usually sexually related and serial: homicide, rape, arson, and bomb attacks. The only thing in common with hacking is the fact that the crime is serial. This does not mean that the same techniques cannot be applied to both. On the contrary, the typically serial nature of computer attacks—in other words, of the criminal behavior (habitual crime)—makes this possible, as it allows an identification of the constants in the behavior of the subject.

The two main constants of interest to the criminologist, as they reveal most of the information on the personality of the subject, are *modus operandi* and *signature*.

The *modus operandi* is the way in which the criminal behaves in committing the crime; this behavior is learned and is dynamic in nature, as it evolves as the technique employed is perfected.

The *signature* is a static behavior that marks out the offender; it isn't necessary for committing the crime but is nevertheless repeated each time the crime is committed.

When dealing with hacker attacks, it must be pointed out that it is very difficult to trace a criminal profile of the attacker on the basis of the *modus operandi;* unless we are talking about a new hacking technique, created on an *ad hoc* basis, we are dealing with a standardized behavior employed by different individuals.

In that case too, it's impossible to say with any degree of certainty that it reflects the personality of the subject who developed it (at least not completely), because hacking techniques have the limitation of having to adapt to the characteristics of the system they intend to "exploit,"* explore, and use.

Hacking is distinctive in that it does not necessarily imply a crime and, more importantly, the criminal behavior is not constant, as varying strategies and methods are employed with only the objective in common: "perforating" a system for many different reasons. It therefore becomes clear that criminal profiling techniques must be re-elaborated if not actually created anew.

The crime scene itself, the primary source of all clues and evidence, is completely different. Furthermore, geographical profiling techniques cannot be applied: the distance between the place from which the hacker is operating and the information system to be violated might be great in geographical terms but becomes irrelevant and meaningless in the context of cyberspace, where "distance" doesn't exist, nor does the distinction between marauder and commuter. Everything is close by—in other words, easily and immediately accessible. It is a hand's breadth—or rather a mouse breadth—away.

The objective of criminal profiling is to try to clarify why a crime has been committed and what are the special traits of the perpetrator. To do this, it becomes necessary to understand what has happened and how.

---

* *Exploit*: neologism deriving from the term *exploit* of French/English origin.

Where there exists a security vulnerability (in an operating system, software application, or whatever), the exploit is a code (software) written by someone to exploit the security vulnerability or vulnerabilities in order to obtain total or partial control of the information system and/or the data it contains or that is in transit. The Wikipedia Web site states, "*Exploit* is a term used in computer science to identify a method which takes advantage of a bug or a vulnerability, to allow privilege escalation or the denial of service of a computer. There are different ways to classify exploits. The most common depends on the way the exploit contacts the vulnerable application. A remote exploit is carried out over the net and exploits the vulnerability without any previous access to the system. A local exploit requires access to the system and usually increases the privileges of the user beyond those specified by the administrator...The objective of many exploits is that of obtaining root privileges on a system. It is however possible to use exploits that start acquiring access with minimal privileges raising them till they reach root level. Usually an exploit can use only a specific breach and once published the breach is repaired and the exploit becomes obsolete for the new versions of the program. For this reason some *black-hat* hackers don't communicate exploits found but reserve them for themselves or their community. This type of exploit is called *zero day exploit,* and their contents are greatly prized by script kiddies—attackers who have no affiliations."

To understand computer attacks, we need the joint know-how of computer security experts, who can tell us exactly "what" has happened and "how," and criminal profiling skills to explain "why" the attack was carried out and what kind of attacker we're dealing with— the "who."

Obviously, the "what" and the "how" are deduced from the crime scene analysis, which in the case of computer crimes is not a physical place but an electronic abstraction, where an analysis of fingerprints and DNA traces left by the perpetrator are replaced by an analysis of the log files* and the audit trail of the violated computer system.

For the purpose of this study, we shall be using a "hybrid" methodology joining the deductive method, applied to analyze data coming in from a new generation honey-net† created especially for this research project, with the inductive method, for processing data obtained from a questionnaire specially prepared for this investigation to define the unique traits of various types of hacker (see Appendix A). This will then be applied to the individual attacker with similar characteristics, as deduced from the crime scene (honey-net).

The honey-net and the questionnaire will be discussed more in detail in Chapter 4, where we will explain the HPP (Hacker's Profiling Project).

---

* A log file is that list actions that have occurred and been carried out (for example, a user, an application, a server, or a command interpreter.)
† Honey-net: a deliberately unprotected (unsafe) information system, constructed and put on line to act as "bait," in order to observe in the field how attacks and violations take place.

2
INTRODUCING "CYBERCRIME"

I've listened to teachers explain for the fifteenth time how to reduce a fraction. I understand it. "No, Ms. Smith, I don't show my work. I did it in my head…"

Cesare Lombroso, in an essay on the Rome banking trials,* stated, "Fraud is a civilized metamorphosis of crime, which has replaced the cruelty and ruthlessness of primitive man, as embodied in the born criminal, with the lies and greed which are sadly becoming common, a generalized trend."

From his late 19th-century viewpoint, the celebrated Veronese scholar saw white-collar crimes—namely financial fraud and larceny—as the fruit of "criminality in evolution," typical of modern times, in contrast with full-blooded, primitive, ancestral, violent crime, which was instead the legacy of an archaic premodern culture, typical of the impoverished illiterate agricultural society of Italy.†

Lombroso's formulations will remain unchallenged over time, shaping one of the axioms of Italian criminology—the delinquent as diseased—and will find their most respected scientific expression in the development of criminal anthropology.

Obviously, an approach of this kind would and will for many years exclude from the scope of its analysis financial and economic crimes, while political crimes in certain cases would be attributed to either individual or social pathological behavior. (Consider, for example, political crime. Studies carried out on anarchists and banditry view them as expressions of a greater or lesser degree of degenerate moral insanity.)

For American criminal sociology, economic and financial crimes are fundamental and become a point of reference. Edward Sutherland,

---

* Lombroso, C., *Sui Recenti Processi Bancari di Roma e Parigi*, Archivio di Psichiatria, Scienze Penali ed Antropologia Criminale, XVI, 1893, 193–210 .
† Martucci, P., *La criminalità economica*, Roma-Bari, Laterza, 2006.

one of the greatest American sociologists, outlined them and gave a first scientific definition to their main characteristics. Even more importantly, he talked about them, using as references notorious cases in the public domain such as General Motors, Chrysler Corporation, Philip Morris, etc.

Sutherland's reversal of trend is enormous compared with the past. First of all, he is challenging the basic assumption of criminological positivism whereby crime is the expression of a physical and/or sociological pathology—the result of destitution, maladjustment, and disease—and therefore the prerogative of the dangerous underclass living in the ghettoes of Chicago and the large American and European cities of the time. Sutherland states that this is a limited view of criminality, which emphasizes certain types of crimes and criminals in a superficial way.

Edward Sutherland defined white-collar crime in this way: a crime committed by a respectable member of the community of high social standing while carrying out professional duties and implying a breach of trust. White-collar crimes therefore take place in the production sector and are committed by abusing the trust that derives exclusively from the social status and the profession of the perpetrator. For this reason, given their complexity and ingeniousness, white-collar crimes can be identified only by someone who has specific skills.

Toward the second half of the last century, connections between the business world, large corporations, and crime are mentioned for the first time, and corporations are no longer considered only as potential victims of crimes or attacks, but also as perpetrators, committing crimes specific to the business world to get a competitive edge in a free market (market rigging, tax fraud, breach of antitrust laws, environmental crimes, etc.).

At the beginning of the 1970s, *computer criminals* made a first appearance in the world of corporate crime: initially low- to middle-grade employees, but highly skilled with computers, they joined the more traditional "white-collar" criminals in perpetrating crimes against corporations.

Technological corporate crime spotlights technical skills and access to computers rather than high social status as distinctive traits of *insider* computer attackers. From the disloyal employee, computer crimes quickly spread to a second, wider type of systems attackers: *outsiders,* i.e., enterprising hackers and crackers who weren't necessarily doing it for financial gain.

From outsiders, attention was shifted to criminal organizations that use information technology (IT)—Internet and cyberspace in the widest sense of the term—for fraud, money laundering, concealing funds, trafficking in pedo-pornographic material, etc.

From this perspective, some telecommunications companies are actually offenders rather than victims, just like the companies that take over a mostly illegal market (e.g., the market for personal data covering thousands of individuals) or use personal and professional data to promote marketing campaigns. In this way, they can create targeted advertisements that are more and more invasive and intrusive, and control people, their habits, contacts, and relations. Thus they are "white-collar criminals."

In the following pages, we will try to draw a comprehensive picture of so-called "cybercrime." It won't necessarily be the definitive picture, but it will explain certain concepts and give you some definitions. All will become clear in Chapters 5 and 6, the heart of this book, where we try to explain everything that is lumped together under the label "hacker," whether cybercriminals or not.

Information Technology and Digital Crimes

The knotty cybercrime question has certainly evolved in a decisive way over the last ten years until it is no longer considered just something to talk about but is actually a serious problem.

Cybercrime, after all, is just a natural development of crime toward new forms of illegal activities. If we believe that "*every new technology leads the way to new kinds of crimes,* * " it becomes self-evident that the use of modern information technologies to carry out illegal activities was actually inevitable.

Think, for example, of the arrival of the automobile on the scene at the beginning of the last century. We are talking about a new technology that allowed people to move from one end of the country to the

---

* Agar, J., *Constant Touch: A Global History of the Mobile Phone,* Chapter 15, Cars, Phones and Crime, Icon Books, U.K., 2003.

other at a much greater speed than in the past. In England, where cars became extremely popular, the government quickly became aware of a side effect: car thieves had made their appearance. Number plates then became compulsory to make it easier to identify stolen cars, and number plates were stolen and used during bank robberies until they eventually were forged.

A hundred years later, the introduction of cell phones and the explosion of the mobile communications market for mass distribution led to "run and steal," where cell phones are stolen on the street while the owner is talking on the phone, actually using it. Any technology usually—if not inevitably—opens the door to new kinds of criminal activity.

If we analyze the social impact of the development of digital technology on everyday life, we can clearly identify the strong dependency and correlations that exist between the *markets* (taken as meaning business, money movements, online shopping, etc.) and so-called *information technology* (IT).

People who, up to a few years ago, would never have used a personal computer find themselves today surrounded by electronic devices—hardware and software that are supposed to make life easier.

Between yesterday's and today's users of the IT world, however, there is a fundamental difference: the early users were few, select, and aware of the pitfalls, whereas today's users are legion: they aren't familiar with the subject and use IT as a simple tool to reach their objective of getting things done at work or in private with as little fuss as possible.

At first glance, this is a minimal difference, but in reality it is fundamental. To give you a concrete example, 15 years ago, companies that were connected to the data transmission networks of the time (the X.25 standard and the packet-switched data networks) were also aware that problems existed, such as hackers, *host scanning*, and *brute forcing* of passwords. In other words, there was the possibility of an attack and a breach of their computer systems. Today's private user in most cases hasn't received any form of specific training, is not familiar with either the terminology or the attack techniques, nor with the swift and exponential dissemination of exploits, viruses, and *zero-day* (0-day) attacks, and hears only the superficial (and often misleading) information supplied by the media.

All of this just multiplies the possibility of crimes linked to the use of technology, because a target that is not aware of the possibility of an attack is *de facto* unprotected, unsafe, and exposed to a greater risk than is a target that is aware of this (and is possibly trained to react, with or without specific types of support).

1980, 1990, 2000: Three Ways of Looking at Cybercrime

Over the last 20 years, we have seen different phases in the evolution of cybercrime. From the first viruses of the 1980s, we quickly moved on to the explosion of malicious code, which was typically aimed at making the attacked system useless and, in most cases, destroying the information it contained.

The 1980s saw a phase in which, on the whole, digital crimes were purely destructive; there was no interest in stealing the information on a system, just to make it unusable.

Conversely, the 1990s saw the dissemination of *intelligent* and self-replicating viruses (for example, the thousands of viruses that are sent automatically by e-mail, copying the address book from the email program of the infected computer), where in these cases the main objective of the attacker is to *be known*—to acquire international notoriety and visibility. Viruses such as "I LOVE YOU," "VERONIKA," and others only made the author famous, often internationally.

From 2000 to date, what we are seeing is the marriage between (a part of) the hacking world and small-time and organized crime, depending on the occasion. Phenomena such as phishing are simply developments of the first viruses of the 1980s, used to exploit the vulnerabilities of operating systems and software applications so as to steal information, with the help of old-fashioned social engineering. This should not be surprising. We are living in a society in which *information* is the primary asset, the ultimate source of power of the 21st century.

Mr. Smith, Hackers, and Digital Crimes in the IT Society

If we start from these premises, we could wonder whether the problem of cybercrime exists only for those who manage large quantities of information. If so, it shouldn't concern the "man in the street." It is highly probable that no one cares what use "Mr. Smith" makes of his computer, but many hackers might be interested in using Mr. Smith's computer as a *launchpad** to initiate attacks against other information systems while maintaining a sort of "anonymity" without leaving traces within the telecommunications networks, such as an IP address or telephone number. At the same time, criminals are certainly interested in Mr. Smith's credit card details, ID, and e-banking information (with the necessary passwords).

But it's not limited to this. Problems for the "man in the street" are called viruses, phishing, spamming, spyware, and bots. For those dealing with *information security* (IS), the real problems are something else again. We're talking about theft of confidential information, attacks against structures critical for national security, continuity and reliability of software applications, theft of credentials for accessing economic and financial services, identity theft, blackmail and extortion, and threats to mobile services (GSM, UMTS, Wi-Fi, Bluetooth, VoIP).

In a word, we're talking about *digital crimes*—crimes carried out by means of, or with the help of, computers and telecommunications networks. The murder weapon in this case is the same tool that should combat and resist these threats, setting up an endless vicious circle where, in most cases, the final user has to bear the brunt.

Furthermore, we must stress how those who should be solving the problems and shoring up the holes in IS are more and more often becoming the victims; recent cases of software code theft from Microsoft and Cisco† are proof of this.

---

* A technical term that identifies a system (or a series of systems such as routers, hosts, etc.) used by hackers as an actual launchpad to launch attacks against other information systems. Let's take A for the aggressor, B for the launchpad system, and C for the system the hacker wants to access. A will connect to B and will launch the attack against C only through B. This approach allows the aggressor to leave no "direct" traces, at least theoretically, of the intrusion (or intrusion attempt) in the log files of server C. As to the B server's security files, a launchpad is generally a system under the complete control of the attacker, who eliminates any trace of his presence from those log files, too, making it impossible (or very difficult) to identify the source of the data call.

† In February 2004, portions of Windows NT 4.0 Service Pack 3 and Windows 2000 SP1 source code were stolen, for a total of 660 MB, and made publicly available on the Internet. In May 2004, about 800 MB of the source code of IOS 12.3, the Cisco router operating system, were stolen and sent to a Web site in Russia. A few months later, in November 2004, copies of the source code of the "Cisco PIX 6.3.1" firewalls were put up for sale in certain newsgroups openly underground and very close to the so-called *black-hat* world.

What is mainly underestimated is the concept of "theft." In IT, nothing is "stolen," as a file is not a physical object but a virtual, digital asset and as such is not physically removed from the server where it resides. Rather, it is copied. The asset itself (in the above-mentioned cases software, but it could be also information, a database, and so on) remains on the attacked information system, which makes it even more difficult (or at the least delayed) for the owner of the asset to detect the criminal activity.

What Mark Weiser wrote in 1991,[*] when he spoke of *ubiquitous computing*, has now come true. "They weave themselves into the fabric of everyday life until they are indistinguishable from it." Patrick Radden Keefe, in the introduction to his wonderful book,[†] discusses this subject—which we believe lies at the basis of the development of the special relationship between digital crime and social life—when, referring to Weiser, he states,

> In the intervening decade and a half, communications technologies have, precisely in this fashion, disappeared. We take for granted our landlines and cell phones, two-way pagers, and wireless-enabled laptops. When Weiser was writing, the telephone was something connected to the wall that teenage children bickered over, and the Internet was for a small few an idea, a rumor, and for the vast majority something closer to science fiction. Today, our relationship with technology is umbilical. My generation was the first to arrive at college to find Internet connections waiting in every dorm room; we cannot live, or even imagine a life, without access to the Web. It is not only that we use this technology daily but also that we transmit more information than ever before through the wires and over the airwaves: pay our bills and our taxes online; meet, date, and converse online; search for the import of medical symptoms online; and type our most embarrassing and revealing questions and quandaries into Google, all online. We have an intuitive sense that this medium, which we have internalized to the point where it is almost an organic extension of our thoughts and words, is vulnerable to interception—which someone might be listening. But for most

---

[*] *The computer for the twenty-first century,* September 1991 (www.ubiq.com/hypertext/weiser/SciAmDraft3.html).

[†] Keefe, P.R., *Chatter: Dispatches from the Secret World of Global Eavesdropping,* Random House, 2005.

of us, this uneasy feeling remains an unsubstantiated hunch, one of the peculiar vagaries of life in a digital age.

Digital Crimes vs. Hacking: Terminology and Definitions

At this point it should be clear how the intrusion of the Internet web and of global communications into our daily lives also cause a "secondary" effect that we must deal with: the increase of computer attacks that today are widespread, standardized, and worldwide.

We are convinced that in order to understand in full the reasoning that lies behind attacks, and consequently today's digital crimes, it's extremely important to know the history and study the development of vulnerabilities and computer attacks. To do this, we decided to use a well-known graph produced by CERT/CC,* which covers the period from 1980 to 1998, analyzing the macro-categories of attacks that were developing.

The following is a list of categories identified by CERT, followed by a detailed description. We believe that this will be extremely useful to the reader, as it gives a better understanding of modern attack techniques.

- Password guessing
- Self-replicating code
- Password cracking
- Exploiting known vulnerability
- Disabling audit
- Backdoor
- Hijacking session
- Sniffer
- Stealth diagnostic
- Packet spoofing
- GUI
- Automated probe/scan

---

* CERT/CC: Computer Emergency Response Team Coordination Center. CERTs are public or private bodies, often within computer science universities and certain government research centers throughout the world. Their task is to study and publicly explain vulnerabilities and attacks when they leave the "0-day-day" circuit and become widespread.

- WWW attack/incident
- Denial of service

Password Guessing

The best-known hacking technique, thanks also to the film "Wargames," is *password guessing*. The definition is self-explanatory: the password is guessed. At the beginning of mass IT and the generalized use of computers in companies, universities, and public bodies, users weren't aware of the importance of passwords (length, type, confidentiality, etc.). Furthermore, anything to do with computers was considered a sort of voodoo, impenetrable to nonexperts.

Consequently, the security level of access passwords was incredibly low. Hackers were aware of this weakness, and whenever they found computers linked to public networks (telephone exchanges, X.25, Internet), they simply tried to guess the password.

Of course, there were certain simple rules to follow to simplify the "search."

- *Use of default accounts.* All operating systems and applications at the time (and things haven't changed that much today, either) contained at installation a series of default user accounts and passwords, from "the factory." These are users that have to exist and should be removed by the installers or the system administrator. At the time, this rarely happened, to the delight of hackers. Here are a few examples: in the VAX/VMS by Digital Equipment Corporation (the system preferred by Kevin Mitnick) you would find the user account SYSTEM with the password MANAGER, which granted system administrator privileges, making the hacker the "virtual owner" of the system. Other accounts were clearly "from the factory," such as "FIELD" with password "SERVICE" used by Digital's technicians for remote assistance. As for UNIX, the "classic" usernames/passwords were "root/root," "test/test," "Informix/Informix," and "oracle/oracle." The last two refer to internationally known and used database applications accounts (Informix and Oracle), common in all kinds of companies and public bodies.

- *Use of common names and surnames in the country of the object of the attack.* Another "classic" is "first name/first name," or "surname/first name" in the username/password field. All the hacker had to do was make a list of common first names and surnames, often taken from a telephone directory, and put them in a file, instructing the password guessing program (often a homemade script or BASIC code) to carry out cross-matched tests or add a sequence of numbers after the password, such as "123." The result was that, for nearly a decade, computer systems of all kinds, large or small, critical or not, were violated thanks to pairings such as "mary/mary," "luke/luke," "john/smith," "white/white123," and so forth.

- *Dictionaries.* With time, some hackers started wondering how to increase their success rate in guessing the correct pair, realizing that all depended on the quality of their user/password list. Dictionaries were born; that is, files containing specific user/password lists, divided by language, system accounts, application accounts, accounts used for the banking system, telecommunications, and so on. Today you can still find thousands of dictionaries on the Internet, as the system hasn't changed and is now applied to password cracking.

Self-Replicating Code

Between 1983 and 1985, the first self-replicating codes made their appearance in the computer world. That period saw an explosion in the market of home computers, so most malignant code was written for *home* systems such as Commodore-64, Sinclair ZX Spectrum, and, soon enough, the first Microsoft DOS versions.

The virus was placed in the software on the floppy disks (at the time this was the only way software could be distributed in the absence of a modem connection, as CD-ROMs and USB keys didn't exist yet, and a hard disk at the time was too expensive for most pockets) and spread through all the users who put that floppy disk in their computers.

It's interesting to note how companies were often free from this type of infection, because the standard systems of the time were *mainframes* (large computers that managed from tens to hundreds or thousands of users at the same time), and the company employees used *dumb terminals*—literally "stupid" terminals without a hard disk or a mass memory—simple monitors (terminals) whose function was to display information coming in from the central system onscreen.

Password Cracking

Password cracking made its first appearance in IT circles around 1986. The idea of cracking a password is very simple, and it arose for obvious reasons in the UNIX operation system world. In the UNIX systems of the time, the *passwd* file in directory */etc* contained a list of all users and their passwords. As this file had to be accessible—in read-only mode—to all kinds of users rather than only to system administrators, the file's structure had a field that contained the password of the user, encrypted with a specific public domain algorithm that was known within hacking communities.

The lines that follow show a series of users on a UNIX NCR system:

```
root:eg9hWn91BdOCc:0:1::/:
va:WIJtWGZ11WJ5s:0:1::/va:/va/obj/vastart
vashell:*no login*:72:100:::
daemon:*no login*:1:1::/:
sys:*no login*:2:2::/usr/src:
bin:*no login*:3:3::/:
adm:*no login*:4:4::/usr/adm:
ncrm:1YtW2mSzlUV0.:0:1::/usr/adm/tally:
uucp:2709wK/ILlk:6:6:uucp administrative login:/usr/
lib/uucp:
nuucp:15Xd7Ibc.A7Yw:7:6:uucp network
login:/usr/spool/uucppublic:/usr/lib/uucp/
uucicosync:*no login*:8:2::/:/bin/sync lp:*no
login*:71:71::/usr/lib:/bin/sh startup:sQHf\
FYAcGgXw:0:1::/:/etc/multi
shutdown:a55STaCX9D96U:0:1::/:/etc/rc6
listen:np:37:4:uucp admin listener:/usr/net/nls:
xsguest:*no login*:126:100::/usr/acct/xsguest:/bin/sh
hpadmgr::0:1::/appl/comm.dir/HPAD:/appl/comm.dir/HPAD/
menu/script/xsmgr.sh
tpmgr:HC7ahZ82BDZLw:0:1::/appl/comm.dir/TPAD:/appl/
comm.dir/TPAD/menu/script/tpm gr.sh
```

```
snax.mgr:Mbq121tJy384E:0:1::/appl/comm.dir/SNAX25:/
appl/comm.dir/SNAX25/menu/script/snaxmgr.sh
lma:f6go\Jb4iHIq6:152:100::/usr/acct4/lma:/bin/sh
lma93::313:100::/usr/acct7/lma93:/bin/sh
fact::110:100::/usr/acct/fact:/bin/sh
sms:QCdCb3kX2PEs.:103:100::/usr/acct/sms:/bin/sh
fund:OD4Xs16J8JrKw:105:100::/usr/acct/fund:/bin/sh
```

In bold we have the account followed by the encrypted password, separated by a colon (":").

If there is no password (quite common in those days and, unfortunately, sometimes today as well), the colon is repeated twice ("::"), as in accounts *hpadmgr, lma93,* and *fact.*

If following the account there is "*no login*," we're looking at accounts that can't access the system as users, and therefore, traditionally, systems accounts. That goes for accounts *vashell, daemon, sys, bin,* and *sync, adm* (abbreviation of *administrator*), *lp* (a system account that stands for *line printer*) and *xsguest.*

Passwords present in the file, as for example WIJtWGZ11WJ5s, actually correspond to a word: it could be "john," "red123," or any other word you like, with or without meaning. As we have already pointed out, though, at the time users had a very fuzzy idea of security, so passwords were nearly always words that meant something and could be found in the above-mentioned dictionaries.

It was necessary, however, to overcome the encryption difficulty: with the technology of the time, it was virtually impossible to guess an encrypted password. It was, however, possible to encrypt a word and compare the result with the encrypted password in the file. The process was quite fast and, yet again, success depended on the quality of the dictionary.

All hackers had to do was feed in their cracking programs both the password file and a good dictionary (John The Ripper* is still the most famous one today, but for Microsoft Windows environment users you can find L0phtCrack or LC5† by the hacker group known as "L0pht Heavy Industries"); at this point it was just a question of waiting, and the hacker meanwhile continued with the intrusion, *chatted* with friends online, or quite simply took a nap or watched TV.

---

* http://www.openwall.com/john/.

† http://www.securityfocus.com/tools/1005.

Exploiting Known Vulnerability

In 1986, Robert Tappan Morris' *worm** caused an uproar in the Internet world: as if by magic, researchers, system administrators, and ordinary users discovered the stark reality and understood that the Internet is not a secure network.

Robert Morris, the son of an NSA[†] researcher, created a self-replicating worm that exploited the known vulnerabilities of UNIX systems to obtain full access to the system, collect new valid username/password pairs, and automatically try to penetrate other information systems.

Then a similar worm, WANK (Worm Against Nuclear Killers), set up to demonstrate against nuclear proliferation, infected most of the VAX/VMS systems present on the DECnet, the international data net distributed by Digital Equipment Corporation (DEC). In this case, too, the worm exploited known vulnerabilities (yet again superficiality in choice of password and the persistence of default accounts in installed systems, as we mentioned earlier).

These two worms opened the era of exploiting known vulnerabilities, when hackers throughout the world analyzed the latest vulnerabilities and went looking for systems that weren't up to date and contained vulnerabilities.

It's worthwhile mentioning that this technique is still largely in use today, both in the case of "0-day" and known vulnerabilities, against systems where for different reasons the vulnerability hasn't been removed. Reasons range from the laziness of system administrators to actual *patching* impossibility due to technical conflicts, such as incompatibility between applications, system scripts, or applications software.

Disabling Audit

Around 1988, hackers started to have a more in-depth knowledge of the operating systems they were violating—often greater than the know-how of the system administrators themselves. By studying the log files, they can understand the company's mindset and policy in the username/password pair and become more and more daring. By

---

* Similar to a virus, as capable of self-replication, a worm, however, doesn't need to be attached to a file in order to spread.
† NSA, National Security Agency, U.S.A.

"daring," we mean that while up to a few years previously the standard approach for an intruder was to keep a *low profile* (that is, avoid actions that could allow system administrators to detect the presence of an intruder), now the approach and view of the "system properties" starts changing, along with its interpretation.

Hackers master the use of the audit files, a sort of daily "journal" containing every action carried out by all users, with levels of detail and traceability defined by the audit system configuration itself.

The widely popular VAX/VMS systems, considered extremely interesting by the hackers of the time, had an *Audit Journal* that contained extremely dangerous information for an attacker: if the audit was enabled, even a simple "access attempt" to a file, if unauthorized by the author, would be flagged.

We must point out, though, that system managers don't usually read the log files daily. They tend to archive them and access them only in the case of an investigation following a security breach, as if they were a flight recorder on a plane. To continue with the flight recorder analogy, the hackers of the time learned to disable the audit function, "interrupting the recording activities of the black box."

Administrators rarely discovered in time that the service was disabled, and during this timespan hackers could copy confidential files, create their own users, change unused or "expired" users' passwords, and reactivate the audit as if nothing had happened, even temporarily changing the time and date of the violated system (usually at night) so that it would be difficult to discover the "black hole" between the previous version of the audit file and the one specifically created by the hacker.

Backdoor

Between 1989 an 1990 some hackers, exploiting known vulnerabilities, started writing portions of code (in other words, software) capable of accessing the violated system more easily and faster than by exploiting the vulnerability step by step. This software code was labeled *backdoor,* meaning "service entry" or "trapdoor."

A backdoor is a program that, once it is launched on the violated system (obviously, the software must be launched by a user having system administrator privileges), enables special functions, such as a listening shell on a high port number (in the case of TCP/IP) or inserting a *magic password* in the system login procedure. The latter was widely used on UNIX and VMS systems of the time, as all it needed was to connect to the "backdoored" information system and insert *any* username, whether it existed or not, and a special password: the magic password.

In the years that followed, backdoors inserted by the software companies themselves became famous, often created by programmers without the company's knowledge or inserted in good faith to make remote assistance easier for companies using a specific type of software.

Hijacking Session

Toward 1992, hijacking of user sessions started. Hackers realized that, depending on the information system in use when users who connected by modem ended the session (either voluntarily or because the connection was lost), the shell remained open, or, in slang, "stayed hanging."

A sort of race started to scan large quantities of targets (IP addresses, telephone numbers, NUA X.25, and so forth) to find "hanging" shells and easily access these systems.

Nowadays, the thought process behind hijacking has evolved, moving around the Web and finding help for *Man-in-the-Middle* attacks (where the assailant places himself between user and server, intercepting everything that goes through the middle, as it were). The approaches used today are extremely sophisticated—so much so that the tacks of the past pale by comparison, seem like Stone Age technology, and even make you smile a little at how simple and naïve they were.

Sniffer

The year 1993 is a milestone in the history of electronic intrusions: the first *sniffer* appeared.

The main difficulty for hackers at the time was that the password of some users was not readily identifiable, notwithstanding full access as system administrator and the massive use of password cracking: either the passwords were too complicated, or the computing power necessary to identify them was not available.

However, on the logic level, TCP/IP* allowed the interception of both the incoming and outgoing data stream on a network card from the server connected to the IP network. With this as a starting point, a "sniffer" was written. This program could ask the LAN's network card to intercept all packets in transit and put a copy on a file. In this way you could intercept, both online and offline, all traffic, including system logins; that is, user connections (local or remote) and their usernames and passwords.

Later, special sniffers were developed which, instead of intercepting the whole data stream, recorded only the beginning of a session (*header*) when access credentials were input.

After installing and activating the sniffer onto the violated system, the attacker could disappear, do something else without fearing exposure, and return some time later to download the intercepted password files.

Stealth Diagnostic

SATAN (Security Administrator Tool for Analyzing Networks) appeared just before the mid 1990s, allowing remote diagnostics of the security level of information systems connected to the Internet. SATAN was written by system administrators to automate, simplify, and speed up the monitoring of vulnerabilities and patches on their systems, but in the hands of a hacker it became an attack weapon, largely used to violate information systems.

Over the years, more of these kinds of tools were developed, up to and including the capability of automatically exploiting discovered vulnerabilities and violating the system under *check* (detailed in the section on *Automated Probe/Scan*).

Packet Spoofing

On Christmas Day 1994, Kevin David Mitnick, probably the best-known hacker on the world level, attacked Tsutomu Shimomura's Sun Solaris server. Shimomura was a researcher at the San Diego

---

* Abbreviation of Transmission Control Protocol/Internet Protocol, which indicates all the transmission protocols used for exchanging data over the Internet.

Supercomputer Center (SDSC) and a U.S. government consultant. Kevin wanted to challenge the government superconsultant, who was guilty of having revealed to Congress that it was possible to intercept cell-phone communications. After watching Shimomura's speech on TV, Kevin wanted, at all costs, to obtain the software operating on Oki cell phones (at the time one of the very few available to intercept cell communications). The quickest way to do this was by violating the research server of the consultant and downloading the software.

In order to accomplish this, Mitnick became the first ever to do what up until then had only been considered a "theoretical possibility, but not applicable in practice." He launched an *IP Spoofing attack* against Shimomura's server; in other words, he appeared with a different IP address—the address of a system known to the attacked server and therefore considered "trusted." In this way, Mitnick *bypassed* the server's defenses, obtained access and full control, copied the file he wanted, and thumbed his nose at Shimomura.

This led to a manhunt in which Shimomura (with the FBI and technological support from telecommunications companies that Kevin violated regularly, including Sprint Communications) hunted Kevin for months, tracking his presence and drawing the net closer. On February 14, 1995 (St. Valentine's Day), Kevin David Mitnick was arrested after having been placed on the FBI's *Most Wanted* list and having become the most famous *fugitive hacker* in history. Two books and a film have been made on the subject, which shows how the popular view of a hacker on the run, part Robin Hood, part criminal, has always fascinated the general public.

GUI

Between 1996 and 1997, the first GUI (graphical user interface) attack tools appeared on the underground scene. These are programs that can be used through a graphic interface (similar to what can be found in a common Web or desktop application) instead of a character-based interface (*command line*) typical, for instance, of DOS environments and UNIX/Linux shells.

Having a GUI available really made it possible for anyone to use the software because, as is commonly known in the environment, software with a GUI is typically software "for the masses," employed by an enormous number of users and therefore not exclusive. Conversely, command line software is stark and basic but comparatively much lighter, often more easily portable, i.e., usable on another operating system. Furthermore, command line software allows a more automated use of the software itself, which is useful for a hacker who has to automate various operations and commands.

Nowadays, command line software continues to exist, as such software provides the classic inevitable support for both programmers and hackers, and is actually proliferating in the case of exploits and 0-day attacks.* However, most tools are managed by means of GUIs, which explains why less-experienced hackers are on the increase, a growing phenomenon over the last few years.

Automated Probe/Scan

Around 1997, the first tool for TCP/IP port scanning and verification of known vulnerabilities was released. This was the period of maximum ferment for the *Internet social and economic boom;* the Internet was spreading by leaps and bounds throughout the world.

In Italy, Internet provider VOL (Video OnLine) had been active for 2 years and offered the option of "try and buy" modem Internet access with a free trial period. Our homegrown hackers soon discovered a username/ password pairing that could be used by an unlimited number of users through a free phone number, without calling costs (local or long distance). The obvious consequence was that many surfed the Web looking for hacker tools for scanning, attacking, and exploiting vulnerabilities.

Universities, small and medium enterprises (SMEs), and public administrations (which were just starting to use the Web) were systematically attacked, usually by *script-kiddies* (inexperienced hackers with a low level of knowledge, more capable of using vulnerabilities found by others than discovering new ones themselves), who tended to replace a victim's homepage (*Web defacement*) or delete system or archive files.

All this was mainly due to the great availability of automated scanning and attack tools.

---

* A 0-day exploit is one that takes advantage of a security vulnerability on the same day—or even before—the vulnerability becomes generally known.

WWW Attack/Incident

The year 1997 marked the beginning of an apparently endless wave of attacks based on Web vulnerabilities, or having as their main objective Web defacement. In the years that followed, especially during the Internet "bubble," Web defacement reached mind-boggling peaks and targets. The case of "Mafiaboy" is notorious; this 15-year-old from Montreal, Canada, brought the stock exchange rates of giants like eBay and Yahoo to their knees.

The start of the Web defacement "fad" marked a second milestone in the macro history of electronic attacks and made extremely sophisticated tools available to inexpert "hackers," so-called *newbies,* lacking the know-how necessary for a proper use of these tools (however "proper" might be defined).

Denial of Service (DoS)

The last category analyzed by CERT/CC takes us up to 1998, the year the first DoS (*denial of service*) attacks started to become popular. In the years that followed (just as with Mafiaboy), these attacks caused incredible damage, both on the private level and to critical Internet structures, costing the violated companies a great deal of money and harming their image, which also suffered from the financial damage incurred.

During a DoS attack, the aggressor tries to saturate the system network with a flow of traffic that will stop authorized users from using it, or to limit if not obliterate their transmissions.

These were by followed by DDoS (*distributed denial of service*) attacks. In this case, it is no longer a single "nozzle" connected to the Internet flooding the targeted company's "nozzle," but rather *n* number of nozzles launching DoS attacks against a single target—in other words a "distributed" flooding.

Today the new trend is *botnets,* actual electronic "robot networks" installed on the victim systems by exploiting known and unknown vulnerabilities through a sort of diabolical marriage between worms and Trojans, but which can be managed by IRC or dedicated interfaces from the safety of your own room.

Another characteristic of *botnets* is that they tend to be installed on workstations and not on servers, using an extremely high number of PCs to launch DDoS attacks from unwitting companies that have a high bandwidth capacity. This is the other side of the coin of the highly acclaimed "wideband."

Conclusions

The final thought we want to leave with the reader is very simple. If we analyze the history of hacking and the more recent attack techniques, changing our way of looking at them and moving toward a point of view more strictly connected to *information security* (*IS*) and less tied to a standard concept of "criminality," we can see how the actions of the so-called *bad guys* are basically always the same, repeating themselves over time: they find the source code of copyright protected proprietary applications (therefore not freely available), identify hardware and software default accounts and passwords, and illegally access information systems and telecommunications networks.

The methods change, but the objectives don't (bearing in mind, of course, developments in technology and the economic system). The only things that have really changed, and quite greatly at that, are the *motivations* for an attacker's actions.

With the help of this brief historical reconstruction and the examples of the macro attacks illustrated in this chapter, we hope to have made clearer the logic that will provide the key to understanding and interpreting present and future electronic attacks.

3

TO BE, THINK, AND
LIVE AS A HACKER

I made a discovery today. I found a computer. It does what I want it to.
If it makes a mistake, it's because I screwed it up. Not because it doesn't
like me...

Society's representation of hackers and definitions describing them
either demonize them or turn them into legends, depending on the
source.

A Robin Hood of the computer era? Electronic pirates willing to
try anything for a few hours of notoriety? Autistic geniuses? Angry
adolescents? Maladjusted nerds? Keen researchers? Political activists?
The plethora of definitions and points of view doesn't give us a clear
and consistent image of hackers, while the many interpretations of
the term lead to an accretion of misleading views that in time become
accepted. Few other groups have ever given rise to such a variety of
definitions that are often incompatible and contradictory.

A classical definition appears in the "Jargon File*" under "how to
become a hacker," giving a description of the correct attitude and
behavior when dealing with technology. Hacking has to do with
"technical adeptness and a delight in solving problems and overcom-
ing limits." To become a hacker, or at least to approach the hacker
world, "only two definitions are really relevant. There is a community
of expert programmers and networking wizards that traces its history
back through decades to the first time-sharing minicomputers and
the earliest ARPANET experiments. The members of this culture

---

* The Jargon File was a document originally written by Raphael Finkel from Stanford
  University and kept up by Eric S. Raymond, one of the greatest exponents of
  the hacker culture in the world. It is basically a glossary of slang used by hackers
  and IT professionals, but it also contains definitions and rules on how to behave
  (*netiquette*).

originated the term "hacker". Hackers built the Internet. Hackers made the UNIX operating system what it is today. Hackers run Usenet. Hackers make the World Wide Web work. If you are part of this culture, if you have contributed to it and other people in it know who you are and call you a hacker, you're a hacker."

The term *hacker* also has a wider meaning, not limited to the sole use of technology. A metaphorical meaning, according to the Jargon File, is "…The hacker mindset is not confined to this software-hacker culture. There are people who apply the hacker attitude to other things, like electronics or music—actually, you can find it at the highest levels of any science or art. Software hackers recognize these kindred spirits elsewhere and may call them 'hackers' too—and some claim that the hacker nature is really independent of the particular medium the hacker works in."

From a dialectical point of view, a concept is defined not only by what it is but also by what it is not. It becomes important to set limits to the concept of hacker, beyond which it becomes something else and different from itself. The Jargon File also defines what hacking is not, and consequently what is not a love of technology:

> There is another group of people who loudly call themselves hackers, but aren't. These are people (mainly adolescent males) who get a kick out of breaking into computers and phreaking the phone system. Real hackers call these people "crackers" and want nothing to do with them. Real hackers mostly think crackers are lazy, irresponsible, and not very bright, and object that being able to break security doesn't make you a hacker any more than being able to hotwire cars makes you an automotive engineer. Unfortunately, many journalists and writers have been fooled into using the word "hacker" to describe crackers; this irritates real hackers no end.

The difference between the two groups is basically that hackers *create,* while crackers *destroy.* On this point, Antifork* defines hacking as "superior knowledge research and ultimate perfection." The act of hacking in effect requires planning and organization as well as acuteness and inventiveness.

---

* Italian hack research group, http://www.antifork.org.

Wikipedia defines hacker culture as a subculture where participation is voluntary, which developed in the 1960s in an electronic academic environment while working at minicomputers. The Artificial Intelligence Lab at the Massachusetts Institute of Technology (MIT), the University of Berkeley in California, and the Carnegie Mellon University are the hothouses from which hacker culture arose. At the end of the 1960s, it merged with the technical culture of the Internet pioneers and, after the 1980s, with the UNIX culture. Since the mid 1990s, it has coincided with what today is called the *Open Source* movement.

Evolution of the Term

To understand the present meaning of the term *hacker*, it might be useful to recap the steps of its development and its various meanings from the Fifties to date. Table 3.1, which summarizes Appendix B of Sam Williams' book, *Free as in Freedom,** illustrates these steps.

We mustn't forget that another subculture exists in parallel that describes itself as a hacker culture—the so-called *computer underground*, a horizontal, nonhierarchical structure for the exchange of knowledge and information to which the media (and consequently public opinion), attribute the meaning of *clandestine use of computer skills*.

The Artifacts of the Hacker Culture

Hacker artifacts arose in 1969 with the creation of ARPANET, the prototype for a series of computers with intercontinental connections developed for military communications by the U.S. Department of Defense. This tool was developed also thanks to the involvement of many universities that were looking for a fast and cheap way to connect geographically far-flung laboratories. One important side effect of ARPANET, however, was that it linked all the hackers of the United States and led to the first intentional culture artifacts, two of which have historical value given the symbolic meaning they possess: "The Jargon File" and "The Hacker Manifesto."

---

* The electronic version is available online at the following address: http://creilly.com/
  openbook/freedom.

Table 3.1   Steps in the Development of the Terms *Hacker* and *Hacking* from the 1950s to Date

PERIOD	MEANING OF THE TERM
MIT: 1950s	Hacking is carefree, for creative and innocent amusement (for example, dismantling a radio).
MIT: Mid 1950s	The connotation is more rebellious: competitive climate, hacking is a reaction to that climate (*tunnel hacking* = unauthorized raids in the tunnels from which later the term *phone hacking* = the same raids but into the campus telephone system).
MIT: Late 1950s	*Computer hacking* = derived from a student group of train model buffs, adept at managing the relays and switches of the electrical circuitry. Their affinity for sophisticated electronic systems and contempt of "no entry" signs led them to getting hold of the TX-0 (one of the first computers placed on the market, and soon available at MIT) in the same spirit of "creative play."
Between 1950s and 1960s	*Hacking* = to put together software programs with little regard for "official" methods or software writing procedures in order to improve speed and efficiency. It also meant writing programs that served no other purpose than to amuse and entertain.
Early 1960s	The MIT hackers developed *Spacewar*, the first interactive video game that was completely free, and a testament to innovation and programming skill. Within a few years, it became a favorite diversion for mainframe programmers around the world.
1960s	The concepts of *collectivity*, *innovation*, and *communal software ownership* distanced computer hacking from tunnel hacking and phone hacking. The latter tended to be activities characterized by secrecy and were carried out alone or in small groups. *Computer hackers*, on the other hand, based their activities on collaboration and open appreciation of innovation.
Mid 1970s	The term "hacker" acquired elite connotations and becomes a sign of respect when used to refer to a fellow programmer.
Late 1970s	To describe oneself as a hacker it was no longer sufficient to write interesting software, a person had to belong to the *hacker culture*. Hackers at elite institutions (MIT, Carnegie Mellon, Stanford) start speaking of *hacker ethics*.
Early 1980s	Computers appear everywhere: "ordinary" programmers start rubbing shoulders with major-league hackers via the ARPANET. This leads them to appropriate the "anarchic" philosophies of hacker culture; however, the native cultural taboo originated by MIT against malicious behavior is lost. Younger programmers started employing their computer skills to harmful ends (breaking into military computer systems, creating computer viruses, crashing machines connected to ARPANET), and the term "hacker" took on a negative connotation. When police and businesses began tracing these crimes back to a few renegade programmers (disowned by the hacker community) who cited *hacker ethics* in defense of their activities, the term took on the connotations it has today. To distinguish themselves from this type of programmer, hackers coined the term *cracker* (whoever applies computer skills maliciously).

The Jargon File

While the "research tribe" in the United States was united and committed to the development of the Internet, on the world scene there were also many parallel independent hacker cultures with a similar background (university campuses) which often weren't aware of each other's existence, dedicated to the promotion of similar ideas: the great value of freedom of information; information sharing; defending the right to use the codes of one project to develop another independent, parallel one (*project fork*); a reciprocal tendency to take serious things with humor and seriously their fun.

All these small separate cultures found, in the Internet and other contexts deriving from it (for example the development of *Open Source*), the end of parallel developments and the birth of a common conscience, characterized by the same views on important questions, a common slang, and shared ethics. One of the moments of greatest awareness in the community is represented by the appearance in 1973 of *The New Hacker's Dictionary*, the first version of "The Jargon File," a dictionary of hacker slang, habits, folklore, and humor. It comes from the experience of institutions such as MIT, Stanford, and Carnegie-Mellon University, Worcester Polytechnic Institute, and is periodically updated according to socio-cultural changes that evolve in the community.

The Jargon File was initiated by Raphael Finkel at Stanford in 1975. However, revisions weren't numbered at the start. The file kept growing right up until the early 1980s. Later, Richard Stallman contributed decisively to its compilation and dissemination, adding many terms that came from MIT slang. This was followed by paper editions, after which the file stopped growing and changing. The intention was to crystallize the existing work so that it would become permanent. In April 1983, however, the conclusion of an important project at Digital Equipment Corporation led to the dispersion of those who periodically compiled the file, which was surrounded by an aura of legend even though it had quickly become obsolete. Only at the beginning of the 1990s, following a 7-year interruption, the Jargon File took on a life of its own. Raymond, the present custodian (his last revision dates back to December 2003) added new terms, and now the Jargon File contains—in addition to various definitions and explanations of underground slang and a portrait of the typical hacker—dress, interests, physical activities and sports, qualifications, favorite foods, politics and religion, communication style, use or not of ceremonial chemicals, sexual habits, personality traits, etc.

Obviously, this artifact does not presume to dictate behavior codes for hackers, who in any case, due to the nature of their activities, tend more toward independent thought and behavior, far from any form of emulation or sameness. The virtue of the Jargon File* lies in its symbolic value of collective creativity, built from the bottom up, with the contributions of anyone who feels up to it.

The Hacker Manifesto

Another historical artifact that still has great emotional impact is "The Hacker Manifesto: The Conscience of a Hacker," signed by "The Mentor" (Lloyd Blankenship), written immediately following his arrest and published for the first time on January 8, 1986, on the e-zine *Phrack*.[†]

The Hacker Manifesto gives us some interesting pointers for analyzing this culture, as it expresses the way the community sees itself, and also its motivations. *To be a hacker means to be constantly looking for challenges.* Breaking impossible (to most people) limits is a passion. As other authors have shown,[‡] adolescent anger and resentment seem to be two emotions that frequently transpire from the verbal reports and accompany the actions of at least one subgroup of hackers. Anger is directed at the *status quo,* at the world of adults, at teachers, at authority with which hackers do not identify (and do not want to), and at grown-ups from whom they have nothing to learn and a lot to teach. What emerges clearly is that they feel misunderstood, and the solution emerges, too: a strong feeling of belonging to the hacker community, which sees beyond any social difference and offers comfort and unconditional solidarity.

The hacker is in conflict with whoever tries to control and therefore limit the innovative scope of discoveries (governments, the holders of

---

* The profile that emerges from the Jargon File is a series of characteristics obtained from a questionnaire compiled on the Net by a hundred-odd respondents and compared with the answers given by a random group of nonhacker respondents.

† You can consult the original document at http://www.phrack.org/. See also Appendix D.

‡ Verton, D., *The Hacker Diaries: Confessions of Teenage Hackers,* McGraw-Hill, New York, 2002.

means of production and distribution, etc.). In a context where information wants to be free, but isn't allowed to be, and education cannot free itself from submission to all that is outdated, hacking becomes a way to go beyond the limits imposed from the outside and discover the limitless possibilities offered by the virtual world.

Being a hacker doesn't mean mindlessly following a movement, nor is it a label. Being a hacker is a lifestyle, an instinct, a shared mindset of how to socialize, remove power from the center, and be "hands-on." The objective is to find inadequacies and loopholes in the Net and repair them, and improve it continuously. To do this, you have to have ethics. A sense of responsibility is the price you pay for your freedom. *Hacker ethics* represents a code of responsibility, a nonwritten value system embedded in the behavioral standards that contribute to forge the psychosocial identity of the individuals who belong to that culture. At the end of the day, the *ethics* represents the backdrop of this culture (*sub-* or *counterculture* as you prefer) which, differently from other cultures, veils instead of parades, and bases its existence on understatement rather than revelation. This is probably one of the aspects that has led to the term *hacker* having "criminal" overtones.

One Code of Ethics or More?

Steven Mizrach,[*] an anthropologist at the University of Florida, points out how a new ethics can be traced back to the hackers of the 1990s. Even though there is a form of continuity with the past, the new ethics seems to contain some contradictions and ambiguities. This could be due to the fact that its members are many more now, and more dispersed compared to the hackers of the 1960s. The ethical debate on whether certain types of behavior are adequate or not is still raging. *Hacker ethics* is not, after all, a code of conduct with established rules but is continuously being revised and discussed internationally in an ongoing debate open to anyone (through mailing lists, online archives, e-zines, etc.).

One of the hottest topics (constantly under discussion in popular mailing lists such as Full-disclosure, Burgtraq, etc.), is whether it is

---

[*] Mizrach, S., *Is There a Hacker Ethic for 90's Hackers?*, http://www.fiu.edu/~mizrachs/hackethic.html.

appropriate to disclose immediately and in full a vulnerability discovered in a system (*full disclosure* approach). The reason for this is the idea that if a vulnerability is revealed immediately, the problem will be solved immediately, too, as the *vendors* have a vested interest, at least in terms of image.

A more moderate approach is that of *responsible disclosure*, where only the vendor and the author are informed so that they can solve the problem without anyone maliciously exploiting it and damaging the system. If the problem could not be solved within a reasonable amount of time (which is also subject to heated debate), the vulnerability would then be made public. As you can see, the concept of a shared ethics appears to be rather an abstract concept instead of a real behavior (at least at this point in time).

Understanding Hackers: How Far Have We Gone?

Up to now, research on hacking has mainly dealt with legal and psychiatric aspects, and sometimes with devising corrective measures. Even though social research has looked at group rules, verbal exchange models, whether groups are homogenous or varied, etc., it has rarely dealt with the psychological aspects of hacking, or, first and foremost, the motivations underlying this behavior. As we have shown, it's very difficult to investigate this reality, for reasons both of organization and of procedure. Given the nature of their activities, hackers remain concealed and, even when they belong to a group, a certain wariness toward the outside world makes it impossible to know this culture in full. One thing is certain: as Voiskounsky* states, the image offered by the media is far from the truth. Scientific and academic clinical-psychiatric literature is interested in the psychopathological behavior in hackers, forms of deviance present in the digital underground (understood as manifestations of adolescent unease), and criminological assessment. Criminological literature, though, is not capable of giving a single definition of hacker and points out the need to establish a taxonomy, stressing the differences in the various subgroups to compare them. The history of the evolution of the hacker mentality indicates

---

* Voiskounsky, A.E. and Smyslova O.V., "Flow-Based Model of Computer Hacker's Motivation," in *Cyber-psychology & Behaviour*, 6, 2003 .

that there have been various succeeding generations of hackers over the years:

- A first generation of pioneers, involved in the development of early software and programming techniques.
- A second generation made up of those who first developed PCs and brought computers to the masses.
- A third generation, who invented computer games and made them available to the public at large.*

Taylor[†] adds a fourth generation, which has started to illicitly access other people's computers. The shift from pioneers to thieves was not spontaneous; influences in cultural innovations were first introduced by *phone phreakers*, then by the gradual dissemination of computers followed by the Internet, and finally by the media reports on "malicious" acts by hackers. All this has contributed to change the image of hackers from sophisticated computer specialists to computer pirates. Rogers asserts, with most international criminological literature, that computer criminals are often erroneously defined as "hackers" and concurs that "classical criminological theories with a psychodynamic matrix are efficient for explaining crimes that derive from unconscious conflicts, but cannot be easily applied to crimes that necessitate great accuracy, planning, and rationality, as is the case with most computer crimes.[‡] In effect, the hacking phenomenon is difficult to interpret using classical criminological theories, mainly due to the great differences to be found in that environment as visible at a superficial glance."

The hacker community is not all the same, and various identifiable subgroups can be classified according to different criteria:

- Level of technical *expertise.*
- Areas of interest (hardware, software, telephones, Internet, etc.).
- Behavioral models/ethics, etc.

---

* Levy, S., *Hackers: Heroes of the Computer Revolution*, Shake Editions, 2002.
[†] Taylor, P., "Hackers: A Case Study of the Social Shaping of Computing," doctoral thesis, University of Edinburgh, 1993.
[‡] Rogers, M., "Modern-Day Robin Hood or Moral Disengagement. Understanding the Justification for Criminal Computer Activity," *Daily Mail & Guardian*, 1999. Chandler, A., "The Changing Definition and Image of Hackers in Popular Discourse," in *International Journal of the Sociology of Law*, 24, 1996. Chantler, N., *Profile of a Computer Hacker*, Infowar, Florida, 1997. Denning, D.E., *Information Warfare and Security*, ACM Press, New York, 1999.

The subgroups can be split into further categories. Rogers[*] suggests a classification based on seven separate categories, even though the last two are grouped together according to aims and skills in the use of technology:

- *Toolkit/newbies,* technology novices, with very low technical skills and know-how; they use ready-made software, preprepared using *how-to* documentation downloaded from the Internet.
- *Cyber-punks,* capable of writing small programs themselves, which they use mainly for "defacing" Web pages, spamming, or credit card theft.
- *Internals,* employees or former employees of an organization or company. They damage the company's system out of revenge. Their attacks aren't based on technical skills but rather on their precise knowledge of the level and type of security present inside the organization.
- *Coders,* who write code aimed exclusively at damaging other systems.
- *Old-guard hackers,* commonly called *hackers,* highly qualified, without criminal intent, who embrace the original ideology of first generation hackers; their interest lies in the intellectual, cognitive side of hacking.
- *Professional criminals and cyber-terrorists,* these are the most dangerous categories: professional criminals specialized respectively in industrial espionage and intelligence operations against governments, national security agencies, etc.

Given this classification, which is based on a progressive increase in the level of competence, which in turn seems to go hand in hand with the level of the crime committed, it appears that there is an "unavoidable" link between increase of technical know-how and *moral disengagement.*[†]

According to Rogers, cyber-criminals are well aware of the fact that their actions are socially and morally reprehensible, and the need to assuage their feelings of guilt makes them to try to rationalize their behavior by developing a self-image as computer-age Robin Hoods.

---

[*] Rogers, M., *The Psychology of Hackers: The Need for a New Taxonomy,* 1999. Available at http://www.infowar.com.

[†] Bandura, A., "Mechanism of Moral Disengagement in Terrorism," in W. Reich (ed.), *The Psychology of Terrorism: Behaviors, World Views, States of Mind,* Cambridge University Press, New York, 1988.

As to hackers, Rogers continues, the ethical aspect of their activities is constantly under discussion, even though there is some support for the idea of looking at a possible psychological explanation for their leanings toward illegality, which in their case, too, are always disguised or presented as prosocial.

Some personality traits that have been studied and reductively used to support a trait theory to explain a type of behavior have to do with the fact that highly narcissistic hackers seem to get a higher score for levels of aggressiveness than hackers who have a low level of narcissism,* just as hackers who are strongly nationalistic become more aggressive when they feel threatened.

Jordan and Taylor,† who were among the first academic researchers to study hacker motivations, refuse any attempt to brand them as pathological and believe that psychological interpretations defining hackers as mentally unstable are reductive and miss the main aspect of hacking: its social basis. They stress rather how this community or collective identity can be defined through six aspects:

- *Technology.* There is a strong tie with technology and the shared idea that it can always lead to new and unexpected uses.
- *Secrecy.* A fundamental ambivalence exists between the need to keep secret an illicit act and the need to share it with the peer group.
- *Anonymity.* Connected but separate from the secrecy aspect, which consists in keeping a hack hidden, while anonymity regards the offline identity of the hacker.
- *Fluid membership.* The hacking world is more of an informal network rather than a formally set up organization, so its borders are rather permeable, and the nature of this kind of network leads to a high level of turnover.
- *Male predominance.* Various factors can explain this aspect. For example, the kind of primary socialization that teaches males a different attitude toward technology from what it

---

* Woo, H.J., "The Hacker Mentality: Exploring the Relationship between Psychological Variables and Hacking activities," PhD dissertation, University of Georgia, 2003.
† Jordan, T. and Taylor, P., A Sociology of hackers, The Editorial Board of *The Sociological Review*, 46, 4, 1998, pp. 757–780. Also on http://www.dvara.net/HK/1244356.pdf.

does to females, computer training, carried out mainly in boys' schools and environments, and a gender bias in computer language.

- *Motivations*. Hackers articulate their collective identity and build up their sense of community, shifting between different motivations and positions:
    - Computer dependency (on the Net) and compulsive need to hack.
    - Curiosity as to what can be found on the Net.
    - Boredom of offline life as compared to the thrill of the illicit offerings of online activities.
    - Acquiring power over systems belonging to government agencies, banks, etc.
    - Peer group recognition, with acceptance within the community or advancement in the hierarchy.
    - Generosity toward future users and society, given that discovering holes in networks leads to more secure systems.

What Are the Motives behind Hacking?

Some research has shown that, even bearing in mind the importance of individual elements (know-how, skill, and temperament), the idea that success in programming is due to the level of competence can be discarded, and it is rather a question of character traits and skills.*

Motivation is the most interesting of personal traits, as it represents the most important characteristic of human behavior. Not enough is known yet of hacker motivations, and this is the aspect that became one of the prime reasons behind the Hacker's Profiling Project (HPP). As explained in the preceding paragraph, Jordan and Taylor reach the conclusion that the most common motivations lead back to a compulsive attraction to hacking, intellectual curiosity, strong feelings of control/power, and finally the satisfaction derived from the feeling of belonging to a group. When interviewed, however, hackers often say that they are fully involved in what they

---

* Dutta, R.D., "Individual Characteristics for the Success in Computer Programming," *Journal of Personality and Clinical Studies*, 19, 1, 2003, pp. 57–61.

are doing and don't think of any kind of gain.* Linus Torvalds confirms this in his introduction to Himanen's† book when he says that, for the hacker, "the computer itself is entertainment," meaning by *entertainment* the mental exercise obtained through an intrinsically interesting and stimulating activity. In any event, even if we consider this statement as our starting point, the motivations behind hacking seem to lead back to a sort of intrinsic motivation; in other words, the tendency to engage oneself in tasks that are gratifying in themselves, are interesting, and can be viewed as a challenge.

Today the most developed theory of intrinsic motivation is Csikszentmihalyi's‡ theory/paradigm of the *state of flow*.

Flow is defined as a state in which all of our processes, thoughts, motivations, and feelings interact and work together smoothly both for our internal needs and to face the challenges of the outside world. The characteristics of flow are: clear objectives to pursue, balance between external demands and personal capabilities of the subject, immediate feedback following an action, full control of the situation without any need for self monitoring, and an alteration of time perception. After a flow experience, the individual develops an increased psychic complexity and consequently looks for greater challenges. This in turn leads to a further increase in the level of skills necessary to face the challenge. In other words, the flow is at a precise level of skill of a person and can be compared to a movable target: in order to match challenges and skills and reach the state of flow, the level of the challenge must increase, but higher skills must also be brought into play. Therefore, the choice of a more difficult challenge leads to an increase in skills. After a learning period, the challenge and the personal skills are again exactly matched, and a state of flow is experienced again. On this point, Voiskounsky and Smyslova§ assume that more highly qualified hackers reach a flow

---

* Taylor, P., Hackers—"Cyberpunks or Microserfs?," in *Information, Communication & Society*, Taylor & Francis, 1999. Hafner, K. and Markoff, J., *Cyberpunks: Outlaws and Hackers on the Computer Frontier*, Simon and Schuster, New York, 1995.

† Himanen, P., *The Hacker Ethic*, Random House Trade Publishers, New York, 2001.

‡ Csikszentmihalyi, M., *Beyond Boredom and Anxiety*, Jossey-Bass, San Francisco, 1975.

§ Voiskounsky, A.E. and Smyslova, O.V., "Flow-Based Model of Computer Hackers' Motivation," *Cyber-Psychology & Behavior*, 6, 2003, pp. 171–180.

state more often than less qualified ones. This assumption hasn't been confirmed yet; flow doesn't increase in a linear fashion with the increase of skills. Periods of flow state alternate with periods of crisis and renewed states of flow. The model is based on a match between the level of skill in computer use (not necessarily hacking) and the level of hacking challenges (or choice of tasks) undertaken. A novice hacker can still find a match between skills and challenges and start to experience flow. The motivation is a strong one, and the beginner experiences a feeling of well-being. A hacker could stay at this level for years, which would, however, imply that no greater challenges are looked for, and no consequently higher skills are employed. Following this theory, the learning curve of a novice can follow three directions:

- A progressive *step-by-step* search for new challenges and higher skills, becoming first a medium-level then a high-level hacker in such a way that challenges and skills are always matched at all steps, and the hacker experiences flow all the time.
- New skills are added, but they are not equaled by a search for new challenges.
- New challenges are looked for, but the subject realizes that the necessary level of skill has not been reached.

These last two lead to periodic flow experiences and only for brief spaces of time. The link between flow motivation and level of skill therefore cannot be so easily theorized; the progression between challenges and skills brought into play requires constant shifts in the development of flow motivation.

The Colors of the Underground

The time has now come to try and describe hackers by classifying them and entering their world—what is commonly called the *underground*.

The term "underground" usually means the subculture of any particular sector. In our case, when we talk of *digital underground*, we mean all those "tribes" that, with different styles and in different ways, lead part of their lives in the world of *information and communication technology* (ICT).

When we speak of *hacker underground*, we are referring to the different categories of hackers who live, communicate, and interact in the part of the digital underground tied to hacking, phreaking, and carding.

Within the hacker underground, different players and figures specific to the hacking world coexist, but before going into this in the next section, we'd like to take a look at a distinction that exists on a higher level—that of *white-hat* and *black-hat*—without going into specific details yet on the meaning of the terms.

Basically, these are an imaginary representation of the "goodies" and the "baddies," the baddies obviously being the black-hats while the goodies are the white-hats. This distinction arose spontaneously in the hacker underground to quickly identify a hacker's approach and use of his skills for constructive or destructive ends, even before the distinction between criminal activities vs. well-meaning actions was made. In the meanwhile, a third term has been added, *grey-hat*, covering those who don't identify with either the white-hats or the black-hats.

To clarify, we can summarize these three terms as follows:

- Black-hats: individuals who violate information systems with or without any personal gain. To all intents and purposes, they have decided to join the baddies and carry out illegal actions, and in many cases go beyond the clear line drawn between "love of hacking" and criminal acts with intent. For them, violating an information system and prying out its secrets, stealing the information, and selling it outside is normal behavior.

- Grey-hats: the common view is that of "ethical hackers" (we'll be coming back to them later). In other cases, they just don't want to be labeled "black" or "white" and, as far as they are concerned, they could even be "pink-hats" or any other color. Mainly, they don't identify with the "goody" or "baddy" distinction. They might have carried out intrusions of information systems in the past but have decided not to follow this approach.

- White-hats: the "hunters." They have the skills necessary to be "black-hats" but have decided to "fight" for the forces of good. They cooperate with the authorities and the police, take part in *anti-computer-crime* operations, and are government and company consultants. But what is more important, they have very rarely in the course of their lives violated an information system, or if they have, it has never been with "criminal intent" or for financial gain.

As to black- and grey-hats, one of their main objectives is to have sufficient access to computers, networks, and hardware or, conversely, enough money to buy what they need. So they can be either wealthy or poor. In the first case, they hack for the thrill it brings. In the second case, thanks to their high technical skills, they often hack for revenge against bad treatment received from someone.

It is, however, to give a foretaste of the following section, important to note that these "unwritten rules" can easily be broken and will not necessarily be considered valid. There are, for instance, various standard subcategories among black-hatters, first among them being *script-kiddies*, whom we'll find again later on. For would-be black-hat script-kiddies, the main rule is "no skills but prebuilt tools," or "no technical skills, only prebuilt tools and programs." These attackers therefore target only weak systems where there are known or presumed specific vulnerabilities, and they don't have the experience and technical knowledge that make "real" black-hatters so dangerous. Furthermore, the category of *black-hat script-kiddies* covers other variants. First of all, there are *basic coders*. These are low-level (if not basic-level) programmers who nevertheless manage to modify existing code to attempt the use of new exploits and possibly discover new security vulnerabilities. At the same time, they depend on tools like *Metasploit** for part of their basic code. Then we have *full-blown coders*, the only difference being that they tend not to use someone else's code if they feel capable of developing one on their own. Lastly, we have *oops! script kiddies;* in other words, people who aren't really black-hats but nevertheless, due to gross programming errors, carry out typically "black" high-impact actions. An example is the "Melissa" worm in its first release, when due to programming errors and the ignorance of the worm's developer, the damage caused was enormous and certainly not an example of a "grey" or "white" hacking approach.

As we have seen, their motivations do have an impact on their attacks and influence their couldn't-care-less attitude and irresponsibility in

---

* Metasploit: a framework for medium- and high-level attacks, thanks to an internal database of standard attack tools and exploits.

the face of the consequences of their activities. Those who don't care about other people and don't feel responsible for their actions will typically use *botnets** to launch their attacks or will write codes to create them. Others will cover their tracks but will use previously violated servers to do this, or will use *hiding systems*† such as Tor. Usually, they are motivated by someone to attack their targets—either an external agent who "encourages" them (pays or lures them) or an insider. When an attack focuses on a single company, they could also be former employees who have been fired, or they may be attracted by a specific operating system used inside the target system.

It is important to stress the fact that hackers focus their attention on software companies because of the licensing systems they use, which are hated by hackers. Many black and grey hackers tolerate hardware limitations imposed by producers but can't stand software limitations and actually hate them. As the *free* concept in Linux operating systems allows hackers to use it in a very flexible way, there is less "hate" against it and therefore greater "hate" against "closed" systems protected by copyright, the consequence of this being a stubborn search for vulnerabilities and programming errors.

If we keep on looking at the various subcategories, we can find so-called *skill testing hackers*. These are people who move around inside an operating system using *checklists* (lists of things to verify), and even though they are violating systems thanks to these searches (a classic phrase is, "oh, yeah, I broke a server there yesterday"), they are more of the grey-hat world, and practically *ethics–based hackers*.

Then there are *firebug hackers*, or "arsonist hackers." This typically is the kind of person who will be in the eye of the storm when a big security incident takes place in a specific computer system. They feed on the emotions of the users who have lost control of their computers, just like an arsonist is excited by the sight of a fire burning. Some of them end up becoming security consultants, but during the first phase of their career they can cause a lot of damage.

---

* A collection of compromised computers connected to the Internet and under the total control of a remote attacker, who will use the enormous band power made up of the sum of power available on each individual PC to launch various types of attacks (for example, DDoS).
† Anonymous communications systems for the Internet.

Now we get to the most dangerous and aggressive black-hat sub-category: *legal black hackers.* They work on commission, signing agreements with contractors to destroy an information system. But before they start, they move to a country where the action is not illegal. They can be firebug hackers, with the difference that they won't hide, and they won't carry out any "illegal" action (in the country where they are residing). This makes them all the more dangerous, as they could return repeatedly to their target, and there's nothing the victims can legally do to stop them.

Location is another aspect that needs to be considered when talking of black-, grey-, and white-hatters. If they have sufficient technical skills, "open" wireless networks are ideal for many black-hatters, and so are places that allow anonymous connections to the Internet. They are capable of crossing a whole city on a bus just to reach a location with these characteristics, and then pass the tip along through their community or group. As their approach implies "not paying" for connection costs, all their actions will be carried out with total disregard for the abused infrastructure. Conversely, if the location and the targeted company are only a small part of a network, they will mainly use viruses and Trojans to reach their objective. The concept of location usually refers to the physical area surrounding a target; if you want to attack a company through a wireless connection, and the company has a public park just opposite, then that is the ideal location for our attackers.

Subcategories also apply to grey-hatters. There are at least two: "traditional" grey-hats and *skill testers.* Your traditional grey-hatters don't care about the definitions and distinctions rife in the hacker scene. They feel above them and hate labels. They follow a personal path where they might take a high profile or a low one. They might show themselves publicly (through papers, tools, research, conferences, posts on mailing lists, and interpersonal relations with other members of the hacker underground), or they might decide to show themselves as little as possible. Skill testers are very similar to black-hat skill-testing hackers. The small but important difference lies in what motivates them and the methods they use to pursue their activities. To give you a real-life example, exploit and virus creators are an excellent example of this category, and referring back to the Metasploit project, the authors of the various tools don't see anything wrong in what they do. They have it in for *OS writers* (programmers who design operating systems), because leaving unresolved (*unpatched**) security breaches certainly doesn't mean "having solved vulnerabilities at the code level," and also because this attitude allows functioning exploits to remain in circulation and cause system crashes.

In the Open Source world, the 30-day limit for solving vulnerabilities discovered by third parties is the maximum acceptable period to be tolerated. Going back to our subcategory, many of these nuisance attacks are caused by the different approach followed by giants like Microsoft as compared with the Open Source world (the number of the attacks could be drastically reduced if there were international legal standards specifying patching deadlines).

Finally, we must remember that there are low-level hackers among grey-hatters too, called *sheep*. They follow in the footsteps of the grey-hats who are high up in the social scale, just like a flock of sheep, often understanding very little about the approach used or the decisions made by others.

We will conclude this section with a last important consideration, this time on white-hats.

Over and above the danger and the threats that can come from the black- and grey-hat underground, even more frightening is the idea of a white-hat who is so simply because he has never had to or wanted to choose what to do with his knowledge, or better still, white because he has never taken other possibilities into consideration.

If hackers of this type are pushed on the psychological level (by an event, or for any other reason) they can turn into a black-hat or grey-hat overnight, a bit like those totally harmless people who for different reasons suddenly become killers (out of self-defense, but also for other uncontrollable reasons). The most common cause in these cases is the developer or the software house not listening

---

* Unfortunately, this is a bad habit many application software and operating systems vendors have. The bitter tirades between David Litchfield—a bug hunter specializing in the Oracle platform—and Oracle itself are notorious in the hacker underground. Litchfield daily identifies—for his own pleasure—no one pays him to do this—many bugs and security breaches in the Oracle database. But often months later, the database multinational has still not solved the problems pointed out by the bug hunter.

to them when warned about a security breach identified by a third party. Another reason is not getting credit for one's discoveries. In this case, an excellent example is the discovery of a code vulnerability, which isn't the simplest of jobs, but rather an activity that requires an enormous amount of time, stress, and brain-wracking activity. After all these efforts, the discovery that there is not even an acknowledgement in the software house *security patch* certificate, or a lack of response on the part of the developers (who were told how to solve the problem step by step) can certainly generate a feeling of rebellion and uncontrolled rage. In the best of cases, the help to the software house will just stop and, in a worst-case scenario, the hacker might decide to keep quiet about the discovered vulnerabilities and use them with criminal intent or to damage the image of the software producer.

Commonly Recognized Hacker Categories

After this lengthy digression on the underground and its population, we can now move on to a description of the more commonly known hacker categories—the most notorious, the most widespread, and the ones that are used and accepted as a general reference by the international underground. These categories were the starting point used to examine, "define," and try to improve the profiling approach for the world of hackers. This led to the results we will detail in Chapters 5 and 6, which deal with the analysis of the HPP working group questionnaires.

In the course of this explanation of the various categories, underground slang and terminology will be used to spice things up a bit and add "color," and also to help you get a feel of this special world. In the next few pages, we will analyze the following categories:

- Wannabe lamer
- Script-kiddie
- The "37337 K-rAd iRC #hack 0-day exploitz" guy
- Cracker
- Ethical hacker
- Quiet, paranoid, and skilled hacker
- Cyber-warrior

- Industrial spy
- Government agent

Wannabe Lamer

This is the most "amusing" category. You can find hackers of this kind practically anywhere on the Net, as they are constantly and publicly asking for help of various descriptions. Their classic question, in pure hacker slang, is, "Yo man! Whaz da b3st way t0 hack www.nasa. gov???? Hey c'mon, explain me man!!!"

Usually all you need to do is navigate to some "low profile" portals to find traces of these characters' comments.

Script-Kiddie

They are "culturally advanced," but it's not a good idea to have one protecting an information system. Their specialty is using tools developed by others to carry out violations they can boast about. Usually, they connect daily to sites from which they can download the latest exploit tool, for example the *BugTraq** mailing list. They're even capable of entering a system and shouting their presence from the rooftops; that's what script kiddies are—a category about which a lot has been said and they'll be talked about a lot more too, given the enormous help they have received from the Internet over the last decade. To give you an idea of the "respect" they enjoy in the hacking world, it's enough to tell you that the less able script-kiddies are labeled *point-and-clickers,* and their attacks are called *point-and-click attacks,* indicating that there's very little reasoning or study involved.

Sometimes, script-kiddies (mainly teenagers acting alone or as a group) fight amongst themselves to get control of chat rooms (as happened between 1994 and 1996, the period defined as "IRC Nuke Wars"). The battle consists in expelling your adversaries from the chat and crashing their systems with *bot* programs (short for "robot"), more commonly known as *ping o' doom or finger o' death* (these are DoS attack tools, used for purely gaming purposes). Luckily, the IRC Nuke Wars period didn't last long.

---

* http://seclists.org/bugtraq/.

"37337 K-rAd iRC #hack 0-day Exploitz" Guy

To ironically paraphrase this cryptic name, we could describe this kind of hacker as "the cool guy who goes on the #hack IRC channel to say he has 0-day exploits available (exactly like *traders* boast on IRC that they are *0-day couriers*).*

Usually. they are characters who would do anything to become "famous." They would sell their souls to have their nickname published everywhere, to end up in the news, and to make sure they are talked about. They are willing to use "brutal methods" to get where they want to be. These aren't hackers who explore; rather, they use what is already available.

Nevertheless, they are cause for concern. They have at their disposal real attack weapons, tools to exploit 0-day vulnerabilities, which are still unknown. Along with script-kiddies, this is the category that launches massive attacks against certain areas of the Internet, seeking the presence of specific vulnerabilities that will allow them illegal entry into a "bugged" information system.

Cracker

First of all, one misunderstanding needs to be cleared up: originally, *cracker* meant someone who removed the protection from commercial software programs. Recently, the term has started to appear in the papers and on mailing lists and has started to mean "violent" hackers, i.e., hackers who are happy to become a nightmare for system administrators, deleting files and causing permanent damage. Compared with the previous categories, these hackers are different, as they really have the know-how to wreak havoc. They try to stay on the system as long as possible, and when they believe they are losing control, they "cancel" it, erasing files, logs, and any kind of trace, whether important or not. This is quite a dangerous category.

---

* A trader is someone who "swaps" pirated software that is copyrighted but no longer protected (cracked). The 0-day courier is the trader's courier, who physically "shifts" the software from one warez site to another and deals only in "0-day"; that is, software copyright recently cracked. Obviously, the 0-day courier who manages to upload newly pirated software first gets brownie points and the attention of all the other traders.

Ethical Hacker

You might even like them. Yes, they enter and violate your system. Yes, they are mischievous, cheeky, curious… but often (there are many reports available on this) they will enter your system, explore it quickly (if it's a big computer or a large net, they might poke around a little "deeper" than for purely "educational" purposes), and they'll even let you know about it, sending you report mails or suggestions once they have finished exploring.

They have a widespread and all-round knowledge of operating systems. Even though it is generally believed that hackers hack only UNIX and LINUX, this is manifestly false. They don't do it for money or for fame. Only passion drives them. Often, they are naïve and speak about their actions publicly, taking for granted that they haven't done anything wrong. If you have the "luck" of having one in your system, don't get rid of him; take the opportunity to learn about all the holes in your corporate network or the bugs in your 10,000-euro *Sun Workstation!*

Quiet, Paranoid, and Skilled Hacker

This one can be fearsome and is possibly the most devious of the non-money-motivated hackers. This doesn't mean your files will be deleted or anything like that, but this hacker is paranoid, so it will be very difficult to detect his presence and virtually impossible to find him.

The paranoid hacker will stay on your system for very long periods of time, doing nothing serious or unpleasant. He will explore it at leisure but will be attracted only by what is of interest (won't read your private e-mails, but will check *syslog files** and similar, one by one). He is not interested in fame. He doesn't "do it for the money." He does it for himself, for his experience and know-how. He is extremely capable and competent on many operating systems; will explore but won't waste any time trying to impress anyone. If you detect this hacker's presence, which is highly improbable, he will immediately disappear.

---

* The syslog files are those files kept by the operating system to keep a log file of the system's activities. Depending on the OS, these logs may include the logon and logoff of the user from the system, the access to a specific file (read, write, or delete mode), and so on.

Cyber-Warrior

These are mercenaries who have acquired very great skills over the years. They probably come from one of the categories described above, and have chosen their way. They are for sale to the highest bidder but refuse certain kinds of requests.

Cyber-warriors keep a low profile, and the targets are low-profile, too. They will very rarely attack a multinational; far more probably, an Internet service provider, the local university, or the registry office.

To some extent these people don't care what system they penetrate or why. They do it for money or for ideals. Rarely do they leave any traces. They are intelligent. Not a hundred percent convinced of what they are doing, cyber-warriors feel "dirty."

Industrial Spy

Money is the motivation. They "do it" for the money. They are highly skilled, with lots of experience, and are dangerous if on the look-out for confidential material. Unfortunately *insiders* are part of this category—people who access sensitive information illegally, inside the company they work for, for personal gain.

Over the last few years, the numbers belonging to this category have increased exponentially, given the high number of white-collar crimes.

Government Agent

Generally, they have a good hacker background and are employed for espionage, counterespionage, and information monitoring of governments, individuals, terrorist groups, and strategic industries (as in the defense sector, or energy suppliers, water, gas, etc.). Think of FBI or CIA agents, or members of Mossad and other intelligence agencies.

In reality, even though it might seem bizarre or excessive to put "secret agents" on a par with the other categories, history shows how cases of this type—a marriage or meeting between the hacking world and the world of intelligence agencies—already existed in the second half of the 1980s.*

---

* Stoll, C., *The Cuckoo's Egg—Tracking a Spy Through the Maze of Computer Espionage*, Doubleday, New York, 1989.

4

THE HPP PROJECT

And then it happened. . . a door opened to a world. . . rushing through the phone line like heroin through an addict's veins. . . "This is it. . . this is where I belong. . ."

The Hacker's Profiling Project (HPP*) began between 2003 and 2004, due to a combination of events. First of all, one of the authors of this book, Raoul Chiesa, started getting involved in criminal profiling. Italian authors such as Picozzi, Zappala, and Lucarelli fascinated him, and when taken in conjunction with John Douglas' analysis methods, mentioned at the beginning of this book, he started seeing definite links and analogies with the world of hacking.

The second triggering factor was a lecture he gave during a criminology master's course held by UNICRI,[†] where "the first Italian ethical hacker" (as Raoul Chiesa is described by national and international media) finds among his students Stefania Ducci. Stefania was intrigued and started looking into *computer crime* and hacking in particular. At the end of the lesson, she contacted Raoul and, in the months that follow, she devours all the literature on the subject she can lay her hands on.

A thorough online search begins, looking for models for *hacker's profiling* as they see it and *understand* it. But nothing of that nature existed—only *parts* of the concept of what a hacker is, with reference to criminology. All they could find is purely criminological research, where the assumption is that a hacker is by definition a criminal,

---

* HPP (http://hpp.recursiva.org/) is an ISECOM project; see http://www.isecom. org/projects/hpp.shtml.
† UNICRI: United Nations Interregional Crime and Justice Research Institute (http://www.unicri.it).

or technological studies such as the Honeynet Project,* or studies dealing with the social† or psychological side. The problem all these studies had in common was that none of them made the connections among different points of view, approaches, and backgrounds.

The HPP was created with one first fundamental rule: don't judge, but analyze. Link up information and sources of widely different origins, open up to the underground communities, and *listen, analyze,* and finally *offer* a view, an interpretation, and a profiling model that will be based on years of research, experience, and passionate interest.

The HPP Working Group (WG) firmly believes in what it is doing, and results obtained to date can confirm our intuition. The WG is made up of hackers (obviously, in all senses of the term), criminologists, psychologists, and sociologists, all contributing their experience and wanting to *practice in the field* their research project.

The HPP has grown over the last two years, but we feel we are still in the start-up phase.

The sections in the chapter that follows will show the reader in detail the single steps that make up the project. However, we must point out from the start—to avoid any disappointment—that, at the moment, we are at the beginning of Phase 3 of the project, whereas the planning of Phase 4 will begin as this book is about to be published.

In a nutshell, we can say that what we are trying to do is "analyze the problem of cybercrime using a totally different approach from what was used in the past, going directly to the source."

The HPP project has the following main objectives (Table 4.1):

- *Analyze* the hacking phenomenon—technological, social and economic—in all its aspects, using both a technical and a psychological approach.

---

* Honeynet Project: the research project of reference for honey-pots and honey-nets. A honey-pot is a system exposed on the Internet which is deliberately unprotected, containing known or unknown vulnerabilities so as to log each step of an attack and analyze it from the technical point of view: how it was done, which code was used, etc. A honey-net is a series of honey-pots that might have different operating systems, applications, and vulnerabilities for each machine. For further information, see www.honeynet.org.

† Dr. Caterina Kertesz's work, carried out at the Universita' della Sapienza in Rome, is particularly innovative and far-sighted.

Table 4.1   The HPP Project, Started in September 2004, Eight Separate Steps

PHASE NUMBER	PHASE	OBJECTIVE
1	Theoretical data collection	Planning and distribution of a questionnaire, with different formats for distinct targets
2	Observation	Participation in "IT underground security"(EU, Asia, USA, Australia)
3	Archiving	Setting up a database for classification and processing of data collected during step 1
4	"Live" data collection	Planning and setup of new generation, highly personalized honey-nets
5	Gap and correlation analysis	Correlation of data collected through questionnaire, data obtained from the honey-nets and profiles derived from literature on the subject
6	HPP "live" assessment (24/7)	Continuous assessment of profiles and correlation with *modus operandi* through data from step 4
7	Final profiling	Definition and fine tuning of hacker profiles previously used as *de facto* standards
8	Dissemination of the model	Final processing of results obtained, drafting and publication of the methodology, dissemination (white paper, conferences, company awareness, training courses)

- *Understand* the various motivations, and identify the various players involved.
- *Observe* (real) criminal acts "in the field."
- *Apply profiling methods* to the data collected.
- *Learn* from the information acquired and spread the information.

The sections that follow will show how we mean to fulfill these objectives by analyzing in detail each step of the HPP project.

The Planning Phase

HPP is based on purely voluntary contributions of time and personal means by the researchers involved in the project. This is important to recognize so that the reader can understand the timing of the entire project.

The schedule that follows summarizes the planning of HPP, and the next one will illustrate the situation at the time of going to print. These are the first two phases, which took place in parallel from 2005 to 2007 (and will continue as "ongoing input" to bolster the method and its dissemination). The third and fourth phases are in progress at the moment and will get to the heart of the matter only next year.

In 2009, further steps will be taken to finish the project within the next three years.

Phase 1: Theoretical Data Collection

During the first phase, the main objective was preparing and distributing a questionnaire tailored to the world we were about to explore: the hacker underground.

The methodology used, as we will show in detail in the next section, had to be different from the "standard approach," and preparation of the questionnaires was a painstaking process, starting out first with three distinct documents and finishing with the present set, made up of two types of questionnaires with three different channels of distribution and dissemination.

In Table 4.2, the planning phase is defined as "completed/ongoing." This means that the planning of the questionnaire has been concluded, but it continues as a *parallel task;* in other words, it can be modified, integrated, and improved if necessary. Meanwhile,

Table 4.2 HPP Roadmap

PHASE	STATUS	DURATION
1. Theoretical data collection	Active (ongoing)	16–18 months + continuous assessment (48 months)
2. Observation	Active (ongoing)	24 (60) months
3. Archiving	Active (ongoing)	Planning: 3–6 months Execution and fine tuning: (E) 12–48 months; (FT) 12–36 months
4. "Live" data collection	Implementation phase	Planning (3–6 months) Execution: 24 months (continuous)
5. Gap and correlation analysis	Not active	9–16 months
6. "Live" assessment	Not active	12 months
7. Final profiling	Not active	6–10 months
8. Dissemination of the model	Not active	2–4 months ISECOM peer-review process

distribution will *carry on,* and so will the analysis; we daily receive questionnaires, suggestions, and advice from people who didn't know us and who learned of our project through conferences, events, simple word of mouth, or articles published online, or who read about us on a friend's blog. After reading this book, someone probably will fill out and send us the questionnaire. That's why we describe this step as a "continuous-input" phase.

What we were looking for with Phase 1 of the HPP was a solid foundation on which to base our research, starting out with the "commonly recognized"* nine categories of hackers. In this way, it became possible to eliminate one category right from the start of the first two phases of the project, the so-called *"37337 K-rAd iRC #hack 0-day exploitz"* guy, which nowadays can be covered by script-kiddies. It also became possible to add a new one, the *military hacker,* or hackers in the service of the armed forces of various countries. This "discovery" was due to two main factors: a careful study and selection of public and confidential texts and literature, which directly or indirectly proved the involvement of hackers in military activities, and also personally meeting people who were or still are in this type of profession during conferences and foreign hack meetings.

As we have repeatedly said during the official presentation of HPP and in articles and interviews given to the media following the official launch of the project by ISECOM (June 2006), HPP *is not based* on the questionnaires but rather wants to use them as a starting point to *verify* whether this knowledge base really gives a true picture of all the different categories of hackers.

As already stated, criminal profiling starts drawing a profile by examining established general profiles, ideas, and concepts, and in this way arrives at the profile of a specific individual. In the case of hackers, though, as there are no predefined models yet, given that this is still a largely unexplored field which is still in evolution, the opposite process had to be followed. Therefore, we started from a study of individual hacking cases and single hacker profiles we had produced on the basis of the literature available on the subject so as to develop one or more general models and profiles, which could then be applied to different types of hackers.

---

* See Chapter 3, section on "Commonly Recognized Hacker Categories."

In other words, *we started from the specific to develop the general.* These general models and theories will allow us to *process and perfect single criminal profiles,* just as in all present cases of criminal profiling.

The data obtained from literature on real hacking cases and from the questionnaires (inductive method) will be cross-referenced with data obtained from the "crime scene" (deductive method), producing, by means of a "hybrid" method, one or more criminal profiles.

In order to do this, the questionnaires were distributed through targeted research partners selected on the basis of criteria that were strategic to the study itself, and with the help of members of the digital underground who are actively participating in HPP. As you will see in the section explaining how the questionnaires were prepared, the approach chosen for the project proved to be fundamental, as was the cooperation between the various participants—some clearly coming from the *underground* (hackers) and others who were more "traditional" researchers (psychologists, criminologists, legal experts)—and their individual way of life. The sum of all these factors, quite an explosive mix, has led to the first, important results.

Even though these are "just" questionnaires, the HPP core team believes that results to date, added to the planning and dissemination methods used, are a definite step forward in observing and understanding the world of hacking, which is *truly* a phenomenon of primary importance that has been underestimated and partly misunderstood in the last few years. It has many facets and has much to contribute to the information and communication society—for better or for worse, some might add.

Phase 2: Observation

The key word for the second HPP phase is "observe." Observe *in the field* is the category we are discussing: hackers. Observe them in the ideal environment, their conferences.

Here, too, the core team had to carefully think through the correct approach, methodology, and strategy to use.

First of all, it was decided that we had to be present from the inside, taking part as speakers at these events, and never as "visitors." This allowed us to be present on the same footing as the other participants and not as *wannabes*.

Our second choice was that of aiming for a comprehensive, international view, so we covered European, North American, Asian, and Australian events.

The third factor was choosing to take part in both declaredly underground events and in *slightly* (not *officially*) commercial ones that were still representative and a meeting point for local communities in certain countries or geographical areas.

For all these reasons, we attended a series of events with rather self-explanatory names such as "Hack in the Box,*" "NoConName," "Hack.lu," "IT Underground," "OpenExp," "PH Neutral," "CCCmeetings & ChaosDays," "Confidence," and "0Sec," plus other more "traditional" market-related ones such as Eurosec, ISACA meetings, IDC, InterOp, and Ticino Communications Forum.

The idea was to identify and establish what relations exist between the more famous speakers from the international security underground and look at their "official" relations during conferences and updating sessions, which are distinct from the official or unofficial meetings within the hacker community.

In all these cases, the core team was represented principally by Alessio Pennasilico, Elisa Bortolani, and Raoul Chiesa as *de facto* members of the underground community, where relational behaviors certainly deserve their own analysis.

Phase 3: Archiving

As already stated, this phase will enter into full force during 2008 and 2009, and it is the more difficult step.

Setting up a database for the distributed analysis and correlation of the questionnaires was not complicated as such; the fields necessary for the database were planned and defined, as were security policies

---

* Hack in the Box (HITB) is an annual event held yearly by the Information Security Community of Malaysia. Internationally famous hackers (coming strictly from the Asian geographical area), professionals, final users, law enforcement, and government agencies spend three days together (the first day is optional and reserved for technical workshops), for seminars, updating, and exchange of ideas at a high technical level in a friendly atmosphere. HITB is held in Kuala Lumpur every year during the month of September, but earlier sessions have also been held in Bahrain. For further information (and minutes of past conferences) see www.hackinthebox.org.

and data management. Then, the questionnaires received (and those sent using a consolidation and validation-check routine) were entered in the first database.

The real problem was the approach to follow for the honey-net database.

On the one hand, as we will see in the next section, the main difference with the key concepts of a "standard" honey-net the WG had to deal with was the different approach: not *how*, but *why*, and *who;* the motives underlying the attack, and not simply intrusion techniques.

This meant splitting the planning phase into two subsections: the fields of the questionnaire on one side and a "protean monster" that keeps changing shape on the other. We define it a "monster," because we believe that the structure of the second database is part of the core of the project; each single action, behavior, *modus operandi*, signature, style, difference, and anomaly was covered and included in the database (DB) so as to allow maximum flexibility during the *post incident* analysis.

In our case, we *deliberately* decided to go further and challenge the so-called science of *computer forensics*, until we could find statistically and objectively more advanced models, relying on the methods and experience of computer forensics only for collecting the technical evidence.

Phase 4: "Live" Data Collection

The fourth phase consists in setting up the systems on new generation, highly tailored, honey-net networks.

What do we mean by "new generation"? Up to now, the minimum common denominator of honey-net systems was the fact that they supplied the analyst with raw data exactly as intercepted from—and typed in by—the intruder, which would then be interpreted with the use of dedicated tools. A sort of "balcony view" of the computer-crime scene, watching firsthand what the attacker was doing as it was happening. Let's face it: it's a dream scenario for a criminal profiler.

The Honeynet.org project was set up a few years ago by Lance Spitzner, a well-known information security (IS) guru. Today, it covers 23 countries,* has a considerable number of research partners, and,

---

* See http://philippinehoneynet.org/ and http://www.honeynet.org/alliance/index. html.

what is more important, analyzes in the field the activities of intruders. All this leads to various results:

- Identify and analyze attacks based on vulnerabilities and exploits, viruses, and 0-day worms.
- Analyze the *modus operandi* of the attacker.
- Observe attack trends.
- Forecast attack trends on the basis of geography, economics, and local spread of IT.
- Demonstrate "in the field" the speed of system violation according to its operating system.

As for HPP, the structure of the database registering the information received from the honey-nets we will implement will be finished in 2008 and will be operational in 2009. We'd rather not add anything more on the subject, as this is one of the "hot activities" of the project.

Phase 5: G&C Analysis

This phase will have strong gap-analysis activities, in the purest risk analysis (RA) tradition, joined with a correlation of the data collected through the questionnaire and present on the database with data collected from the honey-nets, and comparing it all with profiles obtained from the literature on the subject.

This work is necessary to "whittle down" our profiling method, allowing us at the same time to cross-check it with historical, literary, psychological, criminological, and field work information.

The final objective is the creation of a pilot model that can be fine-tuned in the next phase.

Phase 6: HPP Live Assessment (24/7)

The third-to-last phase covers a final assessment of the profiles and a strict correlation with the *modus operandi* derived from the data obtained in Phase 4, a *de facto* application in the field of the profiling model previously defined.

This is an extremely important and critical step, as it will allow us to understand and see with our own eyes whether our methodology is valid. We have called this step "live assessment," as our intention is that of placing HPP in the field, applying it to real live cases in existing companies and functioning IT structures.

Phase 7: Final Profiling

The seventh phase of HPP is a last revision and a final-fine tuning of the profiles previously used as *de facto* standards thanks to the results obtained up to this point.

We will then be able to define hacker categories, and we will probably witness the official birth of new categories that are already under study by our analysts at the moment but haven't yet produced enough material to allow a clear description of them.

Phase 8: Dissemination of the Model

The last step of the project will be the final processing of all the data gathered and, more importantly, we will start to lay down the HPP methodology. This is our final objective: to make available to the world at large a free profiling methodology that can be applied to computer crimes.

Our hope is that once the HPP method has been publicly released, there will be a general increase of awareness throughout all the stakeholders in the information security sector, from the smallest to the largest, which will produce new thoughts to be pondered and analyzed and a new kind of consciousness in all those who not only use the Net—and computer science in general—but to all intents and purposes "live" it.

The Questionnaires

As we said earlier, for the WG the questionnaire is only the first step toward understanding the international hacker underground (Table 4.3) This doesn't mean that the responses obtained aren't important or aren't taken into sufficient consideration, but rather that they are a necessary step along a compulsory journey.

It's also important to stress how the planning of the questionnaires and the approach used to disseminate them—and consequently the results to date—required months of work, suggestions, ideas, and amendments along the way. The reason for this is that, as the WG colleagues

Table 4.3 216 Full Questionnaires Received and Filled Out Completely, Split by Countries

COUNTRY	FULL QUESTIONNAIRES
Australia	8
Austria	2
Belgium	3
Brazil	4
Bulgaria	1
Canada	13
Caribbean	1
Chile	1
Denmark	2
England	15
France	1
Germany	5
Hungary	3
India	3
Ireland	1
Italy	31
Japan	1
Liberia	1
Lithuania	12
Malaysia	7
Netherlands	1
New Zealand	1
Norway	2
Peru	1
Philippines	1
Poland	1
Portugal	3
Romania	1
Russia	1
Singapore	1
South Africa	3
Spain	1
Sweden	1
Switzerland	1
Taiwan	1
Tajikistan	1
U.S.A.	80

returned from the events selected for Phase 2, which took place practically in parallel with Phase 1, different approaches were tried both for the questionnaires themselves and for their distribution method.

The points the questionnaires had in common were and remain the three modules defined by the WG:

- Module A (personal data)
- Module B (relational data)
- Module C (technical and criminological data)

Module A analyzes the personal data of the subject, such as gender, age, social status, family, school, and work environment.

Module B examines relational data, studying, for example, relations with the authorities, teachers or employers, friends and colleagues, or other hackers.

Module C analyzes purely technical data, as well as the crimes perpetrated, employing a criminological approach to interpret many of the answers.

Taken together, the three modules allow the HPP analysts to draw a picture covering background, social relations, character, criminal tendencies, and technical skills of the subjects who completed the questionnaire.

The WG chose unanimously to ensure that all answers in both questionnaires, for all the modules, could be given *anonymously*, even though under certain aspects this could be penalizing.

This was the right thing to do. In many surveys of a similar kind, one of the first questions often is "what is your nickname?" In these cases, it is obvious that whoever compiled the questions hadn't spent time to understand the world of hacking, where the *alias* could be considered practically "public domain," but for many types of personality it is such an intimate part of them that it isn't just handed over to strangers.

Having said this, the following sections will show in detail two of the main operative principles: the format of the questionnaires available to date and the distribution parameters defined and used by the HPP WG.

The Format

The first challenge was establishing the format of the questionnaires: How many and what kind? Very detailed? Similar to others already in use and available on the Net, but in the WG's opinion distant from the real hacker spirit, as they lack the details that show the intervie-wees that we are *really* trying to enter their world?

At this point, three questionnaires were prepared with a different number of questions. We started with a so-called "full" version to move on to a "medium" version and finally a "light" one. Even though it might appear strange, what distinguished each questionnaire was *the time necessary to fill it out.*

Many links and "interesting things" are exchanged daily over the Web, but they are not always examined in depth, especially when the subject matter or the author of the Web page isn't known. For this reason, the level of detail of the questions—implying the length of the questionnaire itself, and the time necessary to read it and fill it out—was the main item under discussion in the WG (remember that it is made up of hackers, criminologists, psychologists, and sociologists, all working together) until we reached an empirical solution (a first series of field tests), at the end of which we opted for *three* different types of questionnaires.

The essential point all members of the WG agreed upon had always been that of not losing sight of the need to identify the characteristics of the targets (interviewees), so it was necessary to calibrate both the distribution and the *version* of the questionnaire, which had to be more comprehensive if aimed at known members of the international hacker underground.

The psychologists kept pointing out the difficulties involved in a "blind" distribution, where completely unknown targets would fill out a presumably large number of questionnaires.

The contacts developed over years of associating with the world of hackers, either on the Net or during meetings, allowed us to circulate the full questionnaire in selected environments so we could keep our eye on the target. However, as it wasn't possible to limit our analysis only to the people we knew, it was necessary to "raise our sights," run-ning the risk of losing the reliability of the data obtained. The danger was that of getting back "distorted" questionnaires, filled out by ego-maniacs for example, which would have meant a great waste of time and risked compromising the first phases of the project.

As we were aware of these pitfalls, after a period of field-testing, the WG decided to use *two questionnaires*. The first was still the full version, though fine-tuned and with added improvements thanks to suggestions and comments received. Those who filled this version out were familiar with the project and/or knew the people who gave them the link to the project itself.

We wanted to identify and draw the attention of subjects we knew would read our questions carefully, responding with criticisms and suggestions; we expected at all events true and constructive responses, possibly also because of the time necessary to fill them out given the length of this version.

The second version was the result of a careful selection of the more significant questions from the three modules, so the questionnaire could be filled out in a reasonable amount of time by subjects who had never heard of HPP but would be sufficient to give us true and reliable answers. This would also weed out the category of intermediate responders, the "not really reliable, but not unreliable either" ones. In other words, our objective in this case was to balance our initial approach, giving a bit more credit to hackers who would come across the Web site of the project or of one of our research partners.

After field testing, we accepted the fact that this kind of questionnaire would be filled out in most cases by people who *possibly* (but not *necessarily*) would like to help the HPP in earnest, even though they had reached our mirror sites* in totally different ways, coming from widely different geographical areas, ages, and social and economic contexts. This will be shown in the section dealing with the distribution of the two versions of the questionnaire and in the following two chapters, which cover the analysis of the questionnaires received over the last three years.

Distribution

Given all this, distribution was a critical factor for our research project—far more than what we expected at the beginning. All our

---

* *Mirror sites* are mirror images of the contents of an entire site. Mirrors are used to increase the traffic speed of a site, as they let users access a closer server. In the case of HPP, we decided to work (also) through mirror sites thanks to local research partners, such as HITB, Web-Hack.ru, and so forth, so as to have a larger distribution of the questionnaires, as the visitors are attracted by the community hosting the mirror.

efforts and work spent in setting the questionnaires up could be wasted by even a single mistake in deciding how to distribute them.

Once again, our activities during Phase 2 proved to be extremely important; they allowed us to present the project to the various communities that make up the underground in different countries* and also allowed a sort of "assessment" (to borrow a term from the information security sector), a critical evaluation on the field thanks to the contacts of the WG members.

We decided to choose and use three different methods for disseminating the questionnaire, with one basic rule: the full questionnaire must not be publicly available, but sent out only after verifying the reliability of the subject, creating a more direct relationship and on the whole letting us know in advance to which category the subject should more or less belong.

The three methods for distributing the questionnaire the WG defined were the following and are used according to the subject analyzed:

- Subjects directly or indirectly known: the restricted link with the full questionnaire is sent or handed over directly (online if, for instance, members of a mirror site or if, after a series of checks by the WG, they show they are seriously interested in supporting or contributing to HPP).
- Subjects *probably* interested in the project, given the careful selection of channels for distributing and making known the HPP questionnaire. In this case, the light version is used, which can be found online at the project's official Web site.†
- Subjects of any kind from whom we don't expect any skills or specific experience in the hacking world, or who could even distort or slow down the processing of some results causing a sort of "background noise." In these cases too, we chose the light questionnaire.

It's important to stress how, in the first case, the QoQ (*Quality of Questionnaires*, the level of quality and reliability of the answers expected) is certainly high.

---

* That's why the questionnaires have been translated in to the following languages: English, Italian, French, Greek, Romanian, Russian, and Albanian.
† http://hpp.recursiva.org/.

In the second case, the expected QoQ is medium, but actually (from first experiments through partners in the press, first online and later paper-based) the result was medium-low. Probably the readers of the *wannabee* press, which aim at introducing their readers to hacking, aren't ready yet to take a test of this type seriously or aren't willing to open up so much for something they don't know.

Incredibly, the Internet grapevine produced unexpected results in the third case: nearly completed light questionnaires, with very few "false positives/negatives." In other words, there was a great show of respect by the "standard" underground community that isn't representative of the elite we are aiming for.

First-Level Analysis

The last section of this chapter aims to offer a first overview of the data received during these three years, which will be commented on further in the next chapters. Here we will consider some basic data necessary to begin building a first idea of the personalities studied up to now, such as geographical origin, and some statistics for specific questions based on fixed answers.

Provenance of the Questionnaires

The geographic provenance of the questionnaires is one of the first points that surprised the WG. At first, we expected contributions exclusively from the U.S.A., but results obtained showed how the gossip surrounding HPP is very widely spread throughout the international underground. Therefore, we got responses from hackers residing in a wide range of countries and could build a *truly* global view.

We will recap the countries from which our interviewees responded and invite the reader to consider this element. We'd also like to point out how the geographic origin of the questionnaires strongly depends on two factors connected to HPP Phase 2.

First of all, we noticed how, when the WG took part in local events in a specific country, the direct consequence was great interest in the research project itself, attention on the part of the local media, and therefore a high number of hits on the HPP website and on the questionnaires themselves. Secondly, and just as important, is the role played by *mirror partners;* that is, associations and communities who agree to host a local language version of the HPP main Web site. At the time of this writing, many mirror partners still have to be activated, so the project is "unknown" in that specific country.

Finally, we need to point out how, for the statistics in this section and the sections that follow, the WG based itself only on the full questionnaires, which were not always entirely* filled out but were nevertheless representative and reliable as far as the information contained is concerned. Given that the survey (compiling and sending out the questionnaires) and the processing of data collected are still ongoing, we think we should mention that, even though the numbers and percentages shown can't be considered definitive, they are still representative of the world we are investigating: the hacker underground.

Basic Statistics

Once we established the geographic provenance of the subjects, the next step was to ask ourselves certain basic questions so as to set down the first statistics. The main questions are self-evident but essential if we want to understand our subjects. We therefore asked ourselves the following initial questions:

- What is the gender of the subjects?
- What is their age?
- At what age did they start hacking?
- How many still hack today?
- How many are hackers and how many phreakers?
- How many have never tried carding?
- What are their technical skills?
- What is their socioeconomic status?
- Do they live in large cities or small towns?
- What qualifications do they have?

---

* The percentages shown here do not consider null or invalid answers, so the sample population of interviewees varies according to the individual question. To date, we have received and processed more than 576 questionnaires from all over the world, out of 700, of which 216 were full questionnaires, completed and valid in all their parts by March 31, 2008.

The first question obviously specifies the gender of the subjects but is also necessary to explode one of the many false myths about the hacking world: that there are no females. In reality, at the moment of writing, 6% of the total responses received from this question (567) came from 32 girls and women who operate daily on the underground scene and are involved with hacking, while 94% (535 individuals) are males.

The second question is very significant, as it allowed us to correlate age with the various subjects. Here too, results were contrary to what is usually expected. Out of 553 questionnaires chosen for this verification, 7% were in the 35–40 (38 answers) and 31–34 (37 replies) age groups, but only 3% are in the 41–45 age group (16 answers).

When we looked at young people, we were frankly surprised at finding 31% in the 10–20 age group (170 individuals); probably a result of the Internet boom that has made exploits and attack tools readily available on the Internet.

Furthermore, if 30% (168 persons) are between 21 and 25 years of age, and 19% (107) are not over 30, that still leaves 16 subjects over age 45 (3%, 16 replies).

Finally, the average age is 27 for females and 25 for males.

The third element is also significant: at what age did they start hacking? This is important, as it shows various aspects such as generation group, is consequently a useful step to verify declared age, and establishes the actual age range when hacking gripped the various generations of hackers.

To do this, we paid a lot of attention to the first result: the fact that 61% of subjects started hacking between the ages of 10 and 15, while 32% started between ages 16 and 20. Only 5% started between 21 and 25, which shows that hacking is usually taken up at an early age, and after age 20 there are very few cases of "first time" hackers. Only 2% declared they started between age 26 and 30, and 1% started after 40 (none declared to have started between 31 and 40).

The results obtained from the fifth question—how many practice or have practiced either hacking or phreaking—were just as significant. On a total of 229 questionnaires, 34% (78 replies) do both, and even though 66% of interviewees (150) focused on hacking and only 0% on phreaking, this mustn't be misleading; it simply indicates that only one of our interviewees to date *exclusively* practices phreaking, not how many *also* do phreaking. The responses seem true and realistic, as we don't see how someone can be a professional phreaker without an ongoing hacking background.

The next question, on carding (234 valid replies), opens up a first fundamental point: whether the subjects at any point of their lives—consciously, we would add—undertake any actions contrary to the original purity of hacking and closer to the actual criminal world. It was interesting to note how, in this case, 87% (203) responders answered "no," leaving a total of only 31 (13%) defrauding credit card users.

The seventh and eigth questions require a self-evaluation and self-criticism: a straight request to estimate technical skills and socioeconomic status. In the first case (273 valid answers), 22% (61 interviewees) described themselves as expert, exactly like the other 22% (61 replies) who claimed high technical skills, 35% (95) average, and 21% (56) low.

In the second case (547 replies), most of the interviewees declared an upper-middle socioeconomic status (44%, 239) compared with 37% (205) who declared lower-middle status. At the two extremes, 11% (59) declared low status and 8% (44) high.

The ninth question (551 replies collected) serves to place the subjects within a large or small urban context, deliberately excluding "middle-sized" towns, as the research carried out showed this to be only a very small percentage. In this case, 45% of subjects (247) declared they lived in large towns and cities, 34% (189 answers) in small towns, and the remaining 21% (115) in very small towns and villages. This result is very interesting, as it shows how the spreading of information and communications technology (ICT) can give rise to an interest in hacking in a number of people who a few years ago would have found it difficult to access the telecommunications systems and the necessary equipment.

Finally, the tenth question covers the last element the WG required to start the first evaluations. The aim of the tenth question (502 total answers) was not just to establish whether they had some sort of formal school diploma or certificate, but rather to show how hacking does not require a standard education and to test our theory that the technical skills of hackers are not tied to a school background and their level of general (or specialized) knowledge. The results showed a wide range of educational backgrounds, revealing that most hackers (37%, 186) were high school graduates, 25% (128) had received vocational training certificates, while 10% (52) had postgraduate degrees (7%, 37) of the interviewees had standard university degrees, 16% (80) had secondary school diplomas, while 4% (19) had elementary school certificates.

Second-Level Analysis

After getting the results for the first set of questions, the WG started analyzing them more in depth. To do this, the answers obtained from different questions were compared and cross-referenced to try to find further nuances.

These are the questions we first examined:

- What is the level of education of the subjects who continue to hack?
- Are they religious?
- What is their relationship with the authorities?
- What type of personalities do they have?
- What motivates them?
- Do they believe in the *hacker ethics*?

An analysis of the answers given to the first question is linked to a certain extent with the last question in the basic statistics (type of qualifications held, regardless of whether the subjects still do hacking or not), with one exception. But let's proceed in the right order.

In this case, 34% of interviewees (44) declared they had secondary school diplomas, and 29% (37) diplomas from vocational schools, while 19% (24) had a secondary school diploma, 7% (9) had completed postgraduate studies, only 4% (5) had stopped at primary school level, and 7% (9) had a university degree, for a total of 128 questionnaires. The exception that struck us is the high drop in the number of university graduates who keep on hacking.

The second question (544 answers collected) was designed to show how professing a religion or being a declared atheist is rarely a problem in the hacker scene. To prove this statement, we found that 61% of interviewees (332) declare they are not religious; however, 39% (212) declare they belong to a religious faith. These two widely different realities coexist quite happily in the underground.

As to the third question (323 replies), the WG "felt obliged" to check a now official and recognized cliché, according to which the hacker world doesn't see eye to eye with law enforcement agencies. We asked them to define their view of the authorities, choosing between "oppressive" and "reassuring," with percentages of respectively 62% (201 answers) and 38% (122).

The next question (1216 answers) was aimed at understanding how the subjects saw themselves, so we asked them to describe their personalities. The most commonly used adjective, with 17% of responses (213), was "inquisitive." Therefore, curiosity is one of the main aspects of a hacker's personality—the same as cheerfulness, at 10% (126).

Two further mutually exclusive adjectives follow with a same rating of 9%: "lazy" (120 replies) and "committed" (113). Of course, if a person is "lazy," it becomes difficult to be considered "committed" at the same time. These are therefore two extremes of the various personalities that exist on the hacker scene, just like being cheerful, or introverted and/or dissatisfied. We have some who blithely describe themselves as "healthy" (7%, 96), but also "introverted" (6%, 82), "dissatisfied" (6%, 74), "well balanced" (6%, 72), or "paranoid" (5%, 65).

It's said that paranoia is a hacker virtue, but of course only when applied to ICT security. In reality, it is actually quite common in the hacker community, as is depression, as evidenced by cases published in some hacker biographies.

Going on with the definitions hackers give of themselves, we have some defining themselves as "anxious" (4%, 55 replies), "manipulative" (55%—which leads us back to one of the talents and traits of social engineers), "naïve" (52), "depressive" (51), and "extrovert" (46), while 3% consider themselves "satisfied" (40) and, lastly, 2% consider themselves "ruthless" (28).

The second-to-last question (716 answers collected) tries to understand motivations for hacking. This is a clear, direct question that simply asks, "What are your reasons for hacking?"

The highest percentage (30%, 213 interviewees) claims inquisitiveness as a reason; the curiosity that leads to exploring an information system, telecommunications, and the most intimate secrets of a society.

In second place, we found a rather significant answer, which agrees with some of the percentages found in the previous answer: 14% (99) answered that they do hacking for the good of the final users, searching for weaknesses in information systems, software, and tele-communication networks.

A further 13% (96) answered "other," which covers reasons for hacking that often have no justification or, more simply, reasons that they don't want to reveal.

Another 12% of responders (86) do hacking because "offline life is so boring," whereas 9% (66) are hacking and phreaking dependent or (another 9%, 64) want to gain power over government agencies, law enforcement agencies, and so on.

A total of 47 interviewees (7%) practice hacking to gain recognition and respect from their group in the hacker underground in general, while 6% (45) do it to increase their level in the internal hierarchy of the hacker group to which they belong.

The last question (225 replies) adds sharing the *hacker ethics*. As we saw in the previous chapter, the *hacker ethics* doesn't just mean "do not steal" (in other words, don't use your hacker skills for criminal ends), but also sharing experiences and know-how, free software, a love for science and broadmindedness, and a veritable way of life. It therefore isn't surprising that 71% (159) answered "yes," while 29% (66) answered no, just as we aren't surprised that 351 subjects—out of 576 questionnaires in this case—deliberately didn't answer this question. This may be because they are more diffident, but more probably is because they profess the grey-hat philosophy that refuses labels or because they want to avoid, at all costs, having to recognize themselves in terms of moral values they don't claim as their own.

Time Spent Hacking

We then analyzed a few short questions about "hacking time:"

- How much time do you spend hacking?
- Which are the best times?
- Has your hacking time increased or decreased over the years?
- If you were inactive for a lengthy period, did you experience withdrawal symptoms?

The intention was to understand how subjects see time in relation to their hacking activity. Here too, existing myths and clichés describe subjects hacking at night, for long stretches of time, never stopping, and often under the influence of drugs. Let's have a look at how our volunteers responded.

On a total of 223 valid questionnaires for the first question, 31% (70 interviewees) "only" hack between 1 and 3 hours a day, 30% (68) between 4 and 6, 21% (46) for more than 12 hours a day, and 14% (31) from 7 to 10 hours. This explodes the myth of hackers who hack into systems for hours on end during mentally and physically grueling sessions (4%, 8 replies, between 10 and 12 hours a day).

The second question (221 replies) aimed to determine whether the night hours are considered the best to operate in, confirming or denying the cliché that shows hackers as night owls. Sixty-nine percent (153) did answer that nighttime is the best time for hacking, followed by early evening and evening (17%, 38). Nine percent (19) hack in the afternoon, which makes us think of teenagers, or at least students, just as the 5% (11) who preferred the morning could, and should, lead us to think of people who are working but at the same time are hacking: insiders or simply system administrators who like to port scan.*

The third question (225 answers) looked at whether there were variations in time spent over the years. Forty percent (89) said that their hacking time has remained unchanged, while 33% (75) indicated that it has decreased. This illustrates why cases where hacking doesn't eventually reach a semipermanent halt are few and far between when hacking time was significant and continued for a period of over 10 years (compared with the crazy time schedule of their younger days). On the other hand, 28% (61) actually answered that it has increased.

The last question (221 replies) of this section looked to establish whether the subjects felt they were to some extent victims of hacking addiction. Apparently, hacking addiction isn't as common as was loudly proclaimed a few years ago, as 47% (103 interviewees) answered, "no, never," 40% (88) "rarely," and 14% (30) "yes, always."

---

* A port scan is a series of messages sent by someone attempting to break into a computer to learn which computer network services, each associated with a known port number, the computer provides. Port scanning gives the assailant an idea where to probe for weaknesses. Essentially, a port scan consists of sending a message to each port, one at a time. The kind of response received indicates whether the port is used and can therefore be probed for weaknesses.

Legal Aspects

In this section, we tried to examine the relationships between the subjects and their countries' legislation on computer crimes. The objective was to understand and interpret some of the main reasons given by the attackers, verifying the deterrent effect of the law, of criminal convictions, and of technical difficulties met on the attacked systems.

- Are hacking and phreaking crimes in your country?
- Do you think you are damaging anyone with your hacking?
- What offenses have you committed with a computer?
- Have you ever been arrested/sentenced for computer crimes?
- Have you ever feared arrest and sentencing for having committed a computer crime?
- If no, or no longer, why?
- Did technical difficulties you met while violating a system have a deterrent effect on you, or did you feel stimulated?
- If you stopped hacking/phreaking, did you continue to be involved in it?
- Did you ever stop hacking and then take it up again after some time?

The first question (224 replies) is necessary to establish the illegality of an action; 81% (182) answered affirmatively, while in 19% (42) of cases, hacking isn't an offense in the country of residence of the subject.

Of course, this makes a difference to various aspects of hacking—first and foremost the *modus operandi*—but leads also to a completely different mental approach compared with the standards in so-called industrialized countries where hacking and phreaking are usually considered offenses.

Those who are operating in countries where these activities are illegal will follow a series of precautions to avoid leaving any traces on the target system or to erase them.

The answers to the second question (219) are significant in that 20% of responders (44) are aware that they are damaging someone or something with their activities, but 80% (175) don't think so.

The third question (586) goes into more detail, asking the subjects which offenses they have committed, with a choice among:

- Unauthorized access to systems and services (31%, 183 answers).
- Unauthorized reproduction of copyrighted programs (25%, 147 answers).
- Damaging and modifying data or programs (15%, 88 answers).
- Computer fraud (10%, 58 answers).
- Forgery (10%, 58 answers).
- Other (9%, 52 answers).

At this point, it became necessary to understand whether the various subjects had already had problems with the law for computer crimes—in other words, whether they had ever been caught for the offenses mentioned. Ninety percent (201) declared they had never been arrested, while 10% had (22 replies), for a total of 223 answers. This is a very high percentage of negative answers, which shows that hacking and fraud cases we hear about—not necessarily due to the victim's* resorting to the law, we might add—are incredibly few.

Next we had to find out whether the fear of arrest ("scared to be busted,"† which characterized the early 1990s in the U.S.A., Europe, and Australia) has any influence on hacking activities and, if so, why. Fifty-six percent of subjects (95) answered that they had never seriously considered the possibility, against 44% of affirmative answers (74), out of 218 replies.

The ones who neither fear arrest nor being charged give the following reasons:

- Inadequacy of investigators (36%, 85 answers).
- Precautions and technical devices employed (35%, 83 answers).
- Other (29%, 67 answers).

---

* We need to point out that victims (especially corporations, banks, and financial companies) don't like to report these events to law enforcement authorities for fear of damaging their image and losing customers. On the other hand, as an example, the customers will rarely find out that their credit card number has been stolen and used without their knowledge.

† This term became fashionable in the U.S.A. in the early 1990s when there were various hacker crackdowns.

Most subjects interviewed are patronizing toward investigators, believing the hacker cliché that often leads them to expose themselves (and run the risk of being identified) just to make fun of those who should arrest them. Many rely on their technical skills, believing their self-image of being smarter and more intelligent than everyone else.

At this point, we decided to find out whether the technical difficulties a hacker meets when violating a system are a deterrent or, rather, a goad toward success.

Respecting in full the definition of "hacker," 73% (111 interviewees) answered that they are stimulated by technical difficulties, and only 27% (42) get discouraged. It's a bit like saying that the more difficult the alarm system, the more the "Beagle Boys" feel the urge to disconnect it—only the Disney characters were regularly caught whereas, in our case, as we saw earlier, the opposite seems to happen.

The reason for the last two questions was to let us better understand certain aspects of dropping out of hacking (or phreaking), whether it is true that you "fall for it" again or remain somehow involved, possibly acting openly by moving into information security.

At least 129 subjects (79%), after stopping, did still dabble in it, against 33 negative responses (21%); conversely, 55% (106) against 45% (88) of cases stopped hacking or phreaking only to start up again after a break.

Here too, it seems quite clear that the laws on computer crime are unsuccessful as deterrents. The problem is, what is the right solution?

Personality

We even tried to gauge the personality of the subjects interviewed, to understand if and how hacking can influence the psychophysical conditions of its practitioners.

- Do subjects have more than one nickname?
- Do the ones who have more than one nickname also have a "split personality?"
- Are they substance abusers (alcohol and/or drugs)?

- Is there any connection between having divorced parents and possible substance abuse?
- What is their psychophysical condition?
- How many have psychophysical problems caused by hacking?

In the "normal" world, the presence of more than one nickname, apart from being the prerogative of people with multiple personalities, can also be a symptom of youth or a search for outside approval. In the world of hacking, it is practically normal to have more than one alias in the course of one's "digital identity," usually until a definitive one that fits is found, after which it becomes the only identifier.

Indeed, 133 subjects (56%) gave an affirmative answer, against 103 interviewees (44%) who declare they use only one nickname. But the answer to the next question, openly asking whether in the case of more than one nickname being used they *also* felt they had more than one personality, was a surprise, too: 65% (67) gave an affirmative answer, against 35% (36) who were of a different opinion, validating (in a sort of severe self-criticism) the equation "double nickname = double personality." However, this must be understood in the right way: hackers have always taken on *at least* one other personality during their online life, whether or not a second nickname is used for hacking purposes.

The third question (543 valid replies collected) looks at substance abuse (alcohol and/or drugs). Exploding yet another myth about the hacking world, 47% (232) declare they do not abuse these substances, 22% (108) say that they drink excessively. The same percentage admits to drug abuse (108) and 10% to both (50).

We must also point out that, of 129 answers, for 47% of subjects (61) the use of drugs and alcohol can be correlated with being part of a family where the parents are divorced and living in a large city. A total of 49 interviewees (38%) have in common alcohol, separated parents, and living in large cities. Only 11 hackers (9%) with separated parents who come from small towns are drug abusers, and 8 (6%) are alcohol abusers.

If we move on to psychophysical conditions, on 276 answers, 34% (94) declare they are insomniacs, 27% (74) suffer from anxiety, 20% (55) are paranoiac, 13% (37) have panic attacks, and 6% (16) hallucinate.

Moreover, 34% of insomniacs (28) believe their condition is caused by hacking, while the percentage for paranoia is 28% (23), anxiety 18% (15), and 10% for hallucinations (8) and panic attacks (8), on 82 subjects. Hacking therefore might influence psychophysical conditions (and for some pathologies strongly), but it is not necessarily so.

Relationships with the Outside World

With this last set of questions, we tried to analyze hackers' relationships with the outside world:

- How many people in the subjects' circle of acquaintance are aware of the hacking activities?
- How many operate on their own and how many in a group?
- Have the subjects ever met the other members of the group in "real life?"
- Where do the group members live?
- How do they communicate with each other?
- How many "sign" their attacks?
- How many inform the SysAdmin after the intrusion?
- How many inform other members of the underground *before* informing the SysAdmin?

The first question is very important, as it allows us to connect the subject with a circle of people they trust.

First of all, we isolated the "traditional" category (parents) from the possible answers, and we learned that in 68% of cases (610), parents are not aware of their children's activities, against 32% who are (290). We then selected the following categories, for each of which we have added the various percentages and totals for the answers (1046):

- Friends (27%, 281 answers).
- Members of the underground (21%, 216 answers).
- Schoolmates (13%, 140 answers).
- Partners (11%, 116 answers).
- Colleagues (10%, 109 answers).
- Teachers (8%, 79 answers).

- Employers (7%, 71 answers).
- Others (3%, 34 answers).

The results obtained didn't particularly surprise us, apart from the 8% for teachers and the 7% for employers (quite alarming to a certain extent, given the recent big scandal at Telecom Italia's security division*).

The second question (256 answers collected) seeks to draw a minimal profile of the subject, looking at whether he operates alone or in a group. Fifty-five percent (141) operate exclusively on their own, but 38% (98) both alone *and* in a group, and only 7% (17) only in a group.

At this point, we asked whether members belonging to the *same* group of hackers had ever met in real life. Out of 182 replies, 37% (67) said they had met all the members of their group (which leads us to think of either small groups or large dedicated hacker meetings), while 34% (61) said they had met only some, and 30% (54)—quite a high percentage—claimed to have never met any of the other members of their group.

This is compared with 54% (97) who declare they neither live in the same city or country as their hacking partners, 35% (63) who live in the same country, and 11% (20) in the same city, out of 180 subjects.

At this point, we wanted to know which were the communication methods of choice within the group to enable us to establish the level of technical skills and of paranoia present (and the various devices used to avoid discovery and arrest). Here are the choices offered and the percentages/totals for the answers:

- Encrypted chat/IRC (66%).
- "Closed," private mailing lists (7%).
- Plain text chat/IRC (7%).
- IRC meetings (7%).
- Other (7%).
- Encrypted e-mails (2%).
- Plain text e-mails (2%).
- Public mailing lists (1%).

---

* Telecom Italia scandal, also known as "The Telecom Italia Watergate," is a history of espionage, secrecy, and corruption, started back in 2003, when the Telecom Italia Tiger Team seemed to launch IT attacks on competitors and private companies. The full explanation is available at http://www.slate.com/id/2146618/.

From the most popular answer, we can deduce how the use of IRC (Internet relay chat) clients and servers with message encryption facilities—both public and private—has become the norm in the hacker community. We also noted how closed, private mailing lists, usually by invitation only and very exclusive, are becoming more and more common, even though old habits persist: IRC (or other kinds) chats in plain text (without text encryption), in real life (IRL) meetings, and an unspecified "other."

The use of encrypted and plain text e-mails is more ore less equal, while fewer hackers write on public mailing lists.

If we move on to signing computer raids, this seems more typical of new-generation hackers and script-kiddies. By asking our subjects whether they usually sign or signed their exploits, it was possible to understand to what age group our volunteers belong.

The 82% of negative answers (204), against a 18% of positive ones (46), lead us to think that, as far as these first years of our project are concerned, we are dealing with a group of hackers who have some years of experience behind them.

The answers to the next question are also a sign, under different aspects, of personal maturity as well as an approach to respectful hacking of a certain kind: 149 subjects (59%) warn the SysAdmin after having found a breach (or, sometimes, after having completed a full attack, without obviously causing any intentional and direct damage), against 104 interviewees (41%) who prefer to let it ride.

The last question (231 answers provided) was intentionally provocative: 53% of the answers (122), "No, I never share the information," frankly surprised us, as did the 32% (75) who do inform the other members of their group, but only after having warned the poor (and lucky) SysAdmin. There are still 15% (34) who unfortunately prefer to share their discoveries, and possible abuses, with other hackers, and only in the best of cases later inform the SysAdmin responsible for the violated system.

5

WHO ARE HACKERS? PART 1

We've been spoon-fed baby food at school when we hungered for steak… the bits of meat that you did let slip through were pre-chewed and tasteless.

The next two chapters are the heart of this book. Here we try to find an answer to the question that gave rise to the HPP research project in 2004: who are hackers? In the pages that follow, we'll show you the results of 2 years of reading, analysis, comparisons, and often "confrontations" where the main arguments focus on real-life experience and the stories of the hackers we studied and observed in our attempt to *understand*.

What Are We Trying to Understand?

This point begs the question, "What we are trying to understand?" Using the HPP questionnaires as a starting point, we decided to analyze different aspects of the hacking world and the psychology of our interviewees.

For the purpose of this study, we started from the similarities and the differences identified through reading the vast bibliography available on the subject, plus what was found through the questionnaires filled out by hackers from different countries such as Italy, Spain, Germany, France, Romania, Russia, the United Kingdom, Malaysia, Australia, Japan, U.S.A., Canada, and Brazil.

Specific texts on the subject* have allowed us to identify some constants in this phenomenon, which, taken together and cross-checked with data obtained from the questionnaires and from different types

---

* For an exhaustive view, look at the Bibliography.

of attack, provide the basis to start tracing a general profile of the authors of these attacks.[*]

Criminal profiling allows us to reconstruct the psychological traits and define the criminal behavior of these subjects starting from elements, concepts, and known general descriptions in order to arrive at an identification of the profile of a specific individual.

As far as our interests are concerned, though, what are lacking are predefined examples. This is a practically unexplored field. For this reason, we have decided to take the opposite approach to the traditional one: we started from a study of individual hacking cases and profiles and, with the help of selected texts, we proceeded to set down various models so that we obtained a series of general profiles that could be applied to a specific type of hacker.

From these general models and theories, it will be possible to develop the single criminal types of behavior, just as in the usual use of criminal profiling. The data obtained through reading the texts will be cross-referenced with what is obtained from the questionnaire and from an examination of the crime scene (honey-net) to obtain various hacker profiles.

As already mentioned, we decided to group the information obtained into three categories on the basis of the HPP questionnaire model, which to date has been applied in three continents (Europe, Asia, and America):

- Personal data
- Relational data
- Technical and criminological data

In the first case, the idea was that of obtaining a sort of snapshot of the personal situation of each individual: information such as age, gender, country of origin and city of residence, physical appearance, personality, psychophysical conditions, use of mood-altering substances (drugs and alcohol), social and family background, education, and last but not least, area of professional activity. This information was essential to "penetrate"

---

[*] The profiles traced in this chapter and the next one were developed by Stefania Ducci, at present employed at UNICRI (United Nations Interregional Crime and Justice Research Institute).

a world that wasn't ours, trying to show the conflicts, dependencies, and problems present in the personal sphere of each subject.

As for the second case, relational data, the focus of our investigation shifted slightly to look in depth at the relationships the single subjects had with the outside world: parents, teachers, and employers, and conflicts with the authorities until we could cover the entire social sphere of the subjects, from friends to schoolmates, colleagues at work, personal relations (friends, partners), and with other members of the underground.

Finally, the third case analyzes the more interesting aspects more closely tied to the hacking world from a purely technical point of view: from nickname use to the age at which hacking is approached for the first time; the possible presence of a *mentor* to single technical specializations; their approach to hacking, phreaking, and carding; the various communications networks (and technologies) against which attacks are brought to bear and the techniques employed; the use of a signature at the end of actions or raids and attack procedures; and actions and reactions to a successful attack. And, of course, the motivations for an attack or for crossing the border between legality and illegality; from simple curiosity to pure entertainment; covering defending freedom of communication and dissemination of knowledge; sharing access and services; the complex questions of privacy; fighting the *establishment* or increasing global security; the inevitable need to defy the authorities; a banal spirit of adventure; the wish for notoriety; or, yet again, boredom, anger, and—why not—the choice of a profession.

The analysis concludes with some of the most topical points we observed: hacking as a power trip (psychological and practical), "ethics," hacking addiction, and, first and foremost, the perception of the illegality of one's actions and the deterrent effect of existing laws on computer crimes.

What you will read in the pages that follow is the result of processing the data obtained through the cross-referencing of all we had expected and actually found in the field, filled out with anecdotes, personal comments, real-life experiences, events that really happened, and characters that have been part of this world for most of their lives.

Appendix A shows the questionnaire on which our research is based. Consulting it will make our starting point clearer, and also illuminate the cross-analysis we carried out between the different answers obtained and existing literature and case studies available to the public.

We believe that what follows is a unique snapshot of a world that has still not been fully explored and is in continuous and systematic evolution. We hope the next pages can give the reader a new perception of this world, which is often painted as "ultratechnical," but which is made up of people—human beings who live their day-to-day life just like everyone else, facing the problems, challenges, doubts, and questions that beset us all.

Without any further ado, it is time now to go into the heart of the matter. In this chapter, we will deal with the information that can be labeled "personal data" and "relational data."

A final note: we don't follow the structure of the questionnaire strictly. In order to avoid being excessively rigid, and to be more clear and exhaustive, we have preferred to group and discuss together blocks of information of a similar nature, which are not necessarily derived from contiguous points of the questionnaire.

Gender and Age Group

The collective view of the hacker world populates it exclusively with males, and for a long time that was the case. After the 1990s, however, the presence of women started to progressively increase and become more and more relevant. The watershed between a male-dominated environment and one in which females are continuously on the increase, maybe even overtaking males, was the year 2001.

In July of that year, Anna Moore (alias "Starla Pureheart")* was the first woman to win the "CyberEthical Surfivor" title during the annual DefCon hacking convention, which is held in Las Vegas, NV. From that moment on, she became the lodestone for female hackers who are approaching this world and a symbol of sophistication and ethics.

From practically no women at all in the 1990–2000 decade, there has been an exponential increase in female presence, which is still continuing. However, a distinction must be made between female hackers

---

* A short interview with Anna Moore is available on YouTube at: http://www.you tube.com/watch?v=sC369CQmrQs

(called *hackse*) and other women who know how to use a computer well and perhaps manage a BBS,* but who don't commit these acts.

As to age, there are no limitations, even though most hackers belong to the *average teenager* age group—basically adolescents. In the last few years, though, the average hacker age has increased, as those who started out 5 or 10 years ago are still part of this world, even though they are now closer to 30 to 35 years of age.

Background and Place of Residence

There are hackers of all nationalities and ethnic groups. In this case, hacking really represents the opposite of the idea of a *digital divide:* from Africa to the Caribbean, and Asia to Russia, hackers come from any country (and social class), whether IT is widespread or not in that area of the world. Most live in large urban areas or at least quite close to one, although a minority of them live in towns far from large cities.

This shows one of the distinctive aspects of hacking: while it breaks down the digital divide barrier, it still tends to be a markedly metropolitan phenomenon. It could therefore be that the possibility of physically contacting and competing with other people, regardless of the Net, might have some influence on the development of new hackers.

How Hackers View Themselves

After collecting the essential data, we asked our interviewees to give a physical description of themselves as if to someone who didn't know them at all.

The aim of this question was to understand whether the traditional image of hackers was true. On the basis of our results, we can say that they are no different from others of their age group, and the cliché that they are all skinny, frail, and wearing thick-lensed spectacles no longer stands. Many are actually very athletic and good-looking. They usually dress casually (a black leather jacket is common), even though they don't have a specific dress code.

---

* Bulletin board systems (BBSs) are electronic bulletins that contain download areas where you can download suggestions and software (games, cracking tools, etc.) and find chats and discussion forums.

A description of their personality, of their *true essence* is rather more complex.

The focal point of this question is the character traits of a person; we wanted to find out whether our interviewees are shy or self-confident, naïve or crafty, sociable or loners, etc.

There are many different types of personality present in the hacker community. Usually, hackers are extremely creative, brilliant people, sharp and bold, rebels and dreamers. Sometimes they can feel frustrated. They are people who want to show the world they are lively and intelligent, capable of taking up any challenge. On the whole, they are unimpressed by what they are capable of doing with a computer.

In their day-to-day lives (when not among other hackers and outside of their hacking activities), some of the analyzed hackers show traits that denote shyness (but also naiveté and sometimes even misanthropic tendencies), only to take on a completely different personality when in their "natural element," cyberspace.

In confirmation of this fact, we found that many hackers declare that they find it very easy to relate to other people electronically (through chats, discussion forums, etc.), whereas they don't feel fully at ease in a one-on-one situation. This can be explained by the fact that the electronic medium is a barrier that hides and *protects* the subject, who therefore feels less vulnerable and so becomes more willing to socialize more and with greater facility.

For instance, some say that they are shy with girls, that they aren't capable of looking inside themselves and expressing their feelings, and that they don't even know how to ask a girl for a date. They have very few friends, and the few that they do have were met through *chats*. Often they have never met them in person or heard their voices.

Here is one example to illustrate this concept better. Let's take the case of Mark Abene (alias "Phiber Optik") from the notorious "MOD" *cybergang*. He says he feels insecure and awkward in his daily life, especially with girls, but when he's in his room hacking away on his computer, he feels like a different person; he becomes the most brilliant, "coolest" guy of the whole underground world. In other words, when he's not hacking or not at his computer (the tool that allows him to have the whole world at his fingertips), he's like any other adolescent, but he really stands out from the crowd when he can use his intuitiveness to understand how the most complex programs and commands work.

A word of warning though: this doesn't mean that we are dealing with people with personality disorders or dual personalities. Quite simply, they only feel comfortable in cyberspace, so their only problem is with relating. But this is not typical of hackers only, as it is a common trait in adolescents in general.

Family Background

When attempting to describe the family background of hackers, we tried to discover not only how many members there are but also the family atmosphere—in other words, the environment in which they live.

Many hackers come from deprived and problem families. A lot have parents who are either constantly on their backs or totally absent; they might be deceased (through accidents or suicide), separated or divorced, or adoptive, but they can also have mental or behavioral problems.

Some have conflicting relations with their parents, while in other cases they might not have seen one of them for a long time. In this case, it is usually the father, and that explains why, often, the male parent is seen as an authoritarian figure to be opposed or with whom it is impossible to establish a relationship. Sometimes parents are alcoholics and show violent behavior, and in these cases it is too often the father. This has led to some subjects having problems growing up, both during infancy and adolescence.

Some have experienced what it means to be abandoned by a loved one, and consequently in adulthood they will avoid deep relationships with other people out of a fear of future loss.

Some hackers were unwanted children, so they didn't receive much attention and care. In other cases, problems are caused by economics: some families live in poverty and are forced to move from one city to the other (usually in the U.S.A., given the greater mobility of labor than in Europe).

Often, the family life of hackers who live in these conditions is colored by fear and insecurity, with the addition of parents who are in conflict with each other. These hackers are typically loners who are left aside by their schoolmates and who have introverted and antisocial personalities. They don't have many friends, and the few they do have are other hackers whom they have often never met in person and whose real identity they don't know. They don't feel accepted by their peers and feel everyone has abandoned them, and often their school-work suffers because of their isolation.

They'd much rather deal with computers, as computers are uncritical and don't discriminate on the basis of class or color of skin. Computers are viewed as an *escape route,* tools that allow them to access virtual worlds they can escape to from a life without any fulfillment. When they become part of the underground community, they feel they *belong* for the first time in their lives.

Usually they are individuals who haven't been nurtured during their development. They have grown up alone, without any guidance or reference points. They have withdrawn to the cyber world, as only there do they feel *empowered*—that they can voice their opinion, break free from a life that is often nasty, and leave behind an ugly reality. They usually have dysfunctional families, or they have been expelled from school, or they belong to a street gang. Hacking and phreaking therefore become a way of escaping, enabling them to develop their personalities and grow into adulthood.

We also tried to find out whether their families, maybe the less difficult ones, helped them at all to follow their interests and whether there were other examples of someone practicing hacking or phreaking.

The case of Anna Moore is quite special and rather the exception: at age three, she was already learning to manipulate DoS (denial of service) files and directories. Anna started getting involved in computers and hacking with the help of her parents. She had her own PC, practically unlimited time to play with it, and the freedom to explore.

Her parents used computers at home for work and had accustomed Anna to use her PC since childhood, monitoring her activities on the Internet. Her parents wanted her to be well versed in hacking. Her mother took her to various hack meetings, including DefCon, which were useful to both mother and daughter.

For Anna, it became a challenge to hide her activities and experiments. She saw her parents' supervision as a problem and an obstacle to her explorations, given that they knew as much about computers as she did.

Anna's parents helped her to develop a moral and ethical sense that allowed her to safely hack without "getting into trouble." They allowed her to be free to act and explore, and make her own decisions, checking that she was capable of setting her own rules and willing to accept the consequences of her actions.

Anna and her parents discussed hacking regularly, which is something we didn't find in any of the previously examined hackers, who were all male. This might be because parents tend to check up on daughters more often than on sons. In addition, boys tend to be more rebellious, refusing to accept parents' advice and leaving home earlier. Anna did not come from a broken family, and her situation would not have been possible had her parents been separated or beset with other problems. Furthermore, their cultural level and their computer know-how certainly helped her a lot.

For other hackers, this role is taken on by *mentors,* who usually teach them *hacker ethics* just as Anna's parents taught her.

Socioeconomic Background

Hackers come from all social classes. Some grew up in deprived areas (like John Lee, alias Corrupt, who lived in Brooklyn), but others come from more prosperous classes, and many are middle class. Often, they are the children of immigrants who live in impoverished suburban areas with financial and maybe racial problems.

The Net has always played the role of great leveler as, both there and in the underground, neither physical situation nor economic and social position is important. What counts is ability—the will to discover and learn.

Many teenage hackers have built their own PCs, because they don't have jobs, because they come from poor families who don't have funds available, or, when lack of money isn't a problem for the family, simply because of a *way of thinking.* In this case, they have bought the various components separately and assembled them piece by piece. This becomes a sort of "never-ending story" in which the computer is never completed and, during our interviews, was left "open and never shut down" in the hacker's bedroom or sitting room, "because I still have one last thing to do, and then it'll be finished."

Social Relationships

To go back to what we said a few pages ago on the view hackers have of themselves, we would like to explode the myth that a hacker—particularly an adolescent hacker—is a "four-eyed wimp," always at his computer, whose social relations are limited to the few friends met online and who has problems with girls—in short, your typical *nerd*.

Actually, it isn't so. Many hackers, even some of the most brilliant, are exactly the same as their peers: sociable, pleasant individuals who get good grades at school, have many friends, practice sports, go to parties, go to the pub or out for a pizza, and have girlfriends (or in the case of social engineers, many girlfriends). In other words, they are absolutely normal; they do not sacrifice their lives to fulfill their hacker objectives (for example "FonE_TonE" from "WoH"). As we have already said, you can't recognize them from their outside appearance; they don't dress in a bizarre way, even though they do prefer casual clothes.

Obviously, you do get the exception who confirms the rule. Kevin Poulsen, for instance, was rather a loner; he liked to go out only with his hacker friends and considered sports a waste of time, especially at a competitive level. But these distinctions are unimportant because, as already stated, hackers are just like everyone else, and therefore some like to do certain things and others don't.

On the whole, some of their closest friends, and the ones they have most in common with, were met on the Internet without ever meeting in person. Psychologists and so-called "hacker experts" label this type of friendship as symptomatic and typical of a twisted hacker personality and of the underground world they define as "alienating." These experts describe hackers as introverts and antisocial persons who feel more comfortable with virtual relationships on the Internet rather than with traditional ones.*

We don't agree with this opinion; in our view, it is distorting and facile. What is *really* alienating is modern society, which forces more and more people, not only hackers, to look for friendship online and discuss all sorts of topics with people never met outside of the Net. All you have to do is browse the Internet and look for any kind of discussion forum, about friendship for instance, to get an idea of the size of a phenomenon that should be studied and examined in depth. Furthermore, there is no doubt that the Net's immaterial world makes it easier to relate with others and break down fears and inhibitions, especially for shyer people.

---

* See Chapter 3.

But this doesn't imply being antisocial. Rather, the Internet makes it simpler to find people who share one's passions or who think in the same way. We don't see anything wrong in this behavior. And this isn't at all *typical* of hackers. Just think of the forums, newsletters, and chats dedicated to all sorts of subjects, and fan clubs. As you can see, these aren't all that different.

Hackers, of course, are undeniably at the forefront of any new thing to hit the Net or computers. Maybe they were the first to use these tools to communicate and relate, but today they certainly aren't the only ones. What is often intriguing is the fact that we are talking of eccentric personalities who also tend to rebel against the symbols and manifestations of authority.*

However, this is no excuse for certain studies† that attempt to describe members of the hacker communities as antisocial drug and alcohol–abusing teenagers. The problem and the limitations of these studies is the fact that they are based only on some segments or fringes of the world they purport to analyze, without looking at the complexities of the phenomenon. As a result, they just repeat the "usual" platitudes without understanding who hackers really are, what their motivations are, and the contribution they are trying to make to society. No doubt, society itself has contributed, either consciously or not, in perpetuating these stereotypes.

Leisure Activities

In order to get a complete picture of hackers, something closer to reality, we tried to find out what their leisure activities are and whether they have passions apart from computers, hacking, and phreaking. Some are not interested in most activities common to their age group, such as music or television, but neither are they interested in sports, which they often consider a waste of time. Furthermore, they don't tend to join clubs or go to concerts.

We can say, though, that an overwhelming majority of hackers love books: both essays and novels, especially sci-fi. Their favorite book seems to be *Lord of the Rings* while, as far as films go, "War Games"

---

* A special section of this chapter will deal with this aspect.
† See Chapter 3.

and "Ferris Bueller's Day Off"* are the ones that, among other things, drove them to start hacking.

Education

To understand where the passion for hacking started, it might be interesting to see how it relates to the kind of school attended and what kind of students hackers make. We can say that many hackers enjoy studying and are particularly keen on scientific subjects such as physics, chemistry, and mathematics. As to courses attended, many study or have studied computer science, and in particular *computer security*.

Notwithstanding what we have just said, hackers on the whole tend to consider school subjects a waste of time. Usually, they get good grades only in scientific subjects and, of course, in computer science.

Even though they are intelligent, often they don't excel at school, because they don't want to give their all in subjects that don't interest them. Many hackers don't make much of an effort at all in school, so their grades are much lower than their real potential deserves, and they appear to be only mediocre students. Often, they don't do their homework, as it would take time away from hacking.

In some cases, their grades suffer from their family difficulties and from the fact that they often are kept at a distance by their schoolmates, so they feel that they don't belong and are abandoned by the others. They are, however, individuals who are interested in all fields of learning, which allows them at least to earn passing grades without too much effort, even if they don't excel. There are also some extreme cases, such as those who "crack" their teachers' accounts to enter the school network where students' personal files are kept. In this way, they can change their grades in their weaker subjects to a passing level. In these subjects, they do not necessarily fail because they aren't any good, but rather because they refuse to comply with the rules imposed by their teachers.

Then again, you can get particularly brilliant hackers who are good in all subjects. They usually consider themselves to be very intelligent, if not among the most intelligent in the world, which is often

---

* In both these films, the hero, played by Matthew Broderick, is a teenage computer whiz, an expert in hacking and social engineering.

true. They hack until the early hours, so they wake up late and don't get to school on time, and then are reprimanded by their parents. However, they are willing to make an effort as long as their parents allow them to keep on using their PCs; often, parents threaten to take them away.

Many hackers, even though they might be doing well at school, go through periods of rebelliousness and start playing practical jokes; in other words, they are rather *difficult* students.

Girl hackers seem to be much better at school than boys, but the same can be said of students who aren't hackers. As an example, Anna Moore followed her high school curriculum and college syllabus at the same time.

Not all manage to attend their courses regularly. There are hackers who are repeatedly suspended from school or expelled for disciplinary problems. They answer back to their teachers, are violent, and turn up without their schoolbooks or without having done their homework.

Some have real personality problems, often caused by dysfunctional family situations. For this reason, they often get into trouble. Some have been expelled for drug possession.

Many others, even though they are doing well at school, don't attend regularly. These are teenage hackers who only stay at home so that they can continue with their explorations. For them, their computer and hacking are much more important. They often get to school late, are totally unprepared, and talk back to teachers who tell them off. They often desert their classrooms to check out computer stores (computer malls, very popular in the U.S.A.), where they are capable of spending hours exploring and studying the latest applications or operating systems as they appear on the market.

At this point, it must be noted that many hackers drop out of school, as they find it too easy, boring, and therefore not stimulating. Others simply aren't interested in the subjects offered. They need constant intellectual stimulation, and school doesn't provide it. School isn't for them, as it doesn't teach the things they want to know and learn about, so usually they get on well only in schools that offer and use computer science.

Many leave the standard school system and enroll in technical colleges, as they don't feel satisfied with basic computer science courses offered by traditional schools. We are talking here of young people who are experts and often know more than their teachers do, so it's quite easy to understand how boring it must be to listen to lessons that to them are simplistic and commonplace.

This doesn't mean that there aren't some who attend school regularly and are very good students, distinguishing themselves without much effort. Usually, they prefer to pay attention in class and learn everything on the spot so that at home they can spend more time on their favorite hobby without "wasting time" with schoolwork. Usually, their IQs are medium-high or high, in all cases above average, and they display exceptional technical and problem-solving abilities and marked creativity. They are lively, smart, shrewd, mischievous, and bold, often considered geniuses. We are talking about intellectually brilliant adolescents who feel suffocated by an inadequate school system and by badly trained or incompetent teachers.

All hackers love to learn, but not all like learning in school. Many dislike, or disliked, going to school because they get bored and are not interested in what school has to offer. They say they can learn a lot more quickly by reading a book, so they don't attend school regularly, as their teachers often explain things they already know; they're always a step ahead of their teachers. Hacking, phreaking, and software cracking offer a lot more intellectual stimulus than a classroom.

Professional Environment

You can find hackers in all kinds of professions even though they show a natural curiosity and aptitude toward *computer security*, whose experts they tend to respect. Some hackers have turned their overriding passion into a profession; for some, this is their greatest ambition. They are often hired by telephone companies, computer security companies, or government agencies (intelligence agencies, police, etc.).

It must be noted that not all of them stop hacking once they are employed. Some work by day and hack at night. They continue to hack, notwithstanding the fact that they might be putting their careers at risk.

Because they want to work in this field, it isn't rare for hackers under investigation to show off their capabilities in the hope of being hired. This is also typical of the adolescent need to be noticed. It can also happen that, in the hope of getting a job, they cooperate with investigators, giving themselves up in the case of solitary hackers. If members of a group, they may give investigators the names of the other members, help them to find evidence, and testify against the perpetrators. In many cases, they start to work in computer security just to prove that they are better than the establishment they had been fighting.

We could say that aspiring to work in this field is part of the natural development of the subject's personality, who, upon reaching maturity and adulthood, wants to turn his overriding passion into a way of earning a living. Yet again, hackers want to make good use of their know-how.

Sometimes a police raid or a conviction leads some of them to open their eyes and see that to continue along the same road in the underground world is too dangerous and is a dead end. They realize that they will only get into trouble if they don't mend their ways.

These experiences help hackers to grow up and decide to turn their passion for computers and hacking into a job; in this way, they start using their talents to a positive end. They stop fighting the establishment, become part of it, and start fighting its enemies.

What we have described is the normal evolution of many hackers as they move toward maturity. There are cases in which hackers continue their illegal activities into adulthood, but these are much less frequent. Most of them want to use their abilities for good, change skins, and move from black-hat to white-hat so as to monitor and "patrol" cyberspace to "protect" the community. With this transition, they are also trying to make up for the negative public image of hackers.

Relations with government agencies are a bit more complicated. Some hackers put their abilities and experience at the service of nonprofit organizations, just as sometimes they supply information and help to the police, but they never inform against other hackers, as this would go against their code. However, many hold antiestablishment ideals and would never work for police forces or other government agencies.

If we take a look at job satisfaction and the effects hacking has on their careers, the picture changes. Many hackers, aware of the crimes they are committing, admit that their activity can damage their careers, especially if they were to be arrested. They are afraid of being placed under surveillance by the police and ending up in jail, which would prevent them from touching a computer or being hired in the industry and working with a PC.

We have already pointed out how not all hackers stop hacking once they have a job, and keep on hacking at night. They keep it up even at the risk of their careers. Some are not interested in their careers, or their lives, or money. They are "out of control" and don't have a social life.

The ones who hack for personal gain instead of in the public interest (see, for example, the prizes won fraudulently for a radio competition by Kevin Lee Poulsen), putting at risk people's privacy and national security, often team up with "traditional" criminals to perpetrate crimes (such as housebreaking), or even checking up on their friends. These are individuals who have the opportunity to leave these circles, have a job they like, and yet continue to break the law, wasting the opportunity for using their abilities well. Often, their first conviction, which should be a warning signal, doesn't have any effect on them.

We must point out, though, that the more capable hackers are often recruited by corporations and government agencies who are interested in making use of their know-how to make their networks safer and, if necessary, take advantage of their programming skills in the event of information warfare.

At 17 years of age, the more skilled hackers already have had some sort of experience working on the most important military intelligence projects. (This goes mainly for the U.S.)

Psychological Traits

After introducing the lifestyle of the subjects we have studied, we can start looking at their main psychological traits.

Some hackers have charisma and are "manipulators," capable of convincing others to do things they wouldn't normally do or would never have taken into consideration. They can convince anyone of anything.

They are seen as fascinating and dangerous (e.g., Kevin Lee Poulsen, John Lee [alias "Corrupt"], or Kevin Mitnick). Often, they are very proud and are so self-confident that they feel no need to get help—even from a lawyer when they are in trouble with the law. This leads them to be arrogant, because they know (or think) that they are the best.

Many have a strong sense of humor. This often comes through online, given that they enjoy playing computer tricks just for the fun of it—think Web defacement with a witty and humorous content.

The majority of hackers are adolescents. If you bear this in mind, and also that they usually have very strong egos, you can understand their need to show off. They want to let everyone know how brilliant they are, especially in the media, so that they can become famous. In the 1990s, this element boosted the development of script-kiddies.

As a rule, adolescent hackers talk a lot, aren't at all discreet, and, to get the attention of the press and television, are willing to claim credit for the actions of other hackers. They may make up exploits to gain respect and fame in the underground world. Unfortunately for them, in this way they often come to the attention of investigators, who will have no problem proving whether a subject who has claimed a hacking action on a BBS or nonencrypted IRC (Internet Relay Chat) is actually the author.

Often, they boast that they have managed to get around and beat the actual computer security experts and antihackers (so-called *hacker-catchers*, or *hacker hunters*), making fun of them to show that they are the ones hunting the security experts and not the contrary. Others (the more mature ones) are discreet, cautious, and don't need to become famous to satisfy their egos. They know they are the best and don't need any outside recognition. They prefer to remain on the sidelines, happily savoring their achievements with no need to tell other hackers about them. They will rarely give away more than necessary about themselves. They're not interested in publicity, and their only concern is to avoid being caught. It is difficult to determine their physical location (whereas script-kiddies will more easily reveal where they come from).

Many of them are aware of the financial implications of their skills. Some offer to be *mentors* for young script-kiddies. Usually, they are employed by computer security companies and are directly involved in the development of "0-day exploits."*

There is no lack of hackers, some of them highly skilled, who feel insecure and have paranoid tendencies. This state of mind is caused by the constant fear of being apprehended and the insecurity of never knowing whom you are dealing with online. This is a constant in

---

* Given the definition of "exploit," a "0-day" exploit is one that is unreleased, that circulates inside a very tight circle of people before it becomes—in a time span difficult to identify—public; in other words, downloadable by anyone familiar with exploit download sites. Only then does the international computer security community become aware of the existence of a software tool that exploits a given vulnerability.

the underground, which can be compared to some extent to a sort of "secret society."

Some hackers who have very strong egos find the idea of being caught by the police amusing, and it gives them the same thrill they get out of hacking. To top it all, it would make them even more famous—practically celebrities.

The satisfaction they get out of challenging the authorities, first among them the police and security professionals, feeds their egos. They are aware of being able to do things ordinary people cannot. The challenge, plus the boost to their ego related to doing something well, is essentially what led them to hacking. This type of hacker never hacks for personal gain.

The challenge and the fun for a hacker consist in managing to enter someone else's system. They spend their nights at it until they get there. However, once inside, their actions and motivations come to an end; once they are inside, they get bored and have no interest in staying in the system or going back unless they are looking for something specific or find something particularly interesting.

Basically, the main satisfaction for a hacker comes from the exploration itself—the process, the study involved, and the journey necessary to enter a given system. That's what gratifies them and makes them proud, not so much what the system itself contains.

It becomes more obvious that hackers hanker after *control* over their actions and their destiny, and they hate the idea of being in someone else's power. As they are mainly adolescents, a certain degree of immaturity shows through in their attacks. Think of "Pr0metheus," who "defaced" Christian Web sites because he hated organized religions and Christianity in particular. This attitude also shows a high degree of selfishness in wanting to impose one's point of view on others.

The need to always be in control explains the fact that hackers like Anna Moore don't see the purpose of, or feel any attraction for, hacking under the influence of drugs and/or alcohol. Actually, these altered states are seen as obstacles to be avoided; however, some do hack under the influence, including some famous representatives of the hacker community.

Anna Moore's words on the subject are quite enlightening. "The party animal mentality is incompatible with my hacker mentality. What is the point of drunken carousing when I could be flying on the wings of code? You have to be sharp, perceptive, and on your toes to hack. Anything that befuddles the mind is a hindrance."*

This kind of hacker considers those who use drugs or alcohol *lamers*, who in this way release their frustration at not being able to compete with the great hackers. It's important, though, to stress how this approach is typically North American, and of the younger generations of hackers.

Later on in this chapter, we'll be dealing with alcohol and drug dependencies, so we'll leave any further analysis to that specific section (Alcohol, Drug Abuse and Dependencies).

To Be or to Appear: The Level of Self-Esteem

We are convinced that hacking, phreaking, and any "art" that allows the demonstration of one's skills and abilities can have a *therapeutic* effect for some. For this reason, we tried to study the level of self-esteem of the subjects and how much they feel understood and appreciated by their families, friends, and acquaintances. We also considered how much they esteem and respect themselves.

In particular, we believe that a high level of self-esteem has an important role to play against the frustration caused by lack of understanding and appreciation from people who don't share their passion (because they aren't into the subject and aren't interested). The frustration also can exist because the subjects don't feel they are as physically attractive as their peers, or they don't enjoy the usual activities (sports, for example) that commonly bind a social group.

As self-esteem is the result of internal and outside dynamics and is mainly the result of the parent/child relations during infancy, we can state that self-esteem develops during the phase of life that molds the personality of a subject. However, it is also true that self-esteem is influenced by relationships with others throughout one's whole lifetime.

It becomes clear that if a subject, no matter how intellectually brilliant and smart, doesn't feel sufficiently appreciated in interpersonal relations (first and foremost with school friends and teachers), their level of self-esteem will suffer a decline. This will lead someone who has a clear view of himself and his needs to react negatively and seek

---

* Verton, D., *The Hacker Diaries*, McGraw-Hill, 2002.

people elsewhere who can appreciate him. This is one of the reasons why hackers tend to socialize among themselves in the underground world, particularly through BBSs, practically cutting themselves off from the rest of society.

A lack of self-esteem can unleash deviant behaviors and make some become violent and destructive against what they view as the source of their disquiet and unease. But not all hackers and phreakers are like that.

For many of them, excessive self-esteem makes it necessary to constantly feed their egos. This concept must be clear if we are to understand why certain individuals launch attacks against bodies such as telephone companies and government agencies or large "symbol" corporations (in other words, against the military-industrial establishment) to express their rage and show the world their power and capabilities.

Some want to prove they are the best by challenging computer security professionals. Others show their rage and aggressiveness by *crashing* information systems (so-called *crackers*). Crackers, however, must be clearly distinguished from hackers, or at least from those who embrace the *hacker ethics*, as they don't share the objective of increasing technical knowledge.

Presence of Multiple Personalities

Some BBS users aren't looking only for intellectual stimulation and new ideas, but also for an identity. In a dimension where neither age nor appearance count, but only technical skills, any visitor can create a new personality.

We have always thought it important to ask our interviewees how they manage these multiple personalities, if they really feel they have more than one, and how they interpret it. We also inquire as to whether this is what they really want, if they would like to be someone else, and if so, who.

Creating a new personality starts with the choice of a "fantasy name," the so-called *handle* or *nickname* (the alias used online, often taken from a cartoon characters, from literature, or from films). This does not necessarily reflect the personality of the subject but is rather an *alter ego*, reflecting how they would really like to be.

Hackers, though, try to increase their power through alternative identities, given that the name becomes a sort of "armor" that protects the privacy of the subject, hiding his true identity not only from the other members of the underground world but also from the police.

Furthermore, it is also a "nom de guerre" under which they can be known in the hope that one day it will be feared and respected by elite hackers. The subjects labeling their discoveries and information acquired with a "trademark," as a sort of guarantee before they are shared through a BBS.

However, the handle doesn't necessarily reflect the personality of the subject. Often, they are nicknames given by friends or names chosen because they are considered important, prestigious, or resonant. They can be fantasy names, inspired by books or films, or the acronym of an electronic device. Think, for example, of "Gandalf," the name of the wizard in *The Lord of the Rings* but also the name of a terminal server (XMUX Gandalf), or "Pad," the acronym for "packet assembler/disassembler" in packet-switching networks on X.25 protocols, and "Parmaster" or "Par," from "Master of Parameter," the name his friends called him because of his skills with parameters (to be inserted in PAD X.28 for the correct viewing of texts). The examples are legion.

We can also observe how nicknames have two tightly linked functions:

- They hide the subject's true identity (no intelligent hacker would use his own identity for online activities, nor his real name as a nickname).
- They reflect the way in which the subjects perceive themselves (or are perceived) within the underground.

We would like to point out that we are not talking about multiple personalities in the pathological, psychiatric meaning of the term. Rather, all hackers lead a double life to a certain extent (and you don't need to be a hacker or deviant to have one). They describe themselves as "quick-change artists," ordinary students by day who at night become the inhabitants of the underground world.

If, however, we consider that hacking isn't just an art or a technique but also a way of life and a perception of reality, it's also clear that you can't separate the two. They often merge to such an extent that the subject ends up having an identity crisis, because obviously the student is still a hacker by day and the hacker still a teenager at night.

On top of this, having two distinct personalities and leading parallel lives, one in the physical world and the other in the cyber world, is natural for them and considered cool and fashionable.

As they feel misunderstood by nonhackers, they try to make two different sets of friends: one made up of their school friends or neighborhood kids (with whom they can share the usual interests of that age group) and one made up of members of the underground (with whom they share their passion for hacking and/or phreaking). These two personalities aren't in competition to attract attention to one rather than the other; neither of them prevails or, indeed, tries to.

So hackers live two parallel lives, full of secrets. It's a way of life. Only a few people are aware of their involvement with the underground, and that they belong to a certain set. In fact, usually only the other members of the same group know. Furthermore, they tell their friends only what they are willing to let them to know about their hacking activities.

Psychophysical Conditions

As already pointed out, all hackers—including the most advanced— have specific psychological traits, often feeling so insecure that they border on the paranoid. These feelings are caused by the constant fear of arrest and the uncertainty caused by never knowing whom they are dealing with online. This is a constant in the underground, which can be compared, as we said earlier, with a secret society.

From an analysis of the questionnaires, it appears that many hackers have neurological or mental disorders. The most frequent is insomnia or the inability to get enough hours of sleep at night. This can also be caused by the use of psychotropic drugs. Other hackers practically never sleep; they alternate hacking with their daytime activities, trying to lead as close to normal lives as possible.

Some are also emotionally unstable and psychologically disturbed. Other pathologies found are anxiety, panic attacks, hallucinations, schizophrenia, maniacal depression, and unipolar personality disorder, as in the case of Electron, described in *Underground*.[*]

---

[*] Dreyfus S., *Underground: Tales of Hacking, Madness and Obsession on the Electronic Frontier*, Random House, Australia, 1997.

Most probably, these mental disorders were already latent sur-
faced following a tragic event (e.g., a police raid or a criminal
sentence), as if post-traumatic stress disorder (PTSD) was the triggering factor.

Alcohol, Drug Abuse and Dependencies

As stated earlier, some hackers, such as Anna Moore, don't see any
use or find any attraction for hacking under the influence of alcohol or
drugs. However, the situation in the field can vary significantly from
country to country. In Dutch, German, Italian, and Spanish hacker
gatherings, it's very common to find the use of soft drugs (marijuana,
hashish) and alcohol (beer, spirits).

It's also important to understand whether and how these substances
impact on the social life, studies, and/or work of hackers, as well as on
their favorite activities—hacking and phreaking. At that point in the
study, we discovered that most North Americans do not overindulge
in drinking. This can be explained as habits learned over the years,
given restrictive laws forbidding alcohol sales to minors in both the
U.S.A. and Canada. In Europe, Australia, and Asia the situation varies from systematic excesses to moderate use.

Usually, it's only the less "skilled" hackers who abuse these substances, given that the lack of clearheadedness stops them from
carrying out an attack without making mistakes and keeps them
from reaching the highest levels of their technical capacities. As
they lack the grounding and the know-how to reach the limits of
their capacities and excellence, they frequently allow themselves "a
couple of beers" during their computer sessions, which often go on
for hours.

Avoiding substance abuse does not mean never using a particular
substance. The difference between these two terms is very important:
abuse implies excessive use.

It becomes important to stress that we can't say that hackers never
take drugs or alcohol, but it is true in most cases that they do not
abuse these substances. This is for a simple reason: it would go against
their very way of life and being, which implies caring about themselves as well as their clearheadedness, without which they couldn't
satisfy their need for knowledge.

The data we collected confirms this: most hackers don't abuse drugs, or at least not "hard" drugs like cocaine or heroin. The use of hashish or marijuana is more common. As to alcohol consumption, here too we can confirm that usually only the less skilled hackers abuse it. It also appears that no hacker has ever used/abused synthetic drugs such as ecstasy.

Among hashish and marijuana users, there are differences as well, which can be geographical or generational. Considering the greater availability of a particular drug on the American or European markets, fads too become important. Others smoke hashish and marijuana to "hold back" their excessive creativity—to stop their brain from working in overdrive, to which they often fall prey. These substances are generally only for very occasional recreational use, as there is little time left over from hacking.

In some cases, substance use has led to being expelled from school for drug possession. If we are talking about adolescent hackers, we mustn't forget that they are still only ordinary teenagers, even though gifted in some ways, who still behave like all the others. It shouldn't be understood that drug use is an expression of deviant behavior connected in some way with hacking.

It can happen that some have been forced to abandon hacking following a detention period, or they have been exposed by the police, or they become aware that it would be too dangerous to continue, or yet again their computers have been seized, so they start drinking and/or taking drugs. In other cases, when drugs were only taken to improve concentration, the drug use stops when hacking is abandoned.

Things change when mental disorders are also present such as, for example (and mainly), paranoia with persecution frenzies. In these cases, they complain they are being harassed by the police and are afraid of being "terminated" because of the importance of the secrets they have discovered during their forays into government systems.

When discovered by the authorities, it appears that they take up drug use to fill the void left by giving up hacking, replacing their "hacking dependency" with a drug dependency. It really seems that they are replacing one addiction with another, even though they don't consider themselves addicts. What they are doing is trying to experience through drugs the same sensations they got from hacking.

The drug abuse is often followed by depression and paranoia. Sometimes this situation can degenerate leading to the edge of madness or, worse still, suicide.

Frequently, persecution paranoia appears, or the fear that what is being said to them isn't true and really means something else. These psychoses are often caused by the drugs themselves (so-called *drug psychosis*).*

These are, however, very rare cases, and we mustn't forget that most active hackers have never abused drugs. A clear head is essential to carry out a computer raid without making any mistakes. Another, even more significant, detail is that they feel no need to take drugs because, for them, there is nothing better than hacking.

Definition or Self-Definition: What Is a Real Hacker?

A last comment has to do with the "name" of our subjects. Do they all define themselves hackers? If not, how do they define themselves?

Hackers rarely define themselves as such; usually, it's other members of the underground or their acquaintances who do so. For them, hacking isn't a way to appear cool, to give themselves identities, or to be labeled as such; it's rather a way of life, a mindset, an instinct, and a sixth sense. As "RaFa" of the "WoH" said, "Either you've got it or you haven't."

Many adolescents think they are hackers simply because they've managed to gain root access to various Web servers. They want to be hackers without really knowing what it is or what it really means to be one.

Hackers are hackers because they have learned programming languages. They know and can master different operating systems, protocols, and programs. They can manipulate the systems in some way, making them do their bidding so they can reach their objectives (even when the systems weren't programmed for that), and exploiting their potentials.

But there is more to it than that. They are hackers mainly because they have been capable of violating not only information systems but

---

* Examples of the destructive relationship between hackers and drugs (referring to members of the Chaos Computer Club, CCC) can be found in Clifford Stoll's book, *Tracking a Spy through the Maze of Computer Espionage*, Doubleday, New York, 1989.

also themselves and their lives, demanding a lifestyle that consists in extending their minds beyond what is written in books or what was explained to them by others.

They are hackers because they have allowed their knowledge to grow without setting any limits, through discoveries and self-learning.

To be a hacker, it isn't enough to be capable of entering a system. This principle is part of both white- and black-hat culture and goes beyond definitions, especially as there isn't even a hacker ranking. This is the most important lesson a mentor can teach his disciple.

For Willie Gonzales,* the difference between a hacker and a criminal is *respect*. A hacker respects both the law and others and sees technology as a mere tool to exploit a system and make it do what you want. According to Willie, one who goes into a Web server and "defaces" its homepage is no better than a common petty criminal or a street vandal. And yet they still describe themselves as hackers, as if this somehow justifies their actions.

True hackers, the ethical ones, always consider Web site defacement *lame,* and damaging someone or destroying information is criminal. Even though they know that when you are young you're not always aware of the consequences of your actions, they do know that these can have repercussions on the lives of other people, either users or the system administrator who is responsible for its proper and secure functioning.

According to Willie, if you want to be a real hacker. you must accept this responsibility, especially if you want to practice on someone else's system. You don't need to break the law or damage people and systems to be a hacker.

Our interviewees are usually considered by their teachers and school friends as computer experts rather than hackers. Some, like Pr0metheus, don't care what they are called or labeled by other members of the underground, whereas others, like "Explotion," identify with the labels applied to them by people they consider more expert than themselves and are concerned about their opinion and the label.

---

* A member of the white-hat community. Willie Gonzales' philosophy is described in Dan Verton's book, *The Hacker Diaries,* McGraw-Hill, 2002.

Relationship Data

In the final part of this chapter, the result of processing the second part of the questionnaire, we will be dealing with how hackers relate with "others," from family to friends, members of the underground, and institutional authorities.

Relationship with Parents

As we have already seen when describing the family of origin, in many cases there are conflicting relationships with parents. Many haven't seen one of them (usually the father) for some time, and this has caused problems when growing up. Others have experienced abandonment at an early age and now have problems having deep relationships for fear of suffering further loss. Some hackers were born to parents who didn't want children, so they didn't receive much nurturing.

A constant element is that the parents don't care about what their children do with their PCs. In fact, they are reassured by the fact that they spend a lot of time at home in their rooms "hacking" and learning rather than in front of the TV set or on the streets where they could fall prey to drug dealers or "bad influences" that would lead them to commit illegal acts, get into trouble, get arrested, and so on.

This attitude can also be explained by the fact that parents usually have no idea whatsoever about what their children are up to with their computers. This is also because hackers, as we have seen, tend to hide their activities.

The result is that parents are more worried about the phone bill than about what their children are actually doing. They often scold them for spending too many hours in front of their computer. In most cases, they don't know that their kids are hacking; they think they're playing computer games, surfing the Web, or chatting.

From this point of view, young hackers are very good at hiding their activities from their parents. The most common technique consists in keeping an unrelated Web page or a videogame minimized as an icon on the desktop, which can be loaded as soon as a parent sets foot in the room.

Relationship with the Authorities

Hackers often consider the investigators studying them to be dumb or actually stupid, because they can't understand all the technical aspects and the personal motivations that inspire them to their deeds. This explains their open defiance of any kind of authority.

We must also remember that, when we are dealing with hackers, we are usually dealing with personalities who have little or no trust in the authorities, who are seen rather as the oppressors of freedom rather than entities there to protect them. This characteristic manifests itself in a form of rebellion against all expressions or symbols of authority.

Sometimes their rebelliousness is expressed rather paradoxically in a keen interest in the instruments of power, such as martial arts, weapons, social engineering, and, mainly, hacking. It is as if they were saying, "We are challenging traditional power with unconventional forms of power."

Hacking offers them the power to challenge "the powers that be." Many hackers have in common an antiestablishment view, showing respect only on the surface.

The antiestablishment view of the underground is mainly aimed at those bodies or organizations that, according to them, hamper or block technological development and free circulation of information by means of a monopolistic management of the market (for instance, telephone companies). This explains why many attacks are launched against them and why "suckering" the telephone system to make free long-distance calls is considered morally acceptable. Hackers believe they are important for the community that is working for Internet security and for its users in general.

Looking at "Genocide's" words, we can say that, according to hackers, there are three different entities in our society—superpowers that are competing against each other: the hacker community, governments, and the Internet community in general. If one of these superpowers is allowed to develop secret hacking attack tools, the risk would be of a shift in the balance of power and consequently concentrating it all in one group's hands. This is unacceptable for hackers, as power should always be equally shared between the three entities. According to Genocide, an imbalance of this kind would be extremely dangerous. Furthermore, stopping the hacker community from accessing knowledge and tools could lead to a revolt inside the underground world, leading to the creation of even more dangerous and destructive tools.

Hackers consider themselves to be the force legitimized, or rather self-legitimized, to act as a counterbalance to power on the battlefield of information security. They believe it is right to enter this sector just like any other group of users, and on a par with government institutions.

It must be stressed that, according to Figure 5.1, hackers have no concept of a hierarchical, authoritarian (vertical) relation between the three entities, but that only an equal relationship (horizontal), peer to peer, can be considered synonymous with true democracy. For them, hacking consists in the search for *truth* and is aimed at not allowing one group to impede the other in this search and their access to it.

For hackers the real crime isn't hacking but rather *hiding the truth*.

Relationships with Friends, Schoolmates, Colleagues at Work

Often, the people we interviewed are loners, kept at a distance by their schoolmates, and are introverts and unsocial; they don't have friends, or the few they do have are other hackers whom they often have never met and whose identity they don't know. They feel they aren't accepted by others and are abandoned by all, and their school grades often suffer from this isolation.

For all of these reasons, they'd rather spend time with computers, which are unbiased and don't discriminate. PCs are seen as a refuge,

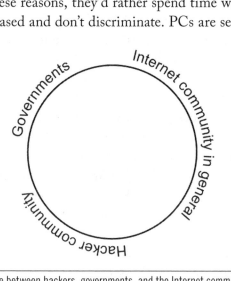

Figure 5.1   Balance between hackers, governments, and the Internet community.

tools that allow them to access many virtual worlds where they can leave behind a life deprived of fulfillment. This is why belonging to a *community* such as the underground, which often represents their main allegiance, becomes important.

Some hackers don't like to cultivate social relations, which are kept at a minimum. This is not only out of shyness but often through a lack of interest and/or misanthropy. Often, they are so hacking dependent, obsessed by the intellectual challenge it represents, that it absorbs them totally, leaving less and less time for their social life, which is often limited to meeting other hackers online.

They also confess that they feel uncomfortable and awkward with the opposite sex. At the same time, only very few others (often only their best friend) outside the underground are aware of their involvement with hacking. That's the price they pay for living two lives full of secrets, as, after all, hackers only tell their friends what they choose to let them know about their hacking activities.

Relationships with Other Members of the Underground Community

Given that they relate mostly in this parallel world, we need to investigate how these relationships work. Is there trust or suspicion? What do they tell each other?

The underground can be seen as a *haven* for these social misfits, as a new world where you aren't judged according to your ethnic group or socioeconomic status. In the real world, prejudice and discrimination run riot, and adolescents in particular are more sensitive and vulnerable. They often have experienced all this firsthand, which is why they feel the need to escape the real world where they don't feel accepted, looking for a different one.

Once these subjects have become part of the underground community, they see their computer as a way of opening up to others without feeling the need to destroy what others have built. In the underground, hackers feel that they are part of something bigger than themselves, a world full of people who think like them and where age does not dictate your social position. In this new world, people are judged only on the basis of what they can do on a computer.

However, the hacker community is very *exclusive* and difficult to penetrate. It isn't easy to be admitted, and it often takes months to prove oneself. The community is made up of individuals who often resort to lies and deceit, both as a defense and as a way of life.

Hackers are suspicious of newcomers, because they are afraid that they might be dealing with investigators from the police. To eliminate any doubt, the more expert challenge newcomers, and tests usually take place in the more reserved chats. To earn respect, it is necessary to prove one's real abilities, and, if it works, the other members will soon enough approach you, either to compete or to ask for advice. If, however, the candidate is notorious for having carried out particularly criminal acts, very few will stick with him, for fear that they might be considered accomplices by the police.

Hackers know each other through their handle. As already stated, they rarely know the real name of the people they frequent on IRCs or BBSs, or what they look like. They love exchanging know-how and consider it important to meet people with their same views. To do this, they employ a special language: they use keystrokes.

They help each other to refine their techniques, for example, for hiding or disguising their computer's IP address, and therefore their identity, so they can't be traced. They view the underground as a fantastic and exciting world, where knowing how to get around the law is considered cool.

The underground is a world where everyone knows each other, even if not in person, and where it is possible to project any image you want rather than what you are in reality. One consequence is that a hacker can take on any appearance, and some have even more than one handle, all belonging to the same person but projecting different personalities.

In this society, hackers share their knowledge and discuss technical questions on IRCs or BBSs, establishing awareness—a sort of "collective consciousness." The only rules are those set down in the *hacker ethics*. We must point out that not all share the same ethic but that there is more than one.

There are also BBSs for elite hackers—for the best. To become part of one, it is necessary to prove that you have special technical skills and also to be sponsored by a member. For obvious reasons, these are very small groups compared to those who go to the other BBSs.

Hackers are eager to share (at no cost) the discoveries, know-how, and information acquired during their raids with other members of the underground. We can say without doubt that for many hackers, this is the fundamental principle. For some, it is the only one of the *hacker ethics*, a corollary of the axiom *maximum freedom of information*, that they strenuously support, because for them acquired knowledge is useless if it can't be shared.

Information sharing is completely free, just as exchanging experiences, skills, and opinions. The objective isn't to get rich but rather gain respect from the other "inhabitants" of the underground. Hackers love freely sharing their knowledge with other reliable hackers and often become mentors to the less experienced, teaching them not only how to hack but also the philosophy of life that is part of it because, as we have already said, hacking isn't just a technique to penetrate systems, but a way of life and a way of being.

There are also *hack-meetings* for learning and keeping up to date. These are meetings where it is possible to exchange knowledge and where some speakers pass on their expertise about their various specialties (computer security, telephone systems, encryption, government systems, etc.).

There are two kinds of hack-meetings. First of all, there are yearly international meetings that usually take place in the same city. After registering online, all experts from the sector can participate: hackers, phreakers, computer security experts, members of government agencies, police, journalists, etc. Both white- and black-hats take part in hacking conferences, and whoever wants to participate must register in one of the two categories (this happens, for example, for DefCon). These are usually well-organized events, with an agenda illustrating the different technical presentations in typical hacker jargon. Good examples of these events are "HITB-Hack In The Box" (which takes place in Kuala Lumpur, Malaysia) and "DefCon," held in Las Vegas, NV.

The second kind of hack-meeting is more restricted. Only hackers and phreakers are admitted, and sometimes system administrators. Examples include those organized by groups called "2600 hacker group." These are national meetings that usually take place in the same location (public centers such as shopping malls, railway stations, etc.) and are monthly events. (In the case of the 2600 hacker group, they take place on the first Friday of every month.)

In this kind of meeting, the participants tend to gravitate toward others they have something in common with and exchange information about, for example, where to download files on hacking, where to find accounts to access other systems, which BBSs give good information, and recently discovered IP addresses of interest. Last but not least, apart from their knowledge, they also exchange "cracked software" (or "pirated software"). During hack-meetings, the general atmosphere is completely relaxed.

Hackers tell only a few trustworthy friends about their exploits. They are very cautious and vague in their conversations on the subject; they don't give away any precise indications of what they have done.

If talking about particularly important challenges, such as their best attacks, they keep the details to themselves for fear of being discovered and caught by the police. They absolutely do not talk about hacking over the telephone, for fear of being under surveillance by the police and ending up in jail, which terrifies them, as they would be unable to touch a computer for years or wouldn't be hired by any company in the sector.

But it isn't always like that. When they are starting out as hacker/phreakers, they need to learn a lot as quickly as possible, so they have to establish contacts with more expert hackers to ask them for technical advice. However, once they have learned the ropes, they can find the information they need for themselves.

Some prefer to keep their hacker life secret and don't tell anyone about it—especially nonmembers of the underground, and even more so when computers belonging to the military-industrial establishment have been violated. That would be too risky; such computer raids are usually shared only with members of the same group unless we are talking about a "lone hacker."

A great degree of solidarity exists not only between members of the same group but between hackers in general when it becomes necessary to cover for each other (for example, during a police raid or when one of them is in trouble, possibly wanted by the judicial authorities*).

Usually, hackers get to know each other in chats and often become great friends without ever meeting or telephoning. Computers are the only means of communication with most of their friends. For this

---

* It's worth remembering that this kind of help can be considered "aiding and abetting."

reason, it is very difficult to leave the underground; the more you go there, the deeper you get into its culture.

The appearance of IRCs and the increase of script-kiddies have partly changed the hacker scene. For many of them, hacking doesn't mean being good with systems but rather boasting about one's exploits.

Traditionally, hacking means first and foremost to gain the *respect* of the other members by proving one's skills and sharing one's experience and know-how. For script-kiddies, however, it consists of destroying data and stopping the spread of information. They use IRCs to boast about "their" success and "their" exploits (especially Web defacing and DoS) without often showing any real abilities. Often, they even lay claim to someone else's feats so as to nurture their egos rather than to share what they have learned.

Many hackers, however, believe that the Web-defacing scene is becoming more and more unimaginative and without skill, and is destined to disappear soon. For this reason, they try to encourage the more intelligent and capable people to become part of the underground.

Finally, there are hackers who would like to involve the whole underground in political activism (so-called *hacktivism*—activism through hacking) without belonging to a particular political party or joining one.

This is typical of the Italian and Spanish hacker scene. The first *HackMeeting* in Italy (Florence, 1997) was characterized by a very strong—and not generally appreciated—marriage between politics and hacking, and today the situation isn't changed.

Spain is going through a similar process where, during local hackmeetings, ideologies and technical aspects merge, encouraging hacktivism and urging a sort of "digital rebellion" aimed at multinationals and telecommunication companies. The goal is to defend freedom of information and speech, often, however, departing from the natural hacking context and moving toward political excesses that aren't always appreciated by all participants. Hacking is by its very nature apolitical, and these excesses are not seen with approval, whether they are left wing or right wing.

6

WHO ARE HACKERS? PART 2

This is our world now…the world of the electron and the switch, the beauty of the baud.

We explore…and you call us criminals.

We seek after knowledge…and you call us criminals.

In this long chapter, which continues and concludes what we started in the previous one, we will examine what has emerged from the questionnaire, but only with reference to information than can be considered "technical and criminological data." When does a hacker become a hacker? How does he increase his knowledge? What motivates him? Is it possible to identify behavioral models while he is hacking? Is it possible to identify patterns? How does he see his actions? Which ones sign their violations and why? Are there common generalized learning procedures everyone has to follow in the world of hacking?

We will try to answer all these questions, which were partly raised in the previous chapters, confirming or refuting what has emerged from other studies and investigations that have already discussed similar topics.

Let's start with the *nickname* or *handle* that usually identifies a hacker.

Handle and Nickname

The main thing about handles is that they have to be unique. They rarely have a specific meaning; usually, they are names that are considered "cool." Sometimes they seek to be evocative of, for instance, the technical abilities of their "owners." For this reason, it doesn't make sense to try to analyze a hacker's personality on the basis of his nickname, and for the same reason the questionnaire doesn't ask for an explanation of the nickname chosen.

However, the *handle* is very important in the underground. It's like a sort of "trademark" covering and evoking various characteristics of the subject, ranging from the user's reputation and enjoyed respect to technical skills and hacking exploits. Newcomers, for example, base their names on those of famous elite hackers to evoke their feats, hoping that something will rub off on them and they will reach their same level of ability and popularity.

It is necessary to point out that hackers don't always use their nickname on chats. They often use a different one and change it quite frequently.

Starting Age

We have seen that hackers are young, but we don't know at exactly what age they first got involved with computers and in particular in hacking/phreaking.

Usually, a hacker's career is an early one. Many start by chance, usually very young (around 11–12, the so-called average teenager). Others, a minority, begin at a later age (18–19 years). The majority, however, start hacking during adolescence, around 13–14 years of age.

Regardless of the starting age, a hacker will manage to violate between 3,000 and 10,000 systems during the course of his activities, and these are his conquests, or trophies.

Learning and Training Modalities

Hackers are very competent technicians, with extremely high-level skills. It is important to understand how they develop these skills and whether anyone helps them along the way.

A hacker's greatest virtues are patience, persistence, and determination. It takes time to learn how to do hacking. Hackers learn the basic techniques very quickly and acquire most of their skills during their first years of activity. They love technology and anything technical but are especially attracted by studying computers and telephone lines, as these are the more technically advanced. They often learn by themselves and have no formal grounding in computer sciences, and, as already stated, they learn very quickly. Some, after 6 months of having been given a PC and a modem, move from knowing nothing at all about computers to possessing great hacking abilities.

They are usually self-taught. They learn by themselves how to program their computer using different languages. They usually start hacking by going to IRCs and BBSs, where they can meet and make friends with someone who is willing to teach. After a period of initiation, if they are good, they might be admitted to a group.

Others have had a mentor who initiated them in the art, but as often happens, the pupil exceeds the teacher and, after learning the rudiments, continues studying information systems alone. The main learning method is by trial and error. Hackers find learning from handbooks boring, because reading makes them want to put what they have learned into practice immediately, and also because they find more satisfaction in trying to learn by experimenting, through a *deductive* method rather than an *inductive* one. They don't want to learn from books, because in that way they would only learn the theory, while computer security can only be learned "in the field."

Furthermore, paper-based documents are updated infrequently and so are not capable of following daily technological developments. One must add to this the satisfaction hackers feel in the knowledge that what they are learning is owned by some computer industry and is *inside knowledge*, and that they are capable of penetrating highly confidential systems. They prefer to learn in the field, reading the necessary documentation but also using their computer. The usual statement is "learn by doing it and by asking a lot of questions" and also "by watching other kids who are very good at experimenting." After all, their aim is to learn and gain knowledge, in a context that allows for "an adrenalin rush."

Recent studies have shown that the most efficient way of learning, which makes it easy to memorize concepts and "fixes" them better in long-term memory, is by *feeling a thrill* during the learning process. But this is easy to understand; it is always easier to learn something you enjoy. It's just as obvious how a deductive studying process and the possibility of putting into practice what one has learned allow for better and faster learning, lessening the probability of forgetting what has been acquired, especially when dealing with adults.

Usually, one starts to practice hacking by learning first how to "crack" protected software (mainly games) and violating one's school's network, possibly to rig tests and homework assignments.

The simpler hacking activities with which one starts to learn are "Windows hacking," consisting of violating the Microsoft Windows operating system (considered one of the most vulnerable), exploiting Web servers' Unicode,* or even experimenting with *Trojans*.

Among the first things learned are user enumerations,† DNS (domain name system) interrogations, techniques for network recognition, and many other *trace-route*‡ tactics.

Given the unavailability of some programming handbooks, as, for example, for VAX (Virtual Address Extension) machines that use the VMS (Virtual Memory System) operating system, some hackers have rewritten them, deducing the programming procedures from the results obtained through their experiments. As these are cutting-edge technology machines, and very expensive, they are accessible only by penetrating networks that connect many computers online.

On the Internet, and on BBSs, it is possible to find actual hacking and phreaking handbooks, and all good hackers read many books on hacking and IT security. The alarming aspect is that many learn to do hacking from handbooks prepared by groups inspired with politically anarchic ideals, where they teach, among other things, how to open locks, make bombs, counterfeit money, create letter bombs, make free phone calls from public telephones, assassinate strategic targets, etc.

Another way of learning that we have already mentioned is that of visiting computer stores and spending hours at the computers made

---

* Unicode is one of the historical vulnerabilities of Microsoft Window systems, more specifically of the Microsoft Internet Information Server (IIS) Web server. Various IISs had this bug, thanks to which it was possible to enter reserved areas of the Web server (protected pages, statistics, administration consoles, databases, etc.) just by "playing" with URL (uniform resource locator) requests. A classic example is GET/scripts/. .%c0%af. .winnt/system32/cmd.exe?/c+ command, which generates— on bugged IIS versions, typically IIS 4.0 and IIS 5.0—an MS-DOS prompt on the attackers PC. The most widely used tools were Unicode Check and the C programme iis-zang.c.

† User enumeration: by using some of the bugs present in the Microsoft Windows operating systems, it's possible to list all users of the authentication domain (active directory or NT 4.0), obtain a list of all existing users, plus other information useful to an attacker (when the password was last changed, is the account still valid or has it been disabled, etc.).

‡ Techniques and applications for tracing and identifying routes followed by information packets on computer networks.

available to customers to explore and experiment. In this way, they learn the details of all new applications and operating systems.

We have already seen how hack-meetings are used to learn and keep up to date through an exchange of know-how and experiences between participants.

The Mentor's Role

The better hackers love sharing their knowledge freely with whomever they consider more committed. Often, they become mentors, guides for the less expert, teaching them not only how to do hacking but also the *philosophy of life* that follows.

Mentors don't teach their disciples everything straight away. When technical questions are asked, they don't give all the answers. The teacher forces a pupil to believe in himself and find answers on his own. He just points in the right direction and gives hints to stimulate the curiosity of his apprentices, forcing them to ask questions. A mentor will give basic definitions and information, allowing the pupil to correlate the data alone, forcing him to explore. A mentor will encourage a pupil to work and learn by himself.

Many adolescents who mentor another aspiring hacker, usually a few years younger than themselves, take on a parental role with their pupils, telling him exactly what to do and not to do. They feel responsible for them, well beyond their duties as simple hackers. They protect them from the dangers of the Web and warn them when they hear about an ongoing police investigation, advising them to keep a low profile until things have calmed down.

Mentors feel responsible for actions carried out by their pupils. For this reason, they follow them step-by-step during raids. They enter the violated systems in the footsteps of the novice hacker in *stealth**
mode and without missing a single keystroke.†

Take the case of Willie Gonzales, who feels he is a role model for his pupil. Often, when hackers become mentors, they feel that they

---

* Stealth: invisible. Mainly on VMS systems, but on UNIX, too, there are programs that allow a user to be invisible (if he has the necessary "superuser" privileges), and that's what mentors do, hiding inside the system violated by the pupil and watching his every move.

† Literally each key hit on the keyboard.

are evolving and maturing because of this role they have taken on. They feel responsible for the future of their pupils. When they see their hacking abilities increasing, they experience the same feelings parents feel when they watch their children grow. There is a real parent/child relationship or a feeling of brotherhood, depending on the age difference between the two and how mature they are. The mentor feels responsible for guiding his pupil in the right direction, often because he initiated his pupil into hacking and helped him launch his "career."

For this reason, it isn't enough to be capable of penetrating a system to be a hacker, and this is part of both white- and black-hat culture (going well beyond definitions). This is the most important lesson a mentor can teach his disciple.

Usually, hacking lessons occur in public places, where it is possible to eat a sandwich and drink something—locations which then become a "meeting place" for mentor and disciple.

It's also interesting to note how in all cases there is a *one-on-one* relationship between teacher and pupil. Hackers usually accept only a single pupil when teaching, rather than many at the same time, and usually they have only one apprentice throughout their lives, with whom they develop a strong friendship, feelings of trust, and reciprocal esteem.

Often, the pupil himself, at the end of his training, and after reaching technical proficiency, becomes the teacher of another hacker.

Technical Capacities (Know-How)

The underground world can be viewed as a microcosm, as a society governed by unwritten rules and customs passed on from generation to generation, and as a social division into *castes*. You mustn't think that all hackers are equal; there is a hierarchy: an elite of the very few, the most capable, and many camp followers—so-called *wannabe lamers*.

"Newbies," or those without special technical know-how, and even those who only practice phreaking, are called *wannabe lamers*, or simply *lamers*. They use hacking techniques without knowing, or bothering to know, what the various commands they give their computer during an attack are for and how they work.

Script-kiddies, too, are unsophisticated and have no technical know-how. Often, they don't even know how to use basic tools and techniques. They don't care how they reach a result, just about the result itself: only the end counts, not the means. For them, hacking consists in downloading software and tools from the Internet and following instructions. They don't care about learning, about knowledge. They only want to crash government or corporate systems. They don't do it out of a love for technology, but just out of anger, to vent their frustrations and aggressiveness, or to attract attention.

Hacking is far more than just identifying usernames and passwords and doing things that can be done automatically with the help of software found online. Many define themselves as hackers, even though they don't have the necessary abilities, and pass themselves of as hackers on BBSs where they leave as many messages as possible in order to get attention. Expert and skilled hackers, *real* hackers in a manner of speaking, see themselves as trailblazers, as they are one step ahead of the majority.

Hacking, Phreaking, or Carding: The Reasons behind the Choice

Let's try to clarify the meaning of the terms that channel hacker activities. Often, *phreaking* and *carding* are assimilated to hacking. By giving a definition, we'll try to see whether they can be associated with certain types of hackers and what differentiates the hackers who practice them.

Phreaking is a technique that consists of using computers or electrical circuits to generate special tones with specific frequencies, or to modify the voltage of a telephone line. Indeed, it's possible to control the functions of a *telephone exchange* (phone switch) by sending special computer-generated tones over the phone line.

Think of the *blue box* developed in the 1970s by Steve Wozniak (one of the founders of Apple, along with another former hacker, Steven Jobs), after John Draper's discovery (alias "Captain Crunch," famous phreaker and pioneer of the phone phreakers movement*).

With the use of a slightly modified plastic whistle found in a cereal box (Cap'n Crunch, hence the nickname), he could produce a sound

---

* In addition to Captain Crunch, we must also mention Trax, the father of phreaking in Australia. See S. Dreyfus, *Underground: Tales of Hacking, Madness and Obsession on the Electronic Frontier,* Random House, Australia, 1997, p. 297.

that would interfere with the telephone system, allowing him to make long-distance and international calls completely free of charge. The blue box simply reproduced electronically the frequency produced by the toy whistle, equal to 2600 Hz, confusing the telephone exchange and making it believe there hadn't been any outgoing call or answers.

With this technique it's possible to make free phone calls in two ways:

- Billing the cost to some other user of the telephone line, to a specific phone number chosen or to a *calling card.*
- Not billing the calls to anyone; the calls are made untraceable, and consequently the cost will be borne by the telephone company.

This is called *blue-boxing* or violation of private telephone exchanges (PBX, private branch exchange) belonging to corporations or telecommunication companies. This technique is useful for hackers, because they can penetrate important systems without being traced.

The objective of phreaking is not simply to make free long-distance calls. It has to do with the skill and the *knowledge* of how to do so, and the study and discovery of how to gain access. And above all, it consists of having the ability to make untraceable calls, experiencing a sort of "power trip."

Phreaking also allows for listening in on telephone conversations or voice mailbox messages. We must point out that *phreaker's phone conferences*, also called *phone bridges*, take place in this way.

Some phreakers aren't aware of the fact that their exploration of the telephone network, seen as a new world without borders that needs to be explored, is actually hacking.

The subjects who answered our questionnaire like phreaking for the power it gives them over the telephone network—the communications system. They like to know they can listen in to telephone conversations and the users' voice mail boxes out of curiosity and also that they can reprogram the telephone system, which is governed more and more by powerful computers, and interrupt the service whenever they like. This is their real power: a power everyone can see, because when they exercise it, they inexorably impinge on everyday life.

Understanding how the telephone or computer system works gives the phreakers power and control to the highest degree.

There are also some who become phreakers out of need rather than choice, for instance, because they live in peripheral areas in the countryside, far from cities. Making free calls is a bonus given that all their calls are long-distance.

Hacking and phreaking aren't mutually exclusive. Some hackers started with phreaking then moved on to hacking, but the opposite can also happen. Some believe that phreaking is hacking's "little brother" because it doesn't require the technical know-how hacking does. If hacking means exploring new computers and systems, phreaking is considered too simple, as it is limited to the ability to go from computer A to computer B. Sometimes phreaking—using the telephone network to connect to the Internet or other networks free of charge—is necessary to keep on hacking.

Carding, "credit card number fraud," is something else again. This is a technique that consists of appropriating credit card numbers, usually obtained by violating the systems of banks or financial agencies, and using them to make long-distance phone calls or to buy goods without the cardholder's knowledge.

"Purist" phreakers don't accept that carding should be considered as part of their activities, the only difference being that the credit card numbers are used for making long-distance calls. For purists, carding is simply theft. But hacking is theft, too, for some—theft of computer resources belonging to someone else. This might seem rather ambiguous, but purist hackers believe there is no theft if you limit yourself to using the system when none of the legitimate users are using it. They believe that in that case it's just "borrowing." Of course, this only applies until the hacker has made the system "his own," appropriating it permanently.

According to purist phreakers, their specialty is the ability to make free, untraceable, long-distance calls. Phreaking requires greater technical abilities than carding, because you need to be able to manipulate a phone switch. That's why it's also called "hacking the phone system." Carding requires very few, if any, technical skills. For this reason, common criminals are also involved in this type of activity. These are people who don't respect anything and have nothing to do with the *hacker ethics*.

Following this line of thought, we can also see how some go from hacking to phreaking and then move on to carding (Figure 6.1). The

Figure 6.1   Decreasing sequence of the level of skills required for the activities practiced.

explanation of this transition is found in the fact that the more skilled hackers, who represent the upper crust of the underground, are members of a small elite, while less able and expert individuals "betray" their hacker identities and become part of the carding community.

We must note, however, that some hackers (not many, to be honest) refuse to use credit card numbers even to make long-distance phone calls to hack overseas systems. They do, however, consider it acceptable when the costs aren't billed to the cardholder but are paid by the telephone company, which, as we have seen, is often their main target.

Finally, for most hackers, using credit card numbers to do hacking is morally acceptable and has nothing to do with ordering consumer goods online, which they consider downright fraud.

Networks, Technologies, and Operating Systems

There are many different types of data networks and technologies available for hacking/phreaking. They include not only the Internet, which is the one most widely known, but also X.25, PSTN/ISDN, PBX, as well as wireless *mobile* networks (GSM, GPRS, EDGE, UMTS), and the newly arrived VoIP.

Cell phone nets (*mobile phone carriers networks*) are being used more and more on the hacker scene in the hope of becoming more "mobile;" in other words, more difficult to trace.

The latest novelty in computer piracy is a game called "node runner." This is a competition where two teams challenge each other as to which one can find the largest array of accessible wireless nodes in town. The team that has physically located a building emitting a wireless signal wins five points. Inside the team, each member has different tasks. One has to find the network signal, another is to photograph the area where the network node has been found, and someone else has to fix the event so as to prove it officially to the jury. The competition consists of moving around with a portable PC. When by car, it's called "war drives," and on foot "war walking." Once a connection to a company's Wi-Fi net has been found, films or software are downloaded from the Internet. In this way, the network is violated. To avoid being traced, IP addresses are hidden.*

Coming back to the subject of this section, we asked our sample what kind of operating systems they liked to practice hacking on; did they prefer Microsoft Windows, Linux, *BSD, UNIX, etc.

The answer is that hackers find penetrating Windows operating system frustrating, because they consider it extremely vulnerable and therefore easy to violate. They prefer to attack more complex systems. Various hackers define themselves *nix boxes* specialists, that is, experts in UNIX and Linux operating systems.

Another interesting point is to understand the "tools of the trade" and whether their own software is used (home-made tools, unreleased exploits, etc.) or developed by others.

Sometimes hackers use codes they have written themselves. Other times they use programs written by third parties and downloaded from the Internet or given to them by other members of the group. They usually *test* all the programs they find. Because of their poor technical skills, script-kiddies don't have any other possibilities. In most cases, they have to use tools developed by more sophisticated hackers.

Techniques Used to Penetrate a System

It would be easy to think that all hackers use standard techniques that are the same for everyone. In reality, all hackers, or at least hackers

---

* Usually the hacking operation isn't harmful to the violated company. From the ISP (Internet Service Provider) logs, where all user activities on the Internet are logged, it is possible to understand whether files are downloaded deliberately or not. There remains the problem that all logs can be altered so it isn't easy to prove whether data has been compromised.

with sufficient technical skills, not only have a signature distinguishing them but also follow a specific *modus operandi*.

A basic rule hackers pass on in the underground is, "Don't foul your own nest." This means that if a hacker has a legitimate account for school or work, he won't use it for attacks. If he cares about his job or about being expelled from the school or university he attends, the hacker will never do anything illegal through this system.

It is, true, however, that school computers are often used to carry out attacks without running the risk of being discovered and without the possibility of tracing the perpetrator of the attack. This is done by violating the accounts of other students—accounts that are then used to complete an attack. Often, hackers hold root permissions for the systems of various companies and universities all over the world, and they use these systems as *launch pads* for their attacks.

It is essential to use a handle to hide one's true identity, but another way to hide is by disguising the IP address, which makes tracing impossible. To hide their identity, they also use *proxy servers,** so network administrators who are monitoring the system (scanning through *pings*)[†] can't trace them easily. Indeed, hackers *spoof*[‡] their identity on the Internet, bookmarking pages that list hidden proxy servers, i.e., e-mail domains and servers they can use as a replacement to make it more difficult to trace their movements.

The favorite time for hacking is at night for two main reasons:

- During the day, hackers are busy at school or at work.
- At night, it's easier to be alone on the target system without running the risk of bumping into a user or the system administrator.

Of course, we must also take into consideration differences in time zones between the hacker and the system under attack.

Another of the golden rules of hacking is entering a system without anyone noticing or letting the administrator become suspicious.

---

* Servers that filter requests sent to other servers, making them anonymous. A search with a common search engine can identify many legal ones, for example http://anonymouse.org/, but we must point out that hackers usually violate corporate proxy servers, using them to cover their tracks.

† See further down, in the section entitled "Attack procedures."

‡ To spoof: fraud, cheat, swindle. These techniques will be described in detail later.

It's also worth mentioning that university computers are used as launchpads for further computer attacks because:

- The cost is that of a local call while the raid into the overseas computer is billed to the university.
- Universities have an Internet connection.
- Universities have powerful computers with minimal or non-existent security (for example, with a default password, etc.).

Some systems are more difficult to penetrate and might require weeks of study and attempts. In that case, hackers try to collect as much information as they can on the target system or Web site, its users, and its system administrator. They then try to identify possible vulnerabilities and establish where the administrator is on the network and what he is doing. To do this, they employ monitoring and identification techniques, collecting data on the target systems and storing them in dossiers that cover country of origin, presence of firewalls, operating system in use, presence of vulnerable ports open to certain types of protocols, connection speed, ISP, and any other information they can collect. The ability to collect information (so-called *intelligence*) is critical for hackers and IT security experts.

Social Engineering

Hackers often make use of *social engineering* to collect information useful for an attack, or just for information's sake, employing persuasion techniques to convince and influence whoever is on the other side.

To access the buildings of telephone companies and other corporations they are interested in, they pretend to be someone else, introduce themselves to other members of the staff as someone just hired and thus obtaining an identification badge, so they can then look for an unused workstation. Still using social engineering, they run password cracking programs or install *Access Point Wireless* (so they can then go outside the company and penetrate its systems far from indiscreet eyes) so as to get root access to the network. To do this, they must be extremely convincing. Their voices must be firm and confident, and their body language must be consistent with what they are saying. They pretend to be looking for help from their "colleagues," flattering them and deceiving them at the same time.* These techniques always work because they are based on the need to trust people, especially if someone pretends to be a colleague having difficulties, triggering a feeling of solidarity.†

Password Search

The key to a system is the password. Sensitive information like this can be obtained in different ways: through a Trojan, with a cracking program,‡ by *trashing*,§ or by intercepting e-mails such as those sent by the system administrator to new users. Furthermore, to gain access to a system with administrator privileges, hackers try out various "standard" logins. In particular, they all know now that there are only a very few default administrator passwords on UNIX systems, which are rarely modified once the new system has been installed (a highly dangerous practice).

Once they've got hold of the desired access, hackers use vulnerable, weak passwords to establish a shell account allowing them to log on to the network in the least obvious way, just like any authorized user, who usually chooses a password that is simple and easy to remember.

---

* See also Andrea "Pila" Ghirardini, *Social Engineering, Una Guida Introduttiva*, 2002, http://www.blackhats.it/it/papers/social_engineering.pdf.

† Kevin Mitnick is probably the greatest social engineer, certainly the most famous in hacking history. His book *The Art of Deception*, Wiley Publishing, Inc., Indianapolis, IN, 2002, can be considered a sort of manifesto of this "attack technique."

‡ L0phtCrack is a well-known password cracking program developed by a group called "L0pht Heavy Industries." It starts out with a common dictionary attack to find weak passwords. It scans a file containing common words in the dictionary and compares them with those chosen by the network users. These are the easiest passwords to find and are cracked very quickly. If the user has used a password not in the dictionary, the program moves on to phase two, a brute force attack, using thousands of combinations of letters, numbers, and special characters. In 20 minutes, it can come up with over 100 passwords, including the system administrator's. At this point, the hacker has root access; he "owns" the whole network.

§ This means going through the trash in a building where the target computers are. The idea is to find notes or draft documents containing passwords or details about the system to be violated. On the Web, you can find actual handbooks teaching all there is to know to go trashing.

Individual and Group Attacks

When hackers aren't acting alone, but in a group of two or three, they use a special *modus operandi* that often allows the police to identify who took part in the computer attack.

Today's hackers are better prepared against police raids, and they encrypt any sensitive data on their hard disk, their connections, and even their voice conversations. During their attacks, hackers are constantly on the phone to keep each other informed and compare notes on the action. That's why they hide their phone conversations too; it would be easy enough for investigators to identify the attackers through their telephone logs showing the connection between them.

Another typical aspect of a group action is a simultaneous attack, maybe using different techniques, so as to be sure the system is penetrated (sometimes this is used as an excuse to compete and see who can violate the system first).

This is typical not only for groups set up to do hacking together all the time, but also for groups of hackers who usually act alone but decide occasionally to join forces for a common target. When they act as a group, they can make it appear that the attack is coming from different parts of the world, getting access to systems all over the globe to mislead possible investigations. They usually employ different levels of "launch pad systems" before attacking the "target system."

A good example of this is the attack carried out by the "Skeleton Crew" on the Pentagon. First of all, they scanned the Net looking for systems that showed known vulnerabilities in the remote procedure call (RPC) code of the Solaris operating system. This allowed them to run commands and programs remotely on the target systems of choice. After doing this, they installed sniffer programs that let them capture hundreds of passwords, giving them access to the network systems through root and SysAdmin accounts. Finally, they installed trapdoors* that allowed them to crash the systems they had taken over.

Needless to say, there are different intrusion techniques and methods, but the possibility of recognizing a personal technique can lead investigators to attribute different attacks to the same person, identifying the author (the so-called "signature," which will be discussed later).

---

* This is a function programmers use to check remotely how programs are running during the testing phase. This function can be reactivated for illicit uses.

The Art of War: Examples of Attack Techniques

Expert hackers are highly sophisticated; they prepare and organize their attacks in advance, leaving nothing to chance. Above all, they are very careful to remove or conceal all possible traces of themselves online.

They are real strategists and tactical experts. One of their cult books is Sun Tzu's *The Art of War*. They are well organized; they write down each step of their action, both to be able to repeat it and also to have an idea of the various steps if things were to go wrong and they were to need to tell someone what happened (especially when entering a phone switching system).

Top hackers aim at installing their backdoor on a new software product before it's released. This technique is called "backdooring a program or an operating system" and shouldn't be confused with the one that allows entering a controlled system at will.*

In a Net browser, a backdoor allows a hacker to connect directly to any privately owned computer, even to home PCs, every time an Internet connection is activated (however, top hackers aren't at all interested in home computers). A famous tool for doing this is the Back Orifice Scanner, a Trojan horse developed by "Cult of the Dead Cow" ("cDc").

We have already mentioned one of the main techniques used, spoofing. There are different kinds of spoofing, depending on the object to "spoof" or use in order to deceive.

You can have IP spoofing, where hackers manage to deceive a system, making it believe that a message is coming from an authorized IP address belonging to a given computer, when in reality it was sent from a different one.

E-mail spoofing modifies the header of an e-mail, making the recipient think the message is coming from a different source. This technique is used mainly by phishers, who "fish" e-mail addresses for spamming purposes or sensitive data (names, addresses, credit-card numbers, etc.) to perpetrate frauds.

Data spoofing consists of adding, modifying, or deleting data present in a packet moving on a Net.

Then there is file spoofing, giving a file a different extension from the real one, thus deceiving the user. This technique is used by viruses,

---

* The term "backdoor" in hacker slang is used both as a noun and a verb.

too, hidden behind "reassuring" file extensions like .jpeg, or .zip, which really contain *executable* files (.exe).

The *modus operandi* script-kiddies use is different. First of all, they scan the Internet looking for systems with known vulnerabilities for which they have written, or copied, scripts that allow them to take it over and exploit it with a root access. Then they start Web defacing; they replace the home page of the target Web site with a new page containing a message informing the system administrator that the server is vulnerable to attacks. They don't usually destroy data present on the violated systems; actually, they nearly always save the original Web page and explain to the SysAdmin where to find it.

The favorite programming language used by hackers to write automated scripts for Web server defacing is PERL (practical extraction and report language), which is mainly used for word processing. This is the first language script-kiddies learn (hence their name).

Hackers consider Web servers running on Microsoft Windows, which have open ports (especially port 80), the easiest to deface. Web defacers exploit a common configuration error various administrators make, running FrontPage Web Server software by Microsoft, on their sites. Given that many administrators often don't configure access privileges correctly, anyone can modify, delete, load, or download information from the server.

On this point, it's worthwhile to describe Pr0metheus' *modus operandi*. He used three different scripts to automate and speed up the attack phases:

- The first was used to carry out a rapid search on Netcraft* so as to identify a first possible target list.
- A second script checked which operating system was used by the servers hosting the chosen sites so as to make a second selection.
- The last script looked for FrontPage systems with open ports (especially number 80) and access controls that allowed anyone to modify the Web site contents.

---

* This is a Web service allowing for identification of sites containing specific terms in their domain names: http://www.netcraft.com.

Attack Procedures

To understand "what hackers do," we will recap and illustrate the more popular techniques and procedures in use.

War Dialing: This is a very popular technique used in the first phase of an attack by hackers with a certain level of technical skills. The computer is instructed through scripts to dial from a list of progressive numbers until the modem of another computer answers. War dialing, a term derived from the film "War Games," is used to find telephone switch systems, which route phone calls, supervise them, and provide the identity of its clients and their numbers. These systems allow users to make calls that are routed all over the world. Basically, all calls go through a central switching system that sorts out both national and international calls.

Ping-of-Death Attack Against Web Servers: The term *PING* (packet internet groper) refers to a method to determine whether a system is present on a network and is operating correctly. To carry out a ping, an ICMP (internet control message protocol) is used to scan or test a connection and locate network accesses.

Networks use ICMP to identify and locate problems; for instance, a router that can't switch data packets at the same speed it receives them. ICMP messages are used to communicate messages between systems in a completely automatic way. When, for example, a user pings a server, he is sending the server an information packet. If the server is on the network, it will send back an answering packet. If, however, a server receives many packets in a short space of time (packet flooding), it might get flooded with information at such a speed that it can no longer respond, crashing and stopping legitimate users from downloading information. This is the classical *ping-of-death attack against Web servers*.

To carry out this kind of attack, hackers use proxy servers to hide their identity. In this way, network administrators monitoring the system through ping scans can't trace them.

NMAP: NMAP is software used for coordinated attacks to map the position, the configurations, and the vulnerability of important military and civilian servers. In its most sophisticated form, NMAP sends one or more data packets, which seem to arrive from different places around the world, to specific servers in a flow made up of millions of packets. NMAP is usually launched from dial-ups,* university systems, or ISP servers. This tool is virtually untraceable by IDSs (intrusion detection systems), as many system administrators will set the IDS alarm system at a higher level than necessary for one or two packets sent by NMAP.

In this way, NMAP makes stealth attacks much easier by scanning and recognizing the fingerprint of the remote operating system. With this tool, hackers are capable of mapping entire networks, even the entire Internet, on the lookout for vulnerable systems. Once they have found them, they can plan their attacks on the basis of the vulnerabilities discovered. In practical terms, hackers carry out scans on network ports, and in a few minutes each system responding to a ping or an *ICMP echo request* can be mapped and its operating system identified. These scans can be considered a clue that coordinated attacks to the systems in question might be in the offing.

Denial-of-Service (DoS): Script-kiddies working against large corporations and companies usually carry out these attacks. These are highly distributed attacks that require the use of many computers, called *zombies* because they are used without the knowledge of their owners and administrators. These vulnerable systems, such as those belonging to universities, are changed into zombies and used as launch pads to carry out DoS attacks with the use of previously installed malicious software.

To carry out an attack of this kind, it is necessary to be familiar with the network and its mapping. For this reason, it is never improvised but always planned and studied at length.

With a DoS attack, the incoming data packet flow exceeds the receiving capacity of the principal companies' router, reaching speeds between 800 Mb and 1 Gb per second.

---

* Dial-up: this term implies that the attacker will rarely if ever launch the NMAP from his PC, but will do it from another, previously violated computer system (usually UNIX or Linux), which is being used to carry out IP address and TCP/IP port scans.

There are also special *denial-of-service tools*. An example of this is Stacheldraht, (the German name for Barbed Wire), a variant of Tribal Flood Network (TFN). When this software is installed on target systems, it overloads them with data requests.

Usually such software is used by script-kiddies who want to know how they work, but they are developed by more sophisticated hackers who consider DoS attacks wrong and criminal. For this reason, they usually warn whoever tries to download these tools with messages such as, "WARNING: Using this program on public networks is highly illegal and they will find you and put you in jail. The author is no way responsible for your actions. Keep this one to your local network!"

Other DoS tools are so-called *bots* (abbreviation of "robots"), more commonly known as *ping o' doom* or *finger o' death*. Sometimes hackers, usually teenagers, either alone or as a group, use them in their battles for the control of chat rooms. As mentioned earlier, the battle consists in kicking one's adversaries out and crashing their systems with the use of these tools.

Another DoS attack tool was the notorious WinNuke, aimed at Windows 95 and Windows NT systems, against which it sent an *out of band* (OOB) packet to port 139 of the target host. This was a digital bomb that caused what is known as *blue screen of death* and was also called, for this reason, *blue screen bomb*.* The system accepting the data packet immediately crashed, and the screen filled with error messages. This was the favorite tool between groups of rival script-kiddies.

Finally, there are DoS attacks carried out by sending a flow of anonymous e-mails that self-replicate all over the network. These are *e-mail bombs*, used by hackers to crash systems and break down Internet connections.

Distributed Denial-of-Service (DDoS) Attack: This is very similar to a DoS attack, but the targets attacked at the same time are so many that it is considered a *distributed* attack.

Until a few years ago, hackers had to penetrate each individual machine and launch single versions of the DoS tool from there, so launching a DDoS was difficult and cumbersome. Today, automated

---

* That is the blue screen that appears on some Microsoft Windows systems when they totally crash.

scripts that even unskilled teenagers are able to use can scan the network, sniffing out vulnerable systems and installing the DDoS software, then ordering these now zombie systems to send floods of information to the other target systems on the Internet or other networks.

Both network bandwidth and number of hosts involved in the attack are essential to DDoS attacks. High-speed networks are the main targets for these attacks, just as university, government, and private company computers are excellent launch pads, thanks to their poor security.

Operating Inside a Target System

In order to discover new vulnerabilities, hackers examine carefully the program source code, then try it out to see if they can enter the system. Once inside, they first try to erase the traces of their intrusion (the log trail) to avoid being discovered. If they were discovered, they wouldn't be able to enter the system again, either because the vulnerability used has been eliminated by the administrator or because the "privileged" account they set up has been erased. Actually, hackers are usually identified and arrested because they don't know how to use *file cleaners*, which remove log files from the target system, as they don't know how these files are created or where they are placed inside the different operating systems.

Immediately after this, a hacker will build a backdoor. This will allow him to enter whenever desired. The advantage of using a backdoor is that the hacker will have access to the machine even if the system administrator has eliminated the initial vulnerability used to enter the system. Thanks to the backdoor, it will be possible for the hacker to log in and have direct access to the machine without the administrator noticing.

Once in the network, the first thing a hacker looks for is the SAM (security account manager) file among the system files if the system is Microsoft Windows. For other operating systems, the files to look for are the *passwd* and *shadow*, though there are significant differences. The SAM file contains information on all users (first and foremost, username and password); furthermore, there is a *SAM report file*, which is the backup copy. They copy either the SAM file or the backup copy (as it's usually encrypted or password protected) into a fake directory they created and use SAMDUMP.EXE, a program that expands the SAM file, putting it into a format that will allow the use of a password cracking program such as L0phtCrack.

To make sure the SysAdmin hasn't noticed anything, they monitor him to see what he is doing. They type the correct commands for the system to show which programs are running and who is present on it, including the SysAdmin. Of course, in order to do this, they must have acquired administrator privileges. In this way, they set up strategies allowing them to remain invisible on the violated system.

Usually, they then start poking around checking for interesting files to read, unless they have a specific target in mind, in which case they'll go looking for it immediately.

Once in the system, they might also decide to install a sniffer to log all users connecting or disconnecting from the system.

Sometimes trapdoors are installed so that the system now under control can be crashed later.

However, once a system or a network has been penetrated, the hacker will go looking for another, more difficult and therefore more stimulating, target.

The Hacker's Signature

Some hackers "sign" their forays into a system, always leaving something behind that makes them recognizable to other hackers. The signature is usually made up of their handle. As an example, when Phoenix creates a root access for himself, he always saves it with the same filename and in the same place inside the computer, or he creates accounts using his nickname.

When a lone hacker or group does Web defacement, they will leave a signature. In this way, instead of the original homepage, a message will appear such as, "*Nickname* was here," "*Nickname* owns you," or simply "Your system was own3d."*

In Web defacing cases, a message is usually left behind. Often, it is of a religious or political-social nature, and is addressed to Web site's users; messages may also be sent to all members of the group or to the site's administrator to let him know that the Web server has been "taken."

---

* Note how "3" often replaces "e" both in handles and during a conversation.

There are also messages announcing a departure from the hacker scene and from Web defacing in particular. This was the case of "RaFa" of the "WoH," who left the following message, "The goal in the community should be common. That is why I am leaving the defacing scene. They all seem to have lost sight of the real goals. I have to admit that what kept me in it so long was the fame and the friends."*

The signature might also be the type of target, or the attack procedure. Look at the Web defacing "World of Hell" group, which practiced *mass defacement* of companies and organizations with headquarters in Mexico or Russia. This was their "trademark." Finally, even the way a program is written, the style used, and the "look" can all be signatures leading back to the author.

Relationships with System Administrators

A certain rapport usually is created between hackers and administrators. It might be an open challenge but, paradoxically, it could also be cooperation. Once new system vulnerabilities have been discovered, a hacker might decide to keep the information to himself, pass it around to other members of the underground, and also inform the administrator. There are also compromise solutions, such as waiting for the SysAdmin to repair the "holes" in the system before revealing the vulnerabilities.

During our research, we met hackers who put themselves in the place of the administrators and understand how unpleasant it is to be under attack. They are aware of the efforts necessary to seek and identify aggressors and correct the faults. They therefore help the network administrator (maybe from their school), seeking out vulnerabilities, informing the administrator, and helping to get rid of them and manage the network.

True hackers warn the system administrator or the telephone company when they find weaknesses in security. Sometimes they even warn the SysAdmin to be more careful and replace the system and router default passwords. They might leave their e-mail address and notes for the system or Web site administrator they have attacked, offering their assistance for security issues. They sometimes tell them which exploits they employed to compromise the system or the Web server.

---

* Verton, D., *The Hacker Diaries: Confessions of Teenage Hackers,* McGraw-Hill, 2002.

The World of Hell group behaved in this way, as they wanted to prove that any Web server is vulnerable and can be penetrated. In this way, the group wanted to help in the repair of the server's vulnerabilities. From their point of view, it was better for companies to be defaced by them rather than by criminals who try to gain an advantage to commit more serious and damaging crimes, causing financial and other types of loss.

There are, however, some hackers who write reports for the members of the underground, where they list the vulnerabilities they know. Their interest lies in showing how easy it would be for administrators to remove the faults found so that if a system is attacked, the blame lies with the careless administrator. In any case, these reports show other hackers how to find companies that haven't yet eliminated their vulnerabilities, sometimes even a year after the information has been published.

Many hackers say that they release so-called 0-day exploits to improve Internet security. These codes make use of known vulnerabilities in commercial software and are released over the Internet by their author, so anyone can download them. According to some hackers, the "public service function" of 0-day exploits is just an excuse, as they believe that there are more appropriate ways to improve security on the Web, and these codes should not be made public.

Motivations

Let's now analyze the question raised in Chapter 3: motives. Why hacking? What did our interviewees answer? Are the motives serial criminals have in the physical world somehow analogous to those that lead a hacker to operate in the electronic world?

The First Step

Usually, an interest in hacking arises out of curiosity; only later does it become someone's main interest, going from being a hobby at first and then becoming a driving passion that can later develop into a job.

Some adolescents just think it's cool to do hacking and belong to the underground. Their search for an identity leads them to join a group, because feeling that they belong to something greater than themselves is for them a need that guarantees protection and safety. They are attracted to this world for the camaraderie present in the hacker community.

It's also clear that some teenagers approach hacking to follow a *fad* rather than through any real conviction. They don't care how things work. They want to learn how to practice hacking quickly, as if they were following a recipe, without being fired up by the passion for knowledge and understanding the various steps in a computer attack. They are interested in the results, not in how you get there. They don't share the spirit of real hackers. For this reason, other hackers call them wannabe lamers or, more simply, lamers.

It also seems that many started hacking after seeing the hacker in the films "War Games" and "Ferris Bueller's Day Off" we already mentioned. Others were fascinated by the sensational actions carried out by hackers who claim, for example, that they managed to shift orbiting satellites.

Finally, many start hacking merely because they have a PC capable of communicating with other computers over a telephone line.

Another recurring motive is escaping an uncomfortable reality—a family with divorced or absent parents, a school system seen as oppressive, or street gangs that they don't believe to be the only "possibility" open to them. Their computer is seen as an escape route, a tool allowing them to access virtual worlds they can run to and escape their unfulfillable empty lives.

Then there are those who do hacking to show that they are smart, brilliant, and capable of winning any challenge. In these cases, hacking is the way to conquer and therefore exhibit their excellence.

Declared Motives

Often hackers can't explain why they do hacking. Their motives can be manifold and not mutually exclusive. Here is a list of the main ones:

- Intellectual curiosity, so as to learn and gain knowledge.
- Love of technology.
- To prove they are smart and intelligent.
- For fun.

- Using a computer the usual way is boring. ("Anyone can do that, so how can I distinguish myself from others? Easy, using it in an unconventional way.")
- They love to solve problems.
- To improve computers, make them more powerful and user friendly.
- To increase the security level of networks and computer systems.
- To defend civil liberties in cyberspace and make information free and accessible to everyone, defeating communication and knowledge monopolies.
- To offer a service, often sharing accesses they believe ought to be free (this is the struggle against telecommunication monopolies).
- To safeguard their own and everyone else's privacy from intrusions by the authorities.
- Antiestablishment attitudes (in particular military and industrial), so the individual can triumph over the community.
- Rebelliousness, challenging the authorities (not only police and government agencies but also system administrators, teachers, parents, and adults in general) so they can show their "hacker power" and feel superior.
- A sense of adventure, the adrenalin rush, the thrill of doing something forbidden, or the fact of *owning* a system, of "defeating" a PC by making it do one's bidding.
- Bored by routine.
- Romanticism, tradition, the "myth;" in other words, because it's "cool."
- To attract media attention in the hope of becoming famous.
- For money.
- Anger and frustration.
- Political reasons.
- Attracted by the camaraderie in the hacker community.
- To escape a conflicting family environment and alienating social reality.
- Professional reasons (computer security experts, cyber-warriors, industrial spies, government agents, and military hackers).

We mustn't forget that motives change with the generations. First-generation hackers (at the end of the 1970s) were fired up by the thirst for knowledge.

The second (first half of the 1980s) were impelled by curiosity, joined with the thirst for knowledge and the fact that many operating systems could only become familiar by "penetrating" them. Later, toward the second half of the 1980s, hacking became more widespread, partly because by now it was a fashion, a fad.

The third generation (1990s) simply wanted to do hacking, which implied wanting to learn and get to know something new, with the intention to violate computer systems and exchange information in the underground community. In this phase, the first hacker groups came on the scene, *e-zine* hackers arose, and BBSs started developing.

The fourth and last generation (of the year 2000) is impelled by anger. Often, they don't have many technical skills but consider being a hacker fashionable; they don't know or aren't interested in the history, the culture, or the ethics of phreaking and hacking. Here hacking is mixed with politics and becomes *cyber hacktivism*.

Let's look in detail now at the main motives listed.

Intellectual Curiosity: Both phreakers and hackers have in common the desire to explore the invisible electronic worlds. They have the curiosity of a child who listens to his parents telling him a fairy tale, visualizes the place where the story is taking place, and enters this new world to be explored. We can say that hackers and phreakers both want to understand *how the machines, the network, and the telephone system work*, so as to understand better the technological world that surrounds them. Obviously, in order to do this, they try to imagine the structure of the system; they map it.

The main reason, the common link, is the wish to learn the telephone system or the network and its architecture and understand how these things work, and to learn computer security. Hacking is seen as a formative growth process—a step in personal development. They want to see "from the inside" how the system works, testing the limits of the machine. To do this, they carry out a veritable autopsy of the machine; they dissect it and examine the individual elements and then look at it as a whole, trying to understand how the various elements work and interact. This is a bit like doctors who in the past used cadavers to understand anatomy and learn about how the human body works and in this way discover new treatments. What impels them is the inexhaustible thirst for knowledge, discovery, and experimentation. It's a veritable craving, a term taken from drug addiction that implies the desire and need to devour the substance in question, in this case, knowledge.

The most famous network among those in existence is the Internet, which remains for hackers an inexhaustible source of information, allowing them to explore the world and go where they want to go, freeing themselves from the bonds of money. The Internet is a *democratic* tool in that it doesn't make any class, ethnic, gender, or skin color distinctions—just like the underground. Hackers feel like scientists (according to Mark Abene, alias "Phiber Optik") using their computers as microscopes to examine the system to which they are connected. They do this to understand the principles of computer security and to share with others what they have learned through hacking.

The words of "FonE_TonE" of the WoH are revealing:

> We like to find new things, see what we can do and what we can't do... Not all defacements are political, but it's still good to know that we do it for a reason. I hack because I love to learn new things about network security.*

So *hackers* want to understand how PCs, or technological machines, work, while *crackers* want to destroy systems. In theory, the distinction between these two categories is clear, but in practice there is a fine line between them. It might be that a hacker, seeking revenge for some wrong he has suffered, or to vent his anger, will decide to crash one or more systems, but a system might also be crashed by mistake through lack of familiarity with a particular system.

According to Explotion, there are three different kinds of attackers on the hacker scene today:

- True hackers: they want to learn, so they are suitable for recruitment in the computer security sector.
- Crackers: they hack with malicious intent, so they aren't suitable to be involved in security.

---

* Verton, D., *The Hacker Diaries: Confessions of Teenage Hackers*, McGraw-Hill, 2002.

- Lamers: they want to become crackers without learning; they are harmless, give up at the first encountered difficulty, and very quickly set aside their intents.

So hackers want to visit new places. They feel the need to conquer new worlds with their PC. The computer is seen as a real "window" on the world, allowing them to go to new places every day and learn something more on their own. The telephone network is seen as a limitless world, which still has to be explored. They are proud of their "work," and they feel they are artists to such an extent that they often sign with their handle. They consider hacking and phreaking to be an *art form*.

Hackers have an uncontrollable need to satisfy their thirst for knowledge and to discover new computers and new systems, because each machine has its own characteristics, its own programming language, and its own secrets. They are also interested in the information contained in them, and this is also part of their thirst for knowledge. Others are not so much interested in the information on a machine but rather in understanding how the information circulates inside the system. All they have to do is understand where these systems are in cyberspace. The objective is that of owning the machine, making it do one's bidding, and having access to it at will.

There are also Web sites where one can practice *legal hacking*. Sometimes hackers who have set aside their illegal activities continue not only as a job, but also for fun or for instruction, practicing on legal hacking sites,* which are also *ethical hacking* sites.

Here you can hack legally. This goes to show how many do it for the love of knowledge and discovery and not just because they want to do something forbidden or break the law.

Ethical hackers limit themselves to penetrating the system. For them it's exciting and satisfying to just enter a system that is considered secure. They have no interest in destroying data or stealing sensitive information; they consider the ones who do so to be criminals. Ethical hackers, who are *true* hackers, have no impure motives; they don't seek personal gain, all they want is knowledge. On the other hand, when hacking isn't for scientific reasons or for learning purposes, it is practiced for economic gain or under the influence of anger.

---

* For example, http://www.progenic.com.

Love of Technology: When the motivation is love of technology, hacking consists in exploring, and this is never destructive. Furthermore, hacking becomes an unconventional way of living, thinking, and viewing things and reality, as well as a means to solve problems that can't otherwise be faced. In these cases, hacking isn't limited to the computer world but moves into other areas. The object might be a PC but could just as well be a car engine, a toaster, or anything else that can be handled and studied. PCs, though, are always the prime object of interest. They are irresistible because they are tools that allow you to discover the world while sitting in your room "playing" with a keyboard.

Fun and Games: Hackers who hack out of curiosity or for fun never do it for money, for the pleasure of damaging someone. For them something clever, which holds technical difficulties, is also fun.

We have said that some hackers do it for fun. With their intrusion, they try to attract the attention of system administrators, forcing them to respond. They enjoy playing "cops and robbers." They get great satisfaction from their forays; they feel fulfilled and proud of themselves. For them, the fun lies not only in working out how to penetrate a system but also how to crack software. These things stimulate them intellectually a lot more than school does. For them, nothing is more attractive than this kind of technological challenge.

For a real hacker, the greatest challenge, and the most fun, consists in getting into someone else's system. Their action and involvement ends there, though, because once they are inside, they get bored and have no interest in staying longer or in returning there unless they are looking for something specific or consider what they have found particularly intriguing.

Some hackers have very strong egos, and they get the same thrill at the idea of being caught by the police as they get from hacking.

There are also hacker/phreakers who do it because they have fun playing tricks on people all over the world. Many have a strong sense of humor, which is reflected in their online activities. Consider Web defacement with funny contents. This kind of motivation is common to nearly all hackers and is very marked in script-kiddies.

In this category, we can also place those who love solving problems. They especially like to create computer problems for not particularly skilled people and then invent a solution.

Making the PC World Safer: Many hackers want to be remembered for having changed things for the better, contributing to improve computers and making them more powerful and user friendly. In particular, they want to increase the level of security of computer networks and systems. We have already seen how many hackers declare it when they release 0-day exploits to improve Internet security.

The case of "World of Hell" is exemplary. They wanted to prove how vulnerable and accessible *all* Web servers are. In doing this, the group wanted to correct vulnerabilities. To understand the philosophy of WoH and many other groups, it's useful to look at how they justified their attacks.

> WoH was about having fun. And we figured that if we defaced a box there would be downtime and maybe a little money lost, but what if we or someone else who hacked the box didn't deface it? What if they erased their tracks and backdoored it and kept coming in and using the box for illegal things and tacking personal and sensitive information from it and no one would ever know? At least when you deface, they know someone has been there, and they fix it so someone else more malicious can't come in and screw things up.*

Public opinion commonly believes that hackers share anarchic ideals. This is true only of some and has to be qualified if the implication is having a political ideology. On the whole, if we look carefully at the hacker world, it's possible to realize how the idea of setting up a sort of cyber "Wild West" is far from their wishes. Actually, the opposite is true: *if anarchy means the absence of all rules, hacker ethics is its antithesis.*

When dealing with hackers, at least with those that share the *ethics*, the objective isn't anarchy but replacing existing rues in the cyber and telephone world (which many consider unfair, as they leave the control of technological means in the hands of the few) with new rules, guaranteeing greater security and equal access to all users. They can be considered "anarchists" only from this point of view, because they are trying to subvert the existing order in telecommunication systems and replace it with a true cyber/telematic democracy.

---

* Verton, D., *The Hacker Diaries: Confessions of Teenage Hackers*, McGraw-Hill, 2002.

They see the "chaos" they create on the Internet as beneficial; the paranoia they generate in the business world and among users is a good thing. After all, apart from being hackers, they are also users—consumers who don't want their credit cards and identities to be stolen and used by others.

Fighting for Freedom: Many hackers, such as RaFa of the WoH, consider hacking as a tool with which to face many political and social problems. Hacking is used mainly to defend oneself from violations of the principles that govern the online world, from the attacks of the physical world they consider morally corrupt, such as the attacks against the civil liberties of both hackers and all other users.

They hate the system and are ready to change it through their activities. Theirs is a veritable mission. However, this is only one aspect of the struggle for freedom. Hackers really want to defend the right to information (which they define as *knowledge addiction*), making information free and accessible to everyone and in this way break the communication and culture monopoly.

Not surprisingly, hacking and phreaking started in the U.S.A., a country with a long tradition of freedom and *conquest*, elements that are directly linked. As Kevin Mitnick says, "In the U.S., we have invented three typically American things: cowboys, hamburgers, and hackers."

Some believe they are offering a real service to society, fighting for freedom of thought in the World Wide Web and freedom in general. Cyber pirates are pursuing the objective of a free share of information. To clarify this concept, we will quote a manifesto written by anonymous Apple employees who founded the "Nu-Prometheus League"*:

> The Nu-Prometheus League has no ambition beyond seeing the genius of a few Apple employees benefit the entire world, not just dissipated by Apple through litigation and ill will.

Furthermore, hackers want to defeat the communications monopoly, bringing to their knees the hated telephone companies. They believe

---

* A group of hackers who in 1989 managed to duplicate and distribute the code of Macintosh systems for controlling the internal chip for managing the screens of Apple machines.

that the media and the population are badly informed. They don't know what hacking is, and they can't understand it and what it means for practitioners—ignorance often breeds fear of what is unknown, mysterious, and obscure. But hackers don't really care that people are afraid of them. They don't view themselves as criminals; they consider criminals the ones who want to censor information and stop the search for truth, for knowledge. They consider themselves as the defenders of these basic human rights and fight with the weapons of intellect and courage. They feel they have a mission that motivates them: a reason of being.

We can say that for hackers, freely sharing acquired knowledge and information with the other members of the underground is the fundamental, if not the only, principle of the *hacker ethics*, as a corollary to the principle of maximum freedom of information.

This is the reason for their claim that they *supply a service*, sharing accesses they believe ought to be free. They admit to using, without paying, an already existing service, a service that ought to be provided free of charge to everyone or at the very least should be less expensive, if it were not for the profit of a few greedy people.

Conflict with Authority: Some hackers believe their privacy is violated by police raids and wiretaps.* They don't think they are invading privacy (which is what wiretapping does), as they claim they only hack to improve their technical knowledge and defend themselves from enemies.

For this reason, the establishment in general, and the military–industrial establishment in particular, are often seen as forms of oppression of the individual.

Apart from curiosity, another *push-factor* can be political or ideological motives (for instance, pacifist, antinuclear, etc.), as is the case for attacks against government agency Web pages.

Here is an example to clarify this concept. In 1989, a worm struck and jammed NASA's computers. The worm was called by its author WANK (Worm Against Nuclear Killers). It was disseminated based on the fear that NASA could use the space programs to put into orbit the first nuclear stellar weapons.

---

* Wiretap: telephone interception, on the "landline," on PSTN or ISDN data lines.

The antiestablishment views of the underground world are usually aimed at organizations and agencies that in their eyes want to hinder technological development and free circulation of information through a market monopoly (e.g., telephone companies).

Antiestablishment views are shared by most hackers, especially Australian, American, and British. In the U.K., Manchester is the city where these views have mainly taken root. This can be explained by the special history of the city, which was the heart of the textile industry during the whole of the nineteenth century, but the economic boom did not mean wealth for the working classes, which was mostly deprived. Even today, unemployment is still rampant.

Hacking therefore becomes a way to challenge the authorities, seen as the oppressor. The "81gm" group, which has been founded by "Pad," a hacker from Manchester, is one of the best if not the top British group.

It's worth remembering again how hackers have no concept of a hierarchical authoritarian (vertical) view of the relationship between the three entities of the Net (governments, hackers, and users) but rather consider a partnership between equals (horizontal), peer to peer, as the sign of a real democracy (see Chapter 5).

Rebelliousness: To defy the establishment, rebelliousness can be added to the open challenge to any kind of authority, therefore not only institutional authorities, such as police forces or large corporations, but in a broad sense, too (system administrators, parents, and adults in general).

For hackers with this kind of motivation, the satisfaction they get by challenging authorities—first and foremost the police and computer security experts—allows them to feed their inflated egos. They feel gratified by using their wits to thumb their noses at experts by penetrating supposedly secure systems, as well as enjoying the action of entering a desired machine and possessing it, knowing that the system is in their power. Even Kevin Mitnick's Web site has been violated, and some of his security reports are now available on P2P networks!

Many also feel that continuing to hack while the police or the system administrator is investigating them is the greatest imaginable challenge. In this way, rebelliousness feeds the *competition* for reaching levels of excellence. These hackers want to become great, elite hackers.

They get satisfaction from defeating the system, the establishment, the upper crust of society.

They often feel the need to hack not only to challenge the authorities but also to challenge themselves and their own capabilities.

Spirit of Adventure and Ownership: Some hackers, usually with a very big ego, feel the thrill of the forbidden; they get very excited at the idea of being caught by the police. This is also because if this were to happen, they would become even more famous—practically celebrities.

Hacking allows them to take over the system, especially if they have obtained accounts with administrator privileges. This is enough to give them an adrenalin rush, because they know that they own the system and they can do anything they want with it—run any process or program they wish to or even delete the users they don't want to allow to use the system.

From this point of view, they are very possessive of the systems they own and which got their attention; so much so that often they make it a personal list. They feel that an administrator accessing "their "system is invading them. For these hackers, it isn't enough to know that if they want the system they can have it, they have to go ahead and do it. They feel the need to see what's inside the system they possess. What makes them really angry is the administrator getting involved with the system's security, because they want him to know that he isn't the one controlling it. From this point of view, the SysAdmin has to be punished for having "dared" to disturb them, by expelling him from the system he is supposed to manage.

They find great satisfaction in penetrating systems that are considered secure and invulnerable (this is the most common motivation for script-kiddies). They keep at it until they get there. Their motivation is the adrenalin rush due to the challenge of hacking—a challenge to their skills, a challenge to the limitations of their machines, and a challenge to systems considered invulnerable.

Hacking really consists in managing to do something others consider to be impossible—solving problems thought to be without a solution. This is what stops them from giving up at the first difficulties. To understand better the concept and the *spirit* of most hackers, here is a quote from Genocide:

It didn't seem like the wrong path. It was adventurous. All of us were adventurous. It was like leaving an etched path to find your own way. We were doing things and going places that most people never even dreamed of. It's sort of the same thrill that a trailblazer gets.*

This attitude is particularly typical of Web defacers who aim at possessing the Internet.

Boredom: If we look at "The Hacker Manifesto" written by "The Mentor," which is considered to be the cyber underworld's "Declaration of Independence," it becomes apparent that boredom with what is taught at school has an important role to play. So the computer becomes a new world to be explored, a refuge from the incompetence of adults. These hackers don't believe they are criminals. They say they are simply curious and are looking for knowledge. They are even bored by what they can learn from their computer science teachers, who usually know less than they do, and they could actually give lessons to them.

Attracting Attention, Becoming Famous: Some hackers feel the need to advertise their successes in the hope of becoming famous and attracting media attention. This goes even if it implies or is the result of a police raid, followed by seizure of the tools used to commit the crime, and even arrest.

Often, media attention and notoriety become the ultimate goal of the hacker (either alone or in a group). This is far more important than the message he wants to pass on. This is the case for RaFa of the WoH, who, on leaving the underground, left the message we quoted above,† which goes to confirm what we perceived.

Anger and Frustration: Cases where hacking, as a tool that gives power, is used to avenge a wrong are not rare. This is the main motivation of script-kiddies who often act alone. Anger and frustration lead them to undertake personal wars. These are of two kinds, outward or inward.

An example of the first kind is that of "Pr0metheus," who defines himself as "Satan's disciple," and under this persona practices Web

---

* Verton, D., *The Hacker Diaries: Confessions of Teenage Hackers*, McGraw-Hill, 2002.
† See the section titled "The Hacker's Signature."

defacing of Christian and religious sites as a personal crusade against organized religions. For the second kind, we can look at "Explotion," who feels irritated by most people because he considers them unintelligent.

So there are two types of character at work here:

- Those who hate a special category of people or of ideals (Pr0metheus).
- Those who are angry at the system in general (Explotion, who is unsure how, where, and against whom to vent his rage).

Pr0metheus is one of the so-called "Satan's hackers" and leader of a Web defacer group called "Hacking for Satan," which destroys only Christian Web sites. The defacement of these sites is not only part of his war against Christianity but also a way to recruit new disciples and disseminate the principles of Satanism and its symbols, which appear on the defaced Web sites. He see his activities as a form of hacktivism; he hacks to give the floor to Satan and, unlike most hackers, to make people more aware of Internet security problems or out of a love for technology. He doesn't feel he is evil; he just hates organized religions and especially Christianity. Pr0metheus doesn't practice defacing because it's easy, nor does he do it to promote better computer security, show off his skills, or gain respect from the underground. Defacing is only a tool to promote his cause, and in doing this he feels fulfilled. For him it is more than just thumbing his nose at Webmasters; he hopes more people will become interested in Satanism. He has stated that, if it wasn't for this, he would have given up hacking long ago.

Then there is a kind of anger that doesn't have a specific target but, as in Explotion's case, is aimed at the system in general. This kind of anger turns to violence and sometimes becomes hate. For example, he doesn't like people who aren't very intelligent, but the problem is that he considers many people "dumb" (such as lamers who keep asking him how to do hacking).

Many hackers, especially teenagers, are impelled by anger. They say they have reasons to be angry and vent this rage through hacking. The feeling is usually caused by the fact that they come from deprived families, and for them computers and hacking are an escape route from a life that is stressful and out of control. In this case, hacking is seen only as a means for revenge.

Other hackers want to send a message through their actions, especially through Web defacement. Think of RaFa from WoH, who was disgusted by an increasingly corrupt and unsafe world, where truth is sacrificed on the altar of corruption and where all resources are depleted by a few governments while there are people dying of hunger every day. The whole system is viewed as corrupted and is the target for their rage, starting with governments that allow unemployment, ignorance, and underdevelopment. Hackers try to get the attention of the media with their raids and then use them to pass on their message (usually on social problems).

Political Reasons: Some hackers try to involve the whole underground in hacktivism (i.e., political activism through hacking) without necessarily targeting members of any political party. Among them we must include those who use Web defacement for purely political motives, attributing a specific meaning to their actions and hoping to get the media attention that can derive from this. Think of the American group, "the Dispatchers," who defaced Web sites as a defense against religious fanaticism. Right after 9/11, they attacked and disabled Internet connections in Afghanistan and Palestine, but they also defaced the Web sites of religious organizations throughout the Middle East. Their objective was to trace the Internet connections of Osama bin Laden's terrorist network Al Qaeda so as to launch attacks against his communications system.

Escape from Family, Escape from Society: We have seen how many hackers come from problem families, living in strained circumstances where parents are fighting or given to alcohol abuse. Often, these subjects find refuge in their passion for computers to get away from a life of isolation and loneliness. They feel they are alone and abandoned by their schoolmates. Because they feel misunderstood, they live on the fringes of society.

Professionals: Up to now, we have mainly traced the profile of people who are impelled by their passion, who hack for the pleasure of discovery or the love of technology, or in any event not for professional reasons. But we mustn't forget that there are hackers among security experts, too: cyber-warriors, industrial spies, government agents, and the military. Think of those who deal with computer security and carry out penetration tests (PenTests) to verify the degree of vulnerability of a system. The difference here lies in the fact that the security violations take place with the approval of the system owner, so the intrusion is no longer illegal, and it becomes an actual profession.

However, there are also government agents, often former hackers from the underground, who attack government systems of other countries (for espionage or counterespionage) or of their own country (to test the vulnerabilities of their own systems), and there are also industrial spies and mercenaries (so-called *cyber-warriors*).

Another category that must not be confused with those mentioned above is that of military hackers. They are still professional hackers, but they are military personnel (or nonmilitary with special authorization), part of the armed forces of a specific country, who are ordered to hack in pursuit of specific military strategies. They fight their wars behind the scenes, using a computer connected to the Net instead of "conventional" weapons.

The Power Trip

What is hacking if not the highest expression of hackers' power? The "primary witness" of this show of power is the machine, and the "secondary witnesses" are ordinary people.

This begs the question of how a computer can be considered not only a tool but also an *audience*. The answer is simple, even though it might not be clear to a nonhacker. The fact of the matter is that hackers feel that they can *rule* the machine. If you know which commands to use ("if you are skilled, if you know what you are doing," as they say in the field), the machine responds to you. It follows you, it doesn't let you down, you have it in your power, and you can make it do whatever you wish. The machine's response, desired and strived for, is like the audience's applause after a brilliant performance of the "hacker artist." Furthermore, this is an always-available "audience;" you can make it "applaud" whenever you want, but at the same time it is uncompromising in case of error.

Speaking of commands, as we said earlier, hackers can be seen not only as scientists or artists but also as leaders of troops and veritable strategists, because all computer attacks have to be prepared down to the smallest details, and nothing can be left to chance.

It might well be that rebelling against the authorities will paradoxically lead to an interest in instruments of power, such as martial
arts, weapons, social engineering, and, of course, hacking. This is as
if to say that *conventional* forms of power are being challenged with
unconventional methods.

But the thrill of power is not without risk. Those who start to hack
because they think it's cool, as if it were a fad, feel all-powerful and
boast of their exploits to arouse awe and reverence in other members
of the underground. For this reason, many feel they must make their
intrusions known to the world at large, informing the media so everyone is aware of their power and what they can do with it. Others,
however, are "satisfied" with advertising their exploits only in their
circle of friends.

The first behavior, typical of teenage hackers who like to show off
so as to be noticed, makes them more vulnerable and easily identified by the police. The authorities won't find it difficult to verify the
authorship of an intrusion when the author has loudly claimed it for
himself. These hackers don't understand the risk they run, or they
don't take it into consideration because they feel they are invincible.

Many hackers have *delusions of omnipotence;* they like to have full
control of computers and, through them, of people's daily lives,
manipulating software, PCs, and the data stored on them. Some like
to show their power by crashing systems or modifying information in
electronic documents discovered during an intrusion. Here we have
a behavior that goes against the *hacker ethics*, which we will discuss
in depth later. For instance, they can modify the financial data of a
bank's customer, giving money to some and bankrupting others. The
feeling that everyone is in their power makes them feel good.

More skilled hackers feel the need to have not only "ordinary"
people in their power but also less expert hackers. This character trait
can be found in Kevin Poulsen and Paul Stira (alias "Scorpion," from
"MOD"), and this aspect is directly linked to their capacity to manipulate the conscience of others. In order to do this, the control technique
they use is to communicate to the others only part of the information
they have.

They are also strongly attracted to the unknown, to what has still to
be explored, and the mysterious, which often leads some to occultism
as well as sinking deeply into the underground. Kevin Poulsen springs

to mind again. He revered the Hungarian magician and illusionist Harry Houdini. From this point of view, magic can also be seen as a form of power, because it allows you to show and make believe things that aren't true and are merely illusory.

But the greatest *magic* of all are computer attacks, because by using special "tricks," they can make you believe one thing rather than another and yet, at the same time, they have the power of being "real."

Lone Hackers

Some hackers prefer to hack alone because they don't trust others, and they believe that in this way there is less risk of being discovered. They believe that when you act as a group, there is always a weakest link. They keep their online activities secret, letting only a few trusted persons know about them, without setting up any intimate collaboration. That way, no one can know much about them and reveal anything to the police. When talking about their exploits, they are very cautious and vague; they don't provide any precise information on what they have done. If it's a really important event, they keep the information to themselves. They never talk about their activities over the telephone out of fear of being under surveillance by the police.

However, this type of behavior might change during a hackers or phreaker's career. At the beginning, they feel the need to learn, so they have to establish contacts with more expert hackers they can turn to for advice. Once they have learned the basics, they can get the necessary information by themselves. To discover new vulnerabilities, they examine program source codes and experiment with them to see whether they can use them to penetrate a system.

Only in a few cases has the increasingly technological complexity of computers led hackers to act as groups made up of different specialists. But this is true only for those who aren't interested in learning and are attracted only by certain specialties.

However, even hackers who prefer to act alone may sporadically operate as a team for special projects and forge links with other underground members, with whom to talk and compare notes and also exchange knowledge and experiences.

We must also stress how the introduction of new, more severe laws against computer crimes has caused a shift in the underground world over the last few years. From being an open and friendly community, it is becoming a more and more closed circle, restricted and exclusive. In the past, its "inhabitants" cooperated among themselves, but now they are more wary and tend to avoid being part of a group. They prefer to act alone (which is why they are defined as *lone hackers*), to reduce the probabilities of being caught. Hackers are more isolated and more reluctant to share information. They act alone not only out of choice but also out of a need to protect themselves.

Hacker Groups

Ever since the so-called hacker crackdowns* at the end of the 1990s, top-notch hackers have been acting alone because of the increased risk of discovery when acting as a group. There are, however, some underground communities frequented by top hackers, even though they are a lot less common and more fragmented than in the past. These hackers have reached new levels of sophistication, not so much in their attacks but in their strategies and objectives.

In the past, elite hackers such as "Electron" and "Phoenix" would try to get copies of "Zardoz,†" which contained a list of security holes discovered by experts from the computer industry. Today, they prefer to find the bugs themselves, reading the proprietary source code line by line from companies such as HP, CISCO, Sun, and Microsoft. Some then sell to competitors the proprietary source codes obtained by means of industrial espionage. These hackers keep the developers in the dark about the original bugs found in their software, so patch releases are delayed. Hackers can use this advantage to enter the system as soon as the product is released. The second favorite target is the *source code development machine*—computer development systems used by programmers to create software code, applications, or operating systems.

---

* This term refers to the first great FBI antihacker operation. Later, many other countries—including Italy, Sweden, Germany, and France—followed their example, launching massive operations against BBS owners and online visitors. Often, searches were targeted to legitimate users who had little to do with the hacking world. The first crackdowns showed the lack of knowledge the law and order agencies had of the underground world. See Bruce Sterling, *The Hacker's Crackdown*, published by Bantam.

† A computer security mailing list with access limited to professionals in the field.

Script-kiddies, too, usually act alone, even when they are part of a group.

There are also hackers who belong to more than one group, and it frequently happens that members of one group dissolve it to create a new one.

Adolescents who approach this as a fad, or because they are attracted by the underground world, often join a group. The reasons for this choice vary from the strictly technical to the more psychological.

Feeling part of something is important for developing a personal identity. The group helps and gives support. In groups, the feeling of belonging and the protection that derives from the other members prevails, so the individual feels more self-confident. These are all important factors for the psychological development of the individual during a certain phase of growth, because following the example of the other members of the group, and of the leader in particular, will help an individual develop his own behavioral model.

The feeling of well-being that comes from being accepted by the other members of the group must not be underestimated, nor should the appreciation for actions undertaken that lead to a more important role within the internal dynamics of the group.

Last but not least, the greatest advantage of acting as a group is that responsibility is shared equally and does not fall to a single member. In other words, acting as a group, the group feels safe. This can be dangerous, as sometimes mistakes are made when one's guard is let down.

Initiation Rites

Usually, only the best hackers are allowed to become part of a group that recruits new members from BBS and IRC regulars. The top hackers set up their own chat rooms that can only be accessed by invitation. To gain access to a group, it isn't enough to claim alleged achievements; one's will and skills must be proven. Many hackers expect to become part of the more famous groups without undergoing any test, without having to prove themselves.

On the contrary, the case of World of Hell is a good example. They looked for adepts among coders, not script-kiddies. They immediately accepted qualified hackers with a list of defacements to their names. All others, if they wanted to be admitted, had to first deface a number of Web sites. All members also had to actively contribute to the actions of the group; otherwise, they would be expelled. The first Web site they defaced was a pornographic one. It was a demonstration, a warning to the underground world that WoH hackers were not script-kiddies but professionals to be feared. They wanted 2001 to be remembered as the year no one could feel safe from WoH.

Restricted access to groups has the dual purpose of preserving the secrets and the knowledge a group has built up over years of activity and also to ensure the quality standards of the group, avoiding access to the group and its knowledge to all and sundry. For this reason too, in the more sophisticated groups, communications between members take place in private chats.

Internal Organization of Groups

It's interesting to note how many young American hackers have spent time as members of street gangs involved in crime, usually robberies, and then moved on to groups involved in hacking. The shift from one kind of group to the other is also due to the fact that they are aware they can't control what happens in the street. In that context, they feel like pawns, but they can control everything that happens on the "electronic network highways." At least this is the reason that led to John Lee's (alias "Corrupt") shift.

This move is also made possible by the fact that there aren't many differences between street gangs and underground groups, as the internal dynamics of the groups are identical. The sense of belonging prevails in both, as well as the protection offered by the other members of the group; the individual feels safe and self-confident.

However, it must be said that, even if a group might appear to be closely knit and supportive, members aren't always united enough to protect each other when the need arises. There have been cases in which one group member has collaborated with investigators, giving them the names of the other members, helping them to collect evidence. The member then testifies against former "colleagues" to save himself and avoid going to jail, or even in the hope of getting a job in some government agency.

But there are also hackers who would never testify against members of their group, preferring to go to jail and keep their dignity and honor. Usually, there is a high degree of solidarity, not only between members of the same group but also between hackers in general when it becomes a question of protecting each other, e.g., during a police raid or when one of them is in trouble.

There is no hierarchy in hacker groups; all members are on an equal level, and the leader is usually whoever founded the group.

The "division of labor" can also be extremely diversified. In an organized group, each member has a particular technical specialty. In this case, though, as we have already mentioned, the individual members aren't interested in a comprehensive view of hacking, or at any rate they don't have any cross-skills. Conversely, more sophisticated groups (like WoH) only recruit hackers with a wide range of skills and knowledge. All must know how to program, even though some members are better than others.

However, the more capable individuals, possessing know-how and skills spanning different systems and networks, usually like to act alone.

Rules and Social Intercourse within the Group

Groups have very strict rules, and if they are broken the transgressor is immediately expelled. The main principle is *sharing* all information gathered during a computer raid.

Furthermore, these groups often have a BBS accessible to members only, who are forbidden to reveal the information circulating on it to anyone outside the group.

Expulsion can also happen if there is no active contribution to the group's activities.

Often, *electronic magazines* (e-zines), with firsthand information on intrusion techniques and vulnerabilities discovered, are accessible only to members of the group to avoid the possibility of less expert hackers employing them and drawing the attention of the police, or allowing a system administrator to correct an encountered breach.

In the more sophisticated groups, members don't meet in person, and very few know the real name, age, or place of origin of other members of the group. They all very carefully control what other members are allowed to know about themselves. The difficulty of access to a group and conducting communication only through chats limits the number of members and safeguards knowledge acquired over many years of activity.

Groups with members scattered around the world interact only minimally. Even though relations aren't personal, they do trust each other and consider each other close friends. In other words, these are *mutual aid societies.* Some hacker groups are very large (more than 100 members) and spread all over the geography of a country as, for example, the "Genocide 2600." Others, as is usually the case for the most notorious, have members from all over the world, as in the case of the "World of Hell." In this case, interactions between members are minimal, relations are never personal, and members have never met face to face.

It's interesting to understand the reasons that lead to the creation of a group. Often, they get together because they feel the need for allies, for instance, after a police raid. However, there might be resentment toward a member who is thought to have been careless and responsible for the raid. In this case, some might decide to collaborate with investigators and testify against the careless member.

At times, members of a group will compete among themselves to solve an argument about their theories. To confirm or refute these theories, they put them into practice, trying them out on a system. An example of this is the so-called *virus writing competitions* in which each member writes a virus using the same code (for instance, Assembly), after which they are simultaneously released on the network. The winner is the developer whose virus wreaks havoc and survives the longest.

Favorite Targets and Reasons

The main targets of computer attacks, especially for Web defacing, are government systems or Web sites, particularly military sites and those belonging to large corporations (mainly financial); those that perform critical functions for security or for the economy; telecommunications companies, Internet providers, and hardware producers; and schools and universities (these, however, are usually used only as launchpads for attacks against other targets).

We can see how a hacker's "career" usually goes through three different phases of target choices:

- *Phase 1*: moderately interesting systems (belonging to unknown companies).
- *Phase 2*: systems belonging to large government and/or financial bodies.
- *Phase 3*: systems belonging to computer security companies.

It's obvious how the choice of targets changes with the increase of technical skills, and this is due to the greater difficulties an attack involves. It shouldn't be surprising that systems belonging to computer security firms are attacked. Think of teenage hackers who want to show off their skills, maybe in the hope of being later hired.

Script-kiddies aim at targets with great visibility, like NASA, the White House, governments, or large corporations. Targets also vary according to the ideals of an attacker; think of terrorist groups, but also hackers like Pr0metheus and his predilection for Christian sites.

On the whole, though, hackers will attack any kind of network (PTT, X.25, mobile phones, or Internet service providers); computer businesses (hardware, software, router, gateway, firewall, or telephone switch manufacturers); military and government institutions in general; banks; security experts; and even systems belonging to other hackers.

When a government or military system, or an important multinational, is attacked, the purpose is often that of attracting media attention and to leave a political or social message. If this is the motive, the hackers don't just penetrate the system; they deface the Web site as well. In these cases, they often lose sight of hacking for hacking's sake, and the ultimate goal becomes media attention.

The situation is different when the message is left for the system administrator, who is simply informed that the Web server has been taken. In this case, the purpose is to attract the attention of the administrator with regard to the need to improve security.

Some groups, like "The Skeleton Crew," have adopted the mission to reveal to the whole world the existing lack of knowledge about computers, and in particular that of the SysAdmin of companies who use the Internet for financial transactions and business. In their opinion, SysAdmins don't know how to adequately protect their systems and customers. These hackers can't stand the lack of security on the Internet.

Specializations

All hackers have their specialties and are particularly good at something. Some are experts at writing code to damage systems, others at configuring operating systems; some at Linux, UNIX, VMS (Virtual Memory Systems) or other operating systems, VAX (Virtual Address Extension) machines from DEC (Digital Equipment Corporation), or the *BSDs. Others are adept at phreaking and telephone systems in general, or hardware architecture, and so on.

Among the hackers we interviewed, some are specialized in setting up coordinated high-speed DoS attacks, and others in surveillance and recognition techniques. Their *modus operandi* is to collect data on target systems without being discovered and file them in dossiers with all the specifications of the system they can discover. The ability to collect and correlate information (in other words, intelligence gathering) is an essential skill for hackers. Others are adept at spoofing their identity on the Internet, keeping to this end some pages ("locally," on their own Linux or *BSD systems, rather than on servers connected to the Internet) that contain lists of proxy servers that can be "abused" or logs of domain zone transfers, or, yet again, e-mail servers they can use to make it more difficult to trace their movements.

Many others are interested in phreaking, showing they also have "old school" telephone skills (that today are mastered only by the more expert hackers), so they can:

- Remove their traces.
- Accept a free long-distance or international call simply by reducing the telephone's voltage.
- Set up a low-cost telephone line between two users.
- Use a public pay phone (token, coin, or card operated) or a "post pay" (billed to the recipient or to a series of predefined contact numbers, usually by means of keypads or special keys) to make free phone calls.
- Generate tones on their computer with frequencies allowing free calls.
- Place domestic landlines under surveillance and intercept calls.
- Steal 12 volts from a telephone cable (in certain countries and depending on the telephone standards in use).

- Collapse a telephone company.
- Cause a phone number to be always engaged.

Web defacement and software cracking are also on the list. We'll now spend a couple of pages more on these two widespread practices, which were previously mentioned.

Web Defacing

There is an American Web site, Attrition.org,* that for many years was a veritable collection of Web defacements and a reference point for script-kiddies. Today, it seems to have been replaced by Zone-h. org,† a community where users—mainly script-kiddies and wanna-bees—send screenshots of the Web defacements they have carried out. Attrition.org has decided to raise its contents to a higher level, giving information on the weak spots of large corporations, information security companies, etc. This is how they introduce themselves:

> Attrition.org is a computer security Web site dedicated to the collection, dissemination and distribution of information about the industry for anyone interested in the subject. They maintain one of the largest catalogues of security advisories, text files, and humorous image galleries. They are also known for the largest mirror of Web site defacements and their crusade to expose industry frauds and inform the public about incorrect information in computer security articles.‡

In the beginning, Attrition.org didn't bother to check who the author of the Web defacement actually was. The only requirement for adding it to the site was that the target had to be a legitimate Web site, not created only for the purpose of the defacement itself (which often happens). However, as reported on Attrition.org some time ago, the defacement collection is no longer constantly updated due to the enormous amount of defacements that take place daily.

Zone-h.org has decided instead to continue with the collection. One of the perverse and hopefully unintentional effects of this work

---

* http://www.attrition.org.
† http://www.zone-h.org.
‡ http://attrition.org/attrition/about.html.

has been to encourage script-kiddies to carry on with Web deface-ment in the hope of becoming famous and of being present in a Web archive with a large number of cases to their names.

As far as the "large number of cases" goes, we'd like to remind you that Web defacing could be carried out on many sites at the same time. The record is held by RaFa, from World of Hell, who in July 2001 carried out 679 simultaneous defacements.

Software Cracking

Software cracking, or software pirating, consists of creating scripts that can crack, or break, the authorization codes of copyright pro-tected software. To do this, crackers must first of all record every moment in which the application interacts with the recording system so as to deduce where the antipiracy protection is located. Based on this information, they must then carry out a detailed examination of the code to remove the protection.

It's possible to crack all kinds of software: games, professional applications, unreleased operating systems source codes, scripting languages, phreaking and cracking tools, software to make BBSs run, etc. Once cracked, the protected software is usually kept in hidden directories, sometimes held on legitimate software shareware and freeware sites managed by the crackers themselves. Only trusted peo-ple can have access to them. Pirated software is also kept on BBSs and is usually downloadable free of charge. Sometimes, though, access to these BBSs requires payment of a fee so as to cover management expenses. Depending on the size of the donation, it is possible to move from limited to full access.

Many BBSs that give houseroom to cracked software have contacts not only with hacker and cracker communities but also with insiders—employees of software industries—who pass on beta copies (*prereleases*) of major applications to outside contacts. These copies are then placed on the BBS for downloading. The best software cracking tools are actually produced inside the applica-tion manufacturing firms themselves. These tools are developed by insiders; by *software testers* who have access to various confidential applications.

It must be said that even someone who has no particular skills is capable of downloading a script and cracking a program. What is a lot more difficult is developing a software cracking script for the first time.

At this point, we need to clarify that the term *cracker* can have two separate meanings, one meaning being "someone who crashes targeted systems" and the other being "someone who pirates protected software." In order to make a distinction between the two, it would be more accurate to call the latter *software crackers* as opposed to the first category, *computer crackers*.

Software crackers get great satisfaction out of their activities. If they are good, their reputation grows, their handle is recognized, and other members of the underground show them respect. They consider software cracking fun because the challenge is intellectually stimulating. However, piracy often leads to very serious hacking offences, with severe legal repercussions.

Some software crackers consider their activity as pure hacking, rather than anything else, because their specialty, too, is managing to "enter" something (a program rather than a system). For them, cracking is hacking without the added risk of being traced on a network.

Principles of the *Hacker Ethics*

We have repeatedly mentioned the *hacker ethics*. We must now explain what this term means to our interviewees and whether there is a single interpretation of its rules.

First of all, there is a series of generally accepted conventions that can be summarized as follows:

- Don't damage penetrated systems, don't crash them. No hacker worth his salt would deliberately damage something. It is more than enough to have penetrated a system, owning it, and having the opportunity to explore it without modifying, deleting, or adding anything. This is the difference between an "ethical" hacker and a cracker.
- Don't modify the information present on the invaded computer. It is, of course, acceptable to modify the log file so as to erase traces of entry.

- Share with the other members of the underground (without any form of payment) discoveries, knowledge, and information acquired during raids.
- Supply a service by sharing accesses that should be free to all.

As we have already pointed out, for many hackers the fundamental principle of the *hacker ethics* is the third one. This ties in with the idea of maximum *freedom* of information they strenuously support. For them, any knowledge acquired is useless if it can't be *shared*. The exchange of information must take place absolutely free of charge, and so should the exchange of experience, skills, and opinions, because the purpose is not to get rich.

That's why hackers like to freely share their knowledge with other trustworthy hackers, and this is the principle that inspires those who become mentors, teaching how to do hacking but also passing on the philosophy of life that derives from this.

Following this principle, industrial espionage, which is selling information about new products or business strategies, is considered contrary to the *ethics*. Consider the use of insider information about markets and prices, or even how a spy can destroy or damage a product or the manufacturing machines by modifying the programs that control an assembly line.

These rules represent the *ethics* with a capital E. *True hackers,* the ethical ones, take as a given that they are acting for the general good. They distinguish themselves from other members of the underground, by being exempt from using shortcuts to get around the *ethics,* as many do in this environment.

True hackers do not steal information and do not damage a system; they are only interested in learning and increasing their skills. Some feel it is their ethical duty to warn other hackers or phreakers of possible dangers (wiretapping or investigations by the police or telephone companies) when they consider them unjustified.

Ethical hackers defend the *ethics* also by showing people the *good* side of hacking and its usefulness. Some, for instance, attack pedophiles in chat rooms, which they also consider an amusing exercise. Others have founded EHAP (*Ethical Hackers against Paedophilia*). This is a nonprofit organization made up of hackers and ordinary citizens who use unconventional and legal tactics to try to combat this phenomenon, helping the police to capture the guilty of online pedo-pornography.

Once again, we can quote Genocide to understand what hackers believe in:

> ...one of those unforgivable things like women being beaten by men, people being denied education, freedom of speech. This is a problem where I might be able to make a difference.*

Ethical hackers see the PC as a way to reach out to others; they have no desire to destroy anything. The ethical development of the individual is a gradual process, molded by the experience acquired in the material world and the immaterial one of bits and bytes. The awareness of right and wrong develops through relating with other people and the events in one's life. This development also coincides with their desire to become adult, mature citizens of the underground.

Willie Gonzalez is a good example of this. He had a profound passion for technology and said that if you really love something, you respect it and don't use it to damage and destroy. Respect also implies exploring the loved object to learn to know it and use it for the good of the community.

This is the hackers' ultimate responsibility and is what Willie and many others who follow the *ethics* believe in: love of technology, the search for truth, and sharing information. They are, however, aware that information can change (for better or for worse) other people's lives. Willie felt that if he hadn't done something good in his life, if he'd gone over to the side of hacker criminals, he would have been like all the others, and he would have become another cog in the wheel of the criminal subculture he had grown up in.

So Willie changed his way of hacking, and he even changed his nickname. Becoming a mentor to another hacker for whom he felt deeply responsible helped his *self* to mature. This attitude is far from that of a simple hacker.

For this reason, according to Willie Gonzalez, whoever defaces a Web site is no better than a common criminal, no matter how much he claims to be a hacker, even if it's only to justify these actions. If you want to become a true hacker, you have to accept the responsibility that goes with handling someone else's work, accepting the consequences of your actions and the weight of the repercussions on other people. You

---

* Verton, D., *The Hacker Diaries: Confessions of Teenage Hackers*, McGraw-Hill, 2002.

don't need to break the law or damage systems or people to be a hacker. Hacking as such is not bad; people are either good or bad. Hacking is a *tool*, and it all depends on how it is used and for what ends.

The *hacker ethics* has evolved with the different generations. The old MIT ethics of the 1950s was based on daring—the boldness that leads beyond any frontier and obstacle to obtain one's desire or fulfill one's needs. "If something is possible, then it must be done." Luckily, today the moral relativism of the first hacker generation has been overlaid with a more sophisticated idea of an ethics, more and careful in the use of technology and aware of the right to freedom of information and privacy.

There are also hackers who declare that there is no *ethics*, and talking about ethics in this context is a contradiction in terms. Usually, they don't care about the problems they cause to the SysAdmins, corporations, or government agencies they have targeted. They feel they are a cut above all others. Some, in open contrast with the principles of the *hacker ethics*, like to show their power over people, crashing systems and modifying information contained in electronic documents. Other hackers develop their *own* ethics, feeling that discovery justifies exploring systems belonging to others. Often, this set of ethics just hides the craving for power and control. It isn't by accident that script-kiddies promote new rules for cyberspace.

Acceptance or Refusal of the *Hacker Ethics*

At this point, it's worthwhile to look again at the distinction between the following:

- White-hats, hackers who never carry out illegal actions.
- Black-hats, hackers who go beyond the limits of what is legally acceptable.
- Grey-hats, who don't identify with either of the two, as they refuse any label.

This classification is very real, and all hackers, either consciously or through denial, feel they belong to one of these three categories, following in consequence the *hacker ethics*.

Grey-hats believe that labels are for lamers, who don't know what hacking is really about. No label can define them, what they do, and why they do it. Sometimes they ironically call themselves pink-hats, or any other color that isn't *grey*, as a protest against these classifications.

Hackers who respect the *ethics* have a constructive, not destructive, approach and want to use their skills to the best of their ability. This *ethics* is shared by all true hackers who act to improve computer security, to make information accessible to all, and to improve computers. They are sometimes considered modern Robin Hoods.

For the "World of Hell" group, not destroying information during an attack was a fixed point. For them, it was a question of pride.

In Las Vegas, during the DefCon yearly convention, among other things, a game called "CyberEthical Surfivor" (the "f" replacing the "v" to imply the use of the Internet) is played, wherein questions are asked on ethical dilemmas. This is a sign that times are changing.

Today, hackers seem to be aware of the consequences of their acts. They consider themselves *netizens* (citizens of the network); in other words, liable citizens of Internet who act with prudence. More and more females are present among this kind of hacker. Think of Anna Moore and the role her parents played in helping her to develop a moral and ethical sense. Allowed to freely act and explore, she had to make decisions, learn to self-regulate, and take responsibility for her actions.

There are also hackers who share the *ethics* but do not respect it in *specific* cases. Think, for example, about a teenage hacker from a poor family who obtains information that, if he were to sell it, could provide money to buy desired things. This is hacking for personal gain rather than in the public interest. Such acts often endanger privacy and national security.

Script-kiddies usually do not follow the *ethics*, as they want to destroy data and stop information and knowledge sharing. However, there are script-kiddies, mainly defacers (for instance, "Pr0metheus"), who follow an ethics of their own. They never destroy data present on servers. When necessary, they save the log file and back up the original files, without copying them to their own computers. Not only do they not destroy data, they also tell the SysAdmin where to recover them.

Many see hacking as the last opportunity for *self-expression* of the individual in the technological era. For them, hacking consists of challenging the power of corporations and governments over knowledge and information.

Some, however, betray their own ethics, as they are willing to work for the corporations and government agencies (i.e., for the establishment they were challenging), giving them the power they intended to put in the hands of individuals. There are many cases of hackers who undertook espionage, selling the information (e.g., military secrets) to foreign intelligence agencies. Think, for example, about Pengo and Hagbard-Celine* who, during the Cold War, along with Markus Hess, Dirk Brezinski, and Peter Carl, sold military secrets to the KGB, the Soviet intelligence service. This is described in *The Cuckoo's Egg*, by Clifford Stoll, who was also directly involved in the story. This is the first public case of hackers employed to carry out electronic intrusions against military and government systems for espionage purposes.

There are also hackers who neither sell nor in any way use the information acquired, but just consider it a *hunting trophy* to be shown to their colleagues and used to prove their skills.

Crashed Systems

Most hackers declare that they have never deliberately crashed or damaged a system and have tried to repair the damage caused. Hackers want to understand how PCs and technical equipment in general work. This is how they differ from crackers, who instead want to destroy them. In theory, the distinction between the two seems clear, but we have seen how, in practice, the dividing line is rather thin. A system can be damaged intentionally or by mistake. This can happen through a lack of experience or skill. A distinction therefore must be made between *malicious hackers* and *look-see hackers*, since the latter don't intentionally damage a system or commit computer fraud.

Script-kiddies are in the malicious hacker category. Most of them want to crash government or large corporation systems, venting their rage and frustration and then justifying themselves by declaring that what they have done is right, without taking responsibility for their actions. They are obviously lying when they justify their activities

---

* The nicknames of Hans Huebner and Karl Koch. The latter was found carbonized in a forest between Hanover and Wolfsburg, in Germany, in June 1989 (see *Phrack* 3, 25, File 10/11, http://www.phrack.org/archives/25/P25-10).

Table 6.1 Purposefulness in Hacker Intentions

MALICIOUS HACKERS	LOOK-SEE HACKERS
Deliberately damage a system (malice aforethought)	Do not intentionally damage a system (fault: negligence, rashness, lack of skill)
Commit computer fraud	Do not commit computer fraud

by saying they were testing the security of the attacked Web sites and that the attacks were necessary to develop and implement new firewalls.

Hacking/Phreaking Addiction

Many questions have been answered by now, but some aspects deserve further thought. For example, given that hacking (or phreaking) can start for different reasons, can it become an addiction?

One way of assessing hacking addiction is verifying the amount of time spent in front of a computer. Often hacking is done for 6 to 8 hours per night during the week and can go up to 12 hours during the weekend. During the day, the hours spent in front of a PC can be 10 to 12 during the week and 18 to 20 during the weekend. Some hackers rarely sleep; they alternate hacking hours with their daily activities, trying to lead as normal a life as possible. Some attacks take days or weeks to complete; it all depends on how much time is spent and the patience and persistence of the hacker.

Hacking is often practiced in the bedroom, where the computer is usually kept (especially if the hacker is a teenager). Often, the bedroom is a veritable laboratory, with various computers and monitors. The choice of place is not made by chance; it must be a place where one feels comfortable and far from indiscreet eyes.

The best hours for hacking are at night, because it is assumed that no user is on the system, and neither is the administrator, who could notice abnormal activities and identify an unauthorized user. But hacking isn't practiced every day; there are also brief periods of inactivity. When one is operative, work usually goes on until the early hours. Many hackers don't start hacking before 2:00 a.m. All hackers have in common an *obsession* with their hobby; they feel the need to increase their knowledge and skills, and most of their time is taken up by this endless exploration. They don't know where their obsession will lead them, but they do know they can't give it up—they can't stop. For many, hacking is an "obsessive-compulsive" behavior, while only for a few can it be considered a real hacking addiction. We aren't talking about *computer addiction,* but *hacking addiction,* because many nonhackers can be computer addicted.

For some hackers, hacking isn't only a way of life but a real dependency; a state of mind they can't get out of. They aren't concerned about having problems with the authorities, because they can't do without hacking—they just can't stop.

Some hackers want to stop but can't, and they try to set limits to their activities. The fact that they can't stop makes them feel even more vulnerable and guilty, and more anxious about the risks they are running. These are all symptoms of addiction.

It becomes even more difficult if they are used to acting with a friend or in a group, because then they egg each other on. This is the same mechanism you get with drug addiction, where it's more difficult to stop if it's done in company (think of so-called "recreational drugs") or when there is someone pushing you to use them.

Hacking addiction often compels one to hack notwithstanding the risks, and for some it can also be a way of seeking someone to help them stop, because they can't say "enough" on their own. In this context, it becomes clear how, for them, a job in computer security becomes not only an opportunity for growth but also a way of avoiding the legal risks involved in hacking activities. This puts an end to the feelings of guilt, allowing them to redeem themselves by creating a positive image and making constructive use of their skills.

According to Dr. James Griffith-Edwards,* hackers are dependent. They are obsessed by the computer, and they can't stop themselves from using it. Therefore, they cannot freely decide their actions or be

---

* Member of a group in the World Health Organization (WHO) who defined "addiction." The term refers to the repeated use of a psychotropic substance or substances, inasmuch as whoever uses them is periodically or chronically intoxicated, showing a compulsion toward the use of the substance (or substances) of choice, shows difficulty in stopping or modifying voluntarily the use of the substance, and is determined to obtain it by any means. It should be noted that the WHO stopped using the term *addiction* in 1964, replacing it with *drug dependence.* The term, however, is still largely in use.

responsible for them. Their actions are totally involuntary and therefore without malice.

From the criminological point of view, this is a sort of determinism
with a vaguely Lombrosian flavor. They are obsessed by the intellectual challenge (obsessive-compulsive behavior) where hacking
becomes their only interest, thus limiting their social lives, which are
often restricted to meeting other hackers online.

Many hackers stop hacking after being raided by the police and
start abusing drugs, replacing one kind of dependence with another.

Many addictive and obsessive behaviors can be found among
"inhabitants" of the hacker underground, even though many hackers
claim they are not dependent and don't feel "unwell" if they abstain
for some time, and that they can stop whenever they want to.

Perception of the Illegality of Their Actions

On the whole, hackers seem to be aware of the fact that violating
someone else's computer system is illegal and is wrong. Often, though,
they are not aware of the *financial* implications of their attacks. They
know that what they are doing is illegal, but "ethical hackers" consider
their activities morally acceptable, as they have internal rules that for-
bid damaging systems and modifying information. They think there
is nothing wrong with poking around, looking at how a system works
from the "inside," and testing the limits of the machine. They don't
think they are committing a crime, because they claim to be motivated by good intentions.

After all, from their point of view, these are "victimless crimes," so
there is no criminal offense involved. According to software crackers,
large, powerful software companies (Microsoft, Apple, Adobe, etc.)
can't be considered victims because, from the cracker's point of view,
they try to manipulate knowledge and profit from something that
ought to be freely accessible without charge. Victims, by definition,
are weak and innocent. Large software companies can't be considered
either, according to software crackers.

Hackers don't see themselves as criminals, nor do they think their
attacks should be considered so. For them, hacking is a legitimate tool
for learning computer security. For this reason, they consider their
forays to be innocent and don't always realize the damage they do.

They actually wonder why people consider hacking a crime, like robbing a bank. They ask what damage can be caused by an individual demonstrating hacking power. Yet again, hacking is only a tool; it depends on how it is used and to what ends.

Most hackers consider themselves *visitors*, explorers rather than *intruders*, as they don't want to do any harm, have no evil intentions, and don't want to damage anyone or anything. In other words, they know that hacking is illegal, but they don't consider it morally wrong, because they don't think they are damaging anyone; no one really knows what they are doing and, in any event, no one should worry about it. They don't think they are committing serious crimes but see their transgressions as unimportant unauthorized forays into someone else's system, nothing more that mere violations of private property.

It is just a "petty crime," one would think. This conviction comes from the fact that they believe governments don't take their attacks seriously. This is demonstrated by the sentences imposed, which are usually mild. Fines for damages, though, are something different—usually very high, and excessive for teenagers still in school. Detentions, on the other hand, are usually limited to a suspended sentence of a few months in jail, probation, or house arrest.

Many think hacking isn't a serious crime and that it's unfair to have to go to jail. Even after arrested, they don't feel any remorse or regret for their actions. They feel they are being accused of crimes that they don't consider to be such: unauthorized access to a computer system, computer vandalism, criminal association to commit telecommunication fraud, hacking, and so forth.

Consider the group, World of Hell, that defaced Web sites to help remove vulnerabilities from Web servers. They think governments shouldn't criminalize hacking or the creation of offensive hacking tools because, if they were criminalized, the computer security experts' community could not study new ways of defense from attacks and make networks and systems more secure. After all, security doesn't affect only hackers.

Many also feel that it is unfair to be blamed and judged when they are adults for acts of bravado they committed when they were still adolescents. While growing up, they changed and are no longer the same people. Meanwhile, they may even have moved into a career as IT security experts.

They think the media and the population at large are unaware and do not and cannot understand hacking, what it means for them, and why they do it. They believe governments and the media are to blame if most people see hackers as "the great evil," especially after the events of 9/11.

According to them, people have a mistaken view of hackers; they feel hated. They don't believe they are a threat to the economy and the well-being of the country but rather a *resource*, because they know they are skilled and knowledgeable. They don't view themselves as criminals; they think that the real criminals are those who want to censor information and stop the search for knowledge and awareness. They feel they are the defenders of these basic human rights.

Clearly, hackers believe there is nothing illegal in trying to understand how computers work. Their intentions aren't criminal in their eyes. They consider the fact that hackers are usually perceived as evil intentioned and criminals as a *waste of talent*.

However, many hackers declare after their intrusion that if they had realized beforehand the problems they caused to the people responsible for the security of the violated systems (who may have risked losing their jobs), or if they had gained any work experience in this field, they would never have acted in such a way.

This last assumption doesn't go for those who don't think there is a *hacker ethics* and don't care about the consequences of their actions. They behave in this way because they think it's easy for system administrators to remove defects, so it's their own fault if they are attacked. They state, "It's not our fault if computers aren't safe." This just goes to demonstrate their *lack of moral commitment* in blaming the victim.

These hackers think that, because the administrator is responsible for security, if he isn't capable of protecting the system adequately, then whoever can enter has a right to do so. They maintain that they don't force anything and, rather, limit themselves to entering the system through doors the administrator has inadvertently left open. That's why they think they are doing "good," allowing administrators to become aware of existing vulnerabilities so they can "patch" security holes. In this way, they want to help the administrators and protect them from computer pirates without scruples. Exactly for these reasons, they consider that attacking a vulnerable system is fair and the right thing to do. In any event, some hackers do have a sense of reality that permeates their activities and keeps them from going too far, but those who set themselves some limits are few and far between.

Some hackers are proud of their activities. They declare they have a right to access other computers, because they entered thanks to their intelligence and "smarts," creating a root access. They believe that corporations and private investigators often violate people's privacy, so why shouldn't they, especially as they see the telephone line as a common property that should be shared?

Offenses Perpetrated with the Aid of IT Devices

Hacking, in a strict sense, consists in unauthorized access to an information system, but it can lead to the commission of other crimes. Some of these crimes are fraud, deliberate damage, receiving stolen goods, theft, bank fraud, and military and industrial espionage. Those crimes *usually* aren't committed by means of computers.

State secrets can be violated when information discovered by chance—or deliberately, where espionage is involved—is passed on to other hackers or sold to the highest bidder. Think, for example, about military secrets regarding new weapons that could interest foreign intelligence agencies or transnational criminal organizations.

For this reason, hackers can be taken for terrorists. Otto Sync* is an example. Since 9/11, hacking has been considered and act of terrorism under the American Patriot Act, the law approved to prevent similar events.

Illicit wire tapping is wildly attractive to some hackers. Computer fraud and carding, fraud through the use of credit card numbers as already described, are also common.

Many commit crimes that don't necessarily require computers. Kevin Lee Poulsen was charged with procuring when, using his technical abilities, he reactivated telephone numbers that were no longer operative and assigned them to a call girl service. So as to avoid a conflict with his ethics, he convinced himself that the girls were just escorts who had freely decided to sell their services. As he was just offering

---

* See Raoul Chiesa's e-book, *La storia di Otto Synk e White Knight,* Apogeo, 2003, freely downloadable at http://www.apogeonline.com/libri/88-503-1079-X/scheda.

a computer service, he wasn't involved in their exploitation. For him, this was a perfect hack, as it was a victimless electronic opportunity.

Offenses Perpetrated without the Use of IT Devices

We must point out that some crimes indirectly linked to hacking do not imply the use of a computer. Examples include breaking and entering telephone companies to steal documents containing usernames and passwords, etc. However, hacking and phreaking are ways of keeping out of trouble, off the street with its dangers and temptations, as for those American teenage hackers who were part of criminal gangs but moved on to hacker groups.

Other times, hackers join up with real traditional criminals, committing crimes such as burglary. Under the influence of paranoia, they even monitor their friends.

Another common crime is aiding and abetting. Through a feeling of solidarity (not only in the same group), hackers usually cover each other's backs when in trouble. Finally, one of the most statistically frequent crimes committed by hackers, without any connection to their hacking activities, is car theft.

Fear of Discovery, Arrest, and Conviction

Hackers don't mind running risks; they feel it is part of the "game." They feel excited, enjoying the adrenalin rush caused by fear of being discovered and love of the "forbidden." Some consider it an honor to have been raided, not so much by the police but by the Secret Service; it makes them feel important.

Furthermore, some are so sure of themselves that they are convinced they will never be discovered. But at the same time, they want to be caught, to become famous and attract media attention. Often they are frustrated and impatient at the low level of competence of investigators and SysAdmins, as they find it more fun to use their skills to defeat a worthy opponent. They find it exciting to know that the system administrator and the police are on their tracks, and they also like to find out about investigations concerning them, possibly by reading their e-mails. They enjoy spying online on investigators and administrators who are trying to understand where the attacks are coming from.

The ones who think the police will never catch them are always surprised if they are discovered, as they believe they have been careful and have taken all necessary precautions. The more confident hackers feel so sure of their skills that they thumb their noses at the authorities, openly challenging them, and boast that they have never been caught (typical script-kiddie attitude). This is perfectly in line with their egos, which are nourished by challenging the authorities. They are aware that they can do things most people can't. What leads them to hacking is really the challenge and the pleasure they derive out of doing something well. They rarely do it for personal gain.

There are also hackers who are unafraid of arrest simply because they believe it is highly improbable someone will bother to investigate them. Even though they are aware they are doing something illegal, they do observe a personal ethics; for instance, they don't destroy other people's data. They feel secure in the fact that, as they aren't appropriating information, it becomes difficult to identify them, even though they are aware of the risks they are running.

Other hackers are frightened by a possible trial. Their main fear is that of going to prison, as in that case they couldn't use a computer anymore or be hired in the IT sector. For this reason, they keep their more successful hacks to themselves, without telling anyone. In this way, they can develop their skills, and they see hacking and phreaking as a responsibility that can lead to loss rather than gain. Therefore, they prefer to stop hacking or phreaking and perhaps undertake a career in IT security. The future is important, and it's not worth compromising it.

Others stop hacking not so much out of fear of going to jail or because of the risk of being discovered, but rather because they feel responsible for the pressure they have brought to bear and the stress they have caused to the administrators of the violated systems. Sometimes it is because they feel disappointed and frustrated by an underground world peopled more and more by poorly skilled script-kiddies.

The Law as Deterrent

Antihacking laws have practically no deterrent value. Usually, hackers are familiar with their country's laws on computer crimes and try to exploit existing loopholes to get around them.

The introduction of stricter legislation for this type of crime has led to changes in the underground. From being an open community, it is becoming a restricted and elite environment. Hackers, who used to live in a world that was by definition hidden, now tend to give even less information about themselves and share as little as possible of what they know. In a world that was based on collectivism, individualism is now prevailing. The new laws and the continuous police raids and operations are changing the face of this world. But instead of making "computer pirates" desist, the stricter laws are just making them more careful and are pushing them into hiding. Furthermore, they have become even more sophisticated and paranoid. Hacking now is less *visible* and identifiable, and this makes the investigators' task even more difficult. This is the paradoxical result of the sometimes excessive severity of these laws.

For some hackers, the fact that they are breaking the law is practically an invitation, an extra encouragement, especially for those who are antiestablishment, even if they are afraid of possible legal repercussions. Hackers think that governments take hacking too seriously. However, today's hackers are able to handle police raids better than their predecessors did, and the frequency of raids hasn't caused them to stop hacking.

Effect of Convictions

Sometimes sentencing doesn't discourage a hacker, especially if a psychological disorder is added to the dependence. Once out of jail, the hacker starts hacking again. Many even do hacking while on the run from the police or on trial. For them, it's a question of principle; they feel invincible and are aware of the fact they have nothing more to lose. Think, for example, about Pr0metheus, who was paranoid, and even during his flight and continuous movements around the U.S.A., he continued his online activities.

Some practice hacking for personal gain. Even though they have the opportunity of "joining the ranks" again, and possibly a job they would like, they keep on breaking the law, wasting the opportunity to use their skills better. Often, the first legal sentence has no effect.

Not all react in this way. Some actually leave hacking forever after the first conviction and want nothing more to do with that experience.

Although some do leave hacking after being raided, arrested, and convicted, they show no repentance for what they have done. Rather, they feel sorry for having damaged the users of the violated systems and the system administrators. But they don't think they did anything wrong, especially if they didn't act to deliberately harm someone.

It is interesting to see that, on the whole, sentences applied to hackers have no deterrent effect on the other members of the underground, who actually see their "colleagues" as "heroes." Their marked egos and unlimited faith in their abilities lead them to believe they will never make the same mistakes that led to the arrest of other hackers.

Leaving the Hacker Scene

Those who have left the hacking and phreaking scene did so when they became aware that the possibility of being arrested by the police or getting into trouble was real and serious. At some point, they start to realize that it isn't worthwhile to risk any longer. An example is "Cowhead2000," who stopped Web defacing after being warned by the police that if he didn't desist, he would be prosecuted. He stopped because he believed that it wasn't worth running risks for the Web defacing scene, full of lamers and kids who don't want to bother with learning.

Like him, many leave hacking not only out of a fear of being arrested but also because they are frustrated and indignant at an underground world that no longer shares their values. Some, once they become of age, start thinking about the future and wondering what to do with their lives and with their hacking skills. They "leave" hacking only to work in the computer security sector.

We have seen how many different reasons there are to stop hacking. Let's recap them as follows:

- They have been caught by the police, or have heard of other hackers being caught.
- Hacking has become too risky.
- The sentence was severe enough to make them stop (for example, huge fines).
- New laws have been introduced criminalizing illicit entry in a computer system or introducing stricter penalties.

- In their country, it's too expensive to use a telephone line (when they aren't capable of phreaking).
- Moral reasons; awareness of doing something wrong and dangerous.

As to this last point, Joe Magee is a good example. Unlike the MOD gang, when he became aware of his power (to "crash" the whole telephone network) and realized that what he was doing was dangerous, he stopped. He realized that if the had interrupted the telephone lines, people couldn't call emergency numbers if needed, and this would no longer have been a game or a victimless joke.

Others only stop hacking temporarily. They might "lose themselves" for a while because they know they are being monitored by the police but, once things calm down, they start up again.

Then there are those who have doubts about what it could mean for them to stay stuck to a computer night and day, or what their life can be outside hacking, and they stop for a while only to return, unable give it up.

Beyond Hacking

We have seen how, on the whole, convictions don't have a deterrent effect, so once out of jail the hacker starts up again. Sometimes, though, a police raid or a criminal conviction lets some open their eyes and realize that to continue on this road would be too risky and would lead nowhere. The fear of arrest helps them grow up; they see hacking and phreaking as a losing proposition. They prefer to stop and begin a career in computer security. The job won't be any different from what they have always done, with the great difference that they aren't committing a crime. They start using their talents for positive reasons; they stop fighting the establishment and become part of it to defeat its enemies.

Even though there are a few cases of hackers who continue with their illegal activities, most want to use their skills for the good, changing identity from black- to white-hat, monitoring and "patrolling" cyberspace for the good of the community, even if according to their own standards, on the basis of unwritten rules that distinguish them. With this transformation, they try somehow to redeem the negative public image of hackers.

What we have described is an obligatory development for many hackers moving toward adulthood. Therefore, hacking is set aside in adulthood, because they grow out of it and start thinking that there is something better to do. As adults, they see a computer as a tool to earn one's living, not a way to fill up spare time. Some are sorry they spent most of their time in the past doing hacking, sacrificing other equally interesting activities.

It's clear how, for them, moving into computer security isn't just a question of personal and professional growth but also a way of relieving their obsession or hacking dependence through their jobs. In this way, the risks tied to an illegal activity are removed, guilt at the inability to stop is exorcised, and there is also a feeling of righteousness.

They follow professional programming courses. Some enroll in computer sciences at a university so they can find a job in the private sector. They often become responsible for computer security in large corporations, or they set up their own companies. It's as if university courses in computer sciences have become the meeting place of choice for all hackers who have a *conscience,* even though they occasionally still dabble in exploring the university's network. Many, however, having no formal professional qualifications, find it difficult to get a job.

Hackers are naturally curious about computer security and usually feel respect for experts in the field. Remember that the skills acquired through hacking are the same needed to become a computer security expert. The only difference lies in the fact that the latter is authorized to access the system.

It can be said, "once a hacker, always a hacker," because a hacker's interest in computers and networks never dies; only the definition changes—the meaning given to the term "hacker."

7
Conclusions

Yes, I am a criminal.
My crime is that of curiosity.

We have finally reached the last chapter of this book, and we hope the journey was as fascinating for the reader as it was for the HPP working group. It hasn't been easy to describe everything that has been done in over 3 years, but it has been exciting.

By now it should be clear how taking a realistic and truthful snapshot of the hacker underground isn't simple. There are many factors that need to be taken into account, and different points of view and approaches to follow in order to examine different situations and motives. Meanwhile, though, the world of hacking is changing, evolving, and growing in a complex way, and hierarchically too, every day, marking the rhythm for the world of information security, which is evolving in turn.

At the end of the line are you, the users, companies, agencies, governments; you all use a PC and the Internet to communicate, work, or study, or simply in your spare time. All of you.

We can't tell you what will happen in the world of information security in 3 or 5 years' time, but we can tell you that hacking will certainly become more and more important in this context.

The dangerous synergism between the world of hacking and organized crime that we have started to observe will certainly increase, and most probably the number of black-hats will, too.

National government stability will become even more dependent on ICT (Information and Communication Technology) security than it is today, as if they were tied by an umbilical cord.

We do know what the history of hacking has taught us over the last 20 or 30 years: we have learned that "nothing is safe," and that things are neither black nor white.

During an interview with *Esquire* magazine given in October 1971, John Draper, alias "Captain Crunch," was asked *why* he defrauded telephone companies by phreaking. His answer, which probably even today offers us the *real* key to understand phreaking (but also hacking and possibly carding), should provide food for thought for many 21st century *telcos* and companies in general:

> I do it for one reason and one reason only. I'm learning about a system. The phone company is a system. A computer is a system, do you under-stand? If I do what I do, it is only to explore a system. Computers, sys-tems, that's my bag. The phone company is nothing but a computer.*

History shows us that, up to now, with a few isolated exceptions, the world of hacking hasn't been linked to criminal actions, but, sadly, it is in part evolving in this direction. This is one of the main reasons why we want to stress—and we will never tire of doing this, explain-ing, teaching, passing it on—how important and necessary it is to study, analyze, and *understand* the hacking phenomenon. We believe we have shown how it is possible to apply a serious profiling method to hacking, without sloppiness, superficiality, or bias. That's what we are doing; it's part of the journey we have embarked upon, notwith-standing the efforts and hard work it requires.

We saw a gap in the world of criminology, and we decided to try and fill it. Throughout our investigation, we never wanted to *judge*, but only *observe* and *correlate*.

We hope this book will be only the first of a series of publica-tions through which we would like to bring to our readers the HPP results and the story of our pilgrimage to the digital underground. We hope that the enthusiasm that distinguishes everyone involved in the research project can be glimpsed behind the lines of the book you have read, and that our ideas and approaches have been use-ful; we hope we have left you with something—food for thought, questions to be answered. This text was written to be understood by people with different backgrounds and training, from the law to psychology, moving through computer sciences and sociology. We have told you about a world that usually can be accessed only by a

---

* From *Secrets of the Little Blue Box*, available on http://myoldmac.net/FAQ/The BlueBox-1.htm.

small circle of people, and we really hope that you found what you have read interesting.

Ethical hackers have always fought for the idea that information must be free. We have written this book to guarantee you one freedom: the freedom to judge for yourselves and without any bias a part of what is out there—in cyberspace.

Afterword: Slaying Today's Dragons: Hackers in Cyberspace

EMILIO C. VIANO

Cyberspace is a world that borders between imagination, dream, and reality; a world that is invisible, imperceptible, silent yet operational, functional and fully interfacing with and impacting on traditional reality, ubiquitous and all encompassing, yet undetected and outside the sphere of our senses' capture and everyday experience. Its absolute novelty, its rapid diffusion, the real impact that it can have on our lives, has transformed it in a few years into an absolute part of our reality and existence. Today we cannot function, operate, communicate, transact, and interact without acting and moving into this invisible world that permeates our existence. Not seen, not heard, not perceived, it is nonetheless as real and necessary as the air surrounding us. The rapid expansion of wi-fi, the growing integration of phone, Internet, video, photography, instant messaging, text messaging, and Web browsing are rendering several technologies obsolete; revolutionizing the world of communications at every level; and introducing new modes of interacting, deciding, researching, selling and buying, conducting international affairs, and even engaging in conflicts and wars that were unheard of and unimaginable until just yesterday. There is already complete portability of phone, video, Web browsing, messaging, and communicating. The cellular phone, expanded and integrated into cyberspace technology, is increasingly the only medium needed to complete transactions that before required disparate and unconnected tools like the fixed-line telephone, dial-up or cable Internet connections, a computer or laptop, a camera, a video camera, and more, now all in one.

As any world we live in would have it, cyberspace has its own innovators, inventors, seers, toilers, visionaries, and futurists.

193

It also has its share of rebels, deviants, nonconformists, and even criminals.

The hacker is the prototype of this new type of deviant who operates in the shadows of this netherworld with at times even more impact than a conventional criminal engaged in street or white-collar crime. The problem is one of perception. As in many cases of white-collar crime, this type of criminality is taken lightly and considered either not really existent or inoffensive. The reality is quite different, of course.

This volume depicts with bold and vivid strokes, based on first-hand experience, painstaking research, and detailed analysis, this world that goes unperceived and unnoticed by most but whose effect and consequences can and do in reality affect and impact us all.

The authors of this volume have brilliantly described an international assortment of at times highly skilled and motivated people who often toil alone, painstakingly penetrating complicated and well-protected software systems that constitute the operating force of cyberspace. Their motivation, preparation, background, reasons why, objectives, hierarchy, and even mutual recognition systems are reconstructed and presented to the reader in a credible, plausible, and eminently readable manner.

To write on this arcane, difficult, and complicated but real subject with authority and to objectively, yet persuasively, describe the hackers' operations and motives requires not only high skills and a well-disciplined mind but also firsthand knowledge of the very reality being portrayed. One of the authors did at one time belong to the world of hackers and thus has firsthand knowledge and experience with that reality. Moreover, all of the authors did participate in a well-designed and rigorous study, and they contributed to the patient and incisive analysis of its results.

But nothing remains static for long these days. What it took centuries to accomplish and introduce in years past changes in seconds today. No doubt in a few years, contemporary technology and hacking may seem as quaint, naïve, and frankly "behind" as we look with bemusement and a sense of benign compassion on the science, technology, and medicine of centuries past.

This book lays strong foundations and clear premises for continuing to pursue and monitor developments in this area. It is a classic field manual for those who want to pursue serious research and successful monitoring of this field. No doubt it marks an important and essential milestone in the study of cybercrime and of hackers. There are few credible and serious works in this area. Many are impressionistic in nature, repeat journalistic and hearsay accounts, and do not have strong empirical foundations. This work is definitely different. It is based on high-quality empirical research and sharp, laser-like analysis, finely honed by field experience.

One can expect not only that there will be updated editions of this work in various languages in the future but that it will spur more interest and effort in discovering, penetrating, and monitoring this invisible but real world. This is not an easy task, given the ever-changing permutations of those involved in it. However, this volume provides clear and well-marked guideposts that will make perceiving, understanding, and comprehending hacking and cybercrime doable and successful.

Cybercriminals and hackers represent a serious challenge for our society. Just as piracy at one time threatened international commerce and travel, and still does in certain lawless areas of the world, and had to be eradicated, so does cybercriminality. Cyber-connected hijackings, kidnapping, extortion, and thefts are just as real and disruptive. They are only going to increase in number, sophistication, frequency, depth, and amounts stolen in the future as more and more of the world becomes dependent on the Internet and on Web access for an ever-increasing number of transactions. Soon almost 100% of what we do, from banking to communicating, from buying to selling, from investing to voting, will be done in and through the cyber world. Thus, the imperative to have it closely under control, and to maintain it well policed and protected is clear and unavoidable. Our private lives are not the only ones in danger here. National and international security, the welfare of nations, and even war and peace will increasingly depend on cyberspace transactions and their security, confidentiality, and proper functioning.

Thus, this book opens for us the vision of a world increasingly dependent on invisible and silent operations that have a real and palpable impact on world affairs. The sensitivity, importance, and relevance of cyberspace transactions are clear and undeniable. Hence the absolute need to have clear knowledge, a sharp image, to be fully prepared and to have excellent operational capabilities for understanding, intervening, and preventing this new type of deviance and criminality.

What favors cybercrime and permits it to continue expanding and operating with relative impunity and freedom of operations is the difficulty that most people have, with some reason, to perceive its very existence existentially and not just intellectually, and to understand the gravity and seriousness of its threat. Many people have a distorted and unrealistic image of the hacker as a harmless and nerdy adolescent, generally male, boring, uninteresting, and obviously not successful in more exciting and manly pursuits like sports, business, and chasing after the opposite sex. There are, no doubt, hackers like that, but many are quite different—articulate, perceptive, intelligent, sharp, and, yes, not like most people their age. Many are quite worldly, mature, and deeply engaged in a highly rewarding pursuit. Some are company, law enforcement, security firm, or government employees. Like any avocation, hacking can bring fame, notoriety, respect by peers, and most of all monetary, political, or ideological rewards. Hackers can work with white-collar crime using these new and very helpful Internet technologies. But they can also be motivated by political or religious reasons and even extremism. There are hackers supported, funded, and encouraged by the state for positive or negative reasons. On the positive side, we can think of detecting, understanding, and fighting hackers who are disrupting the system violating databanks, manipulating financial transactions, and stealing. On the negative side, there are governments who sponsor hackers for spying on other countries and their political and business leaders, or for attacking them electronically, or for disrupting their communications or other essential grids. There are hackers who are spies for political, industrial, and private reasons. Like paparazzi, there are hackers who try to break into private Web sites, files, and e-mails to find juicy information about famous people, be they politicians, actors, actresses, singers, writers, or otherwise notables. This information can then be sold for publication by the insatiable gossip press, tabloids, or "legitimate" magazines. We live in a world of instant communications, "live" images of tragedies taking place thousands of miles away, and constant hunger for more news, more information, more gossip. There are no limits, no boundaries, no ethics for many hackers when financial, political, religious, or extremist gains beckon. Clearly, the most dangerous forms of hacking are those sponsored and supported by countries. Some of them may be so-called rogue states, but others are respected, influential, and powerful countries. The potential for conflict, conflagration, and war is real and menacing. Hacking is not just an individual's pursuit. It can be a state pursuit as well.

This is why this book is such an important, original, and needed contribution to the literature, research, policy-making, counter-terrorism, and diplomatic activities in general, and also specifically on cyber threats. This work does not just deal with "new wine in old containers" but with new forms of thinking, relating, deciding, communicating, and operating. It is at the cutting edge of becoming progressively aware, cognizant, and well-versed on the rapidly changing forms of cybercrime that can be subject to quick and chameleon-like metamorphoses. Too much is at stake from the individual, business, research, security, and societal levels not to take what this volume portrays seriously and develop, propose, approve, and enact appropriate policies and measures. Thus, this book is very much future oriented, opening up new views, new perceptions and realizations, and new forms of intervention. It is a must reading for anyone interested and working in e-commerce, e-government, e-business, or simply through the Internet. Only if the book is read with attention, studied with care, taken into account by the legislator, and translated into action can we effectively prepare for the growing presence, pervasiveness, and threat of the hacker at all levels. Taking a bold look forward, this trailblazing book tells us what the future will look like and gives us ample opportunity to prepare and intervene to ensure a safe world for all of us.

The translation of this book into different languages is welcome and propitious, because it contributes in a significant way to the best literature in the field and provides a firm foundation for a clear understanding, a sharp awareness, a well-targeted approach, and an informed capability to identify, isolate, prevent, and combat the problem.

Raoul Chiesa, Stefania Ducci, and Silvio Ciappi are true pioneers in presenting such a clear, convincing, and well-documented study of hackers worldwide. No doubt they will inspire others to expand and deepen this type of analysis, contribute to further research, and most of all outline appropriate policies and propose concrete steps, on the one hand, to prevent and neutralize this piracy of the 21st century and, on the other, to support the continuing development of the positive, useful, and helpful ways in which the Internet and the cyber world have immensely improved our lives.

About the Author

Emilio C. Viano [Ph.D., Ph.D., LLB (Hon.), LLM, LLM] is a professor in the School of Public Affairs, American University, and adjunct professor in the Washington College of Law, Washington, DC. He has published more than 30 books and 120 scholarly articles. He is a member of the Board of Directors of the International Society of Criminology and an alternate member of the Board of Directors of the International Association of Penal Law.

He has lectured at various universities worldwide, has organized several international conferences and meeting, is often invited as a consultant by various governments and non-governmental organizations, and regularly appears as an analyst on CNN, BBC, Voice of America, and many other television and radio programs, as well as printed media.

Appendix A: HPP Questionnaire

This appendix presents the questionnaire at the basis of the Hacker's Profiling Project. The responses are shown and discussed in chapters 4, 5, and 6 of this book.

The questionnaire can only be filled out online on a dedicated Web site. It is split into three sections (A, B, and C).

Section A collects the personal data of the interviewee, section B relational data, and C technical and criminological data.

To filter the information obtained and be certain that the compiler is a real hacker and not a mythomaniac, various strategies were employed, one of which was distributing two versions of the questionnaire—a full one (shown in this appendix) and a light one, which can be found online (http://hpp.recursiva.org/).

The full version is distributed exclusively to people who are proven members of the underground, and subjects interested in filling it out were found through the underground grapevine itself. The subjects who filled out the full version were used as a control group for those who compiled the light version.

Each section has an introductory comment that gives a general idea of the objectives and the type of questions covered.

Each section is split into subsections.

Section A—Personal Data

This information is necessary to understand the hacker world and, added to the relational data, to understand its background. It is also useful when correlated with technical data, as it becomes possible to understand better both motives and *modus operandi*.

> *Gender*
>> Male
>> Female

Age

Place of residence

Country and city of residence

Do you live in:

A large city (over 500,000 inhabitants)

A small city (under 500,000 inhabitants)

A town

How far are you from a large urban center?

Within a radius of 5 km

Between 6 and 10 km

Between 11 and 20 km

Over 20 Km

Socioeconomic status

What is your socioeconomic status?

Low

Lower-middle

Upper-middle

High

Studies

Qualifications (tick the most recent)

Primary certificate

Secondary certificate

Professional qualification

High school diploma

University degree

Graduate studies (MA, PhD, specialization, etc.)

What kind of studies did you follow or are following now (*multiple answers*)?

Humanities

Art

Science

Technical/computer science

Are you (or were you) good at school?

Yes

No

Do you (or did you) attend school regularly?
Yes
No

Do you (or did you) enjoy going to school?
Yes
No

If no, why not (*multiple answers*)?
Because it isn't/wasn't very stimulating
Because we learn/learned nothing new
Because the teachers are/were too rigid in following the curriculum
Other

Do you (or did you) enjoy studying?
Yes
No

If yes, which subjects do you (or did you) enjoy most (*multiple answers*)?
Humanities
Arts
Sciences
Technical/computer science

Did you ever interrupt your studies?
Yes
No

If yes, why (*multiple answers*)?
Because it isn't/wasn't very challenging
Because we learn/learned nothing new
Because the teachers are/were too rigid in following the curriculum
Other

Did you ever resume your studies?
Yes
No

Professional sphere

Are you in work at the moment?
Yes
No

If yes, are you working in the computer sector?
Yes (*please specify*)
No

Would you like to work as a computer security expert for government agencies such as law enforcement, intelligence service, military agencies, etc.?
Yes
No

In either case, please explain why you would or wouldn't like to work for some or all of the above-mentioned institutions.

Do you think your hacking/phreaking activities can damage your (present or future) professional career (or have they already damaged it)?
Yes
No

Does/did the possibility of it happening ever worry you?
Yes
No

If no, why not?
Because I never thought of it
Because I thought (and it happened) that it would help
Other (*please specify*)

Interests

Do/did you have any other interests apart from hacking/phreaking?
Yes
No

If yes, which? For example: hobbies, sports, etc.

Religion
>Do you belong to any religious denomination?
>>Yes
>>No

Description of physical aspect
>How would you describe yourself? For example: tall, short, slim, stocky, etc. (max. two lines)

Description of personality
>Try to describe your character

>Did you ever feel you had multiple personalities?
>>Yes
>>No
>If yes, try to describe your alter ego/egos

Self-definition
>Do you define yourself as a hacker?
>>Yes
>>No

>If you do not, how do you define yourself?

>Do others (or could others) define you as a hacker?
>>Yes
>>No
>Why?

>In your view who is a hacker?

Psychophysical conditions
>Do you (or did you ever) suffer from the following complaints (*multiple answers*)?
>>Insomnia
>>Paranoia
>>Anxiety
>>Panic attacks
>>Other

If yes, do you think their appearance is linked with your hacking/phreaking activity?
Yes
No

Alcohol and/or drug dependency
Have you ever abused alcohol?
Yes, in the past
Yes, I still do
No, never

If yes, why?

If yes, what kind and how much?

Have you ever taken drugs?
Yes, in the past
Yes, I still do
No, never

If yes, why?

If yes, what kind and how much?

Did you ever feel dependent on any of those substances (*multiple answers*)?
Yes, alcohol
Yes, drugs (*please specify*)
No, never

Has alcohol and/or drug consumption ever influenced:
  – your social life?
     Yes
     No

  – your studies/work?
     Yes
     No

  – your hacking/phreaking activities?
     Yes
     No
If yes, in what way?

Family background

Are/were your parents:
Living together/Married
Separated/Divorced

Are you living with your parents at present?
Yes
No

What job does/did your father have?

What job does/did your mother have?

Do/did you come from a happy family background?
Yes
No
If no, please explain why.

Describe your relationship with your parents (for example reciprocal communication, understanding, support, conflict, hostility, etc.). If the relationship is/was conflictual, explain why.

Do/did you hide your hacking/phreaking activities from your parents?
Yes
No
If yes, what tactics do you (or did you) use?

Have/did your parents become aware of your hacking/phreaking activities?
Yes
No

If yes, how do/did they react to your hacking/phreaking activities?
Permissive
Repressive

With which members of your family do/did you share your interest in computer sciences and/or hacking/phreaking?

Did you start hacking/phreaking thanks to this person(s)?
Yes
No

Are/were you this person(s) mentor?
Yes
No

Perception of esteem/respect/acceptance
Do you feel esteemed/respected/accepted by
   – Your parents
   Yes
   No

   – Your friends
   Yes
   No

   – Your acquaintances (in general)
   Yes
   No

Section B—Relational Data

This information is necessary to understand how hackers relate to the outside world and, with the personal data, they give us a picture of their background. It is also useful to the study, because when we correlate it with the technical data, we can understand better motives and *modus operandi*.

Awareness of your hacking/phreaking activities
   Among the people you know, who is/was aware of your hacking/phreaking activities [teachers, employer(s), schoolmates, colleagues, friends, other members of the underground world, partner, etc.]?

Relations with the authorities
   What is your attitude toward the authorities: Do you respect them or do you challenge them and feel rebellious towards them? In this case, why?

According to you, the authorities are:
Reassuring
Oppressive

Do you feel the authorities are a guarantee or a danger for the freedom of individuals? If a danger, why?

Relations with teachers and/or employer
Please describe your relationship with your teachers (trouble-free, well-balanced, tense, conflictual, etc.). If it is/was tense, conflictual, etc., explain why.

Please describe your relationship with your employer (trouble-free, well-balanced, tense, conflictual, etc.). If it is/was tense, conflictual, etc., explain why.

Relationship with partner
Does/did your present (or former) partner feel neglected because of your hacking/phreaking activities?
Yes
No

Did you meet any of your partners (present or former) in the underground world? (BBS, IRC, etc.)?
Yes, all of them
Yes, some
No

Relationship with friends
Have you (or did you have) any friends outside of the underground world?
Yes
No

Relationship with the other members of the underground world
Have you (or did you have) friends among the members of the underground world?
Yes, many
Yes, a few
No

Do you (or did you) trust them?
    Always
    Sometimes
    Never

Do/did you boast about your computer raids?
    Always
    Sometimes (*please specify when*)
    Never

Do/did you share with them what you learned during hacking/
phreaking?
    Always
    Sometimes (*please specify when*)
    Never

Do/did you believe you have/had enemies in the underground world?
    Yes
    No

If yes, who are/were they and for what reasons?

How do/did you react to them?
    I ignored them
    By counterattacking them
    Other (*please specify*)

Section C—Technical and Criminological Data

This is the "heart" of the questionnaire and the essential "core" of the
Hacker's Profiling Project. Correlated with the data obtained from
the previous two sections, they give us a "3D" view of how hackers
behave and the different typologies of hackers.

Nickname/handle
    Have you (or did you have) more than one nickname/handle?
      Yes
      No

    If yes, why have you chosen (did you choose) more than one?

Age at approaching computer sciences

At what age did you start getting interested in computer sciences and/or computers?

At what age did you start getting involved in hacking/phreaking?

At the moment do you practice hacking/phreaking?
Yes
No

Learning modalities of hacking/phreaking techniques and level of technical skills.

How did you learn hacking/phreaking techniques?
Completely alone
Thanks to a mentor

If you had a mentor, describe how he/she taught you to hack/phreak

What level are your technical skills?
Low
Average
High
Expert

Did the increase of your technical skills bring an increase in the "severity" of the consequences of your attacks?
Yes (give reason)
No (give reason)

Hacking, phreaking

Do/did you practice:
Hacking
Phreaking
Both

Did you start with hacking and then move on to phreaking or vice-versa? Why?

Do you believe phreaking requires greater or fewer technical skills than hacking?
Greater technical skills
Lower technical skills
Equal technical skills

How do you view hacking/phreaking?
A way of life
A tool to reach certain objectives

Have you ever practiced carding?
Yes
No
If yes, what for?

Types of data networks, technologies and operation systems, and tools employed
On what kind of data network and technologies do/did you hack/phreak? For example, Internet, X.25, PSTN/ISDN, PBX, wireless, "mobile" networks (GSM/GPRS/EDGE/UMTS), VoIP.

On what kind of operation systems do/did you mainly hack? For example: MS Windows, Linux (which distribution), *BSD (state which one(s)), commercial UNIX (state which one(s): Sun Solaris, HP/UX, and so on) Firewalls, Routers, Wi-Fi APs, etc.

When you hack/hacked do/did you use:
Your own tools (homemade, unreleased exploits, etc.)
Software/tools developed by third parties
Both

Technique employed to penetrate a system and signature
What technique do/did you use to penetrate a system? Please describe it.

What do/did you do once you gain/gained access to a system?

Do/did you sign your raids on a system? In other words, do/did you leave some mark behind that distinguishes/distinguished you from other hackers?
Yes
No

If yes, what do/did you do exactly and what is/was its significance?

Why do/did you leave a signature?

When you discover/discovered new vulnerabilities on a system do/did you warn the SysAdmin?
Yes
No

Vulnerabilities discovered:
You keep/kept them to yourself
You share/shared them with other members of the underground

If you usually warn/warned the SysAdmin, you share/shared the vulnerabilities with the other members of the underground:
After informing the SysAdmin
Before informing the SysAdmin

If you share/shared with other members of the underground after warning the SysAdmin, do/did you wait for the "holes" to be patched?
Yes
No

Motives
What led you to become a hacker/phreaker?

What are/were the reasons for practicing it?

Your motives for practicing over the years are/were:
The same
Changed

Does/did hacking/phreaking make you feel powerful?
Yes
No
If yes, why?

Lone or group hacker/phreaker
Do/did you practice/practiced hacking/phreaking:
Alone
In a group
Both

Why do/did you prefer to act alone and/or in a group?

If in a group, what is/was it necessary to prove to be able to become a member?

What are/were your targets (for example: military or government systems, producer/industry, research institutes, etc.)?

Is/was there a message you or your group want/wanted to send through hacking/phreaking?
Yes
No

If yes, what?

What are/were your aims?

What do/did you do (for example: Web defacing, developing unreleased exploits for known and/or unknown vulnerabilities, etc.)?

Is/was there an internal hierarchy in the group? If yes, please explain what it is/was based upon (for example experience, technical skills, initiative, charisma, seniority, etc.).

Do/did you all have the same level of technical skills and know-how, or is/was there anyone more advanced?

In this case, is/was the more skilled member also the leader of the group?
Yes
No
Sometimes (*please specify*)

Do/did you all have different specialties (for example: hacking/phreaking; data network types, operating systems and technologies; Web defacing; development of unreleased exploits for known vulnerabilities; development of exploits for unknown vulnerabilities)? Please specify.

Are/were there any rules the group members have/had to respect?
Yes
No
If yes, which?

What measures do/did the group members take against any transgressor?

Have/did you ever met/meet with other members of the group in person?
Yes, but only with some
Yes, with all of them
No

Do/did you know their real identity, age, and place where they live/lived?
Yes, but only some
Yes, all
No

Do/did the members of your group live in your same city and/or country?
Yes, same city
Yes, same country
No

How do/did you communicate with each other (*multiple answers*)?
Plain text e-mail
Encrypted e-mail
"Open" mailing lists
Encrypted mailing lists
Plain text Chat/IRC
Encrypted Chat/IRC
IRL meetings
Other (*please specify*)

Describe your relationship with the members of your group (friendship, trust, competition, confrontational, etc.).

Meaning of the hacker ethics
Do you think a hacker ethics exists?
Yes
No
If yes, what do you mean by this term? What are the principles that compose it?

Do/did you follow it?
Yes
No
Sometimes (*please specify*)
If no, why not?

Crashed/damaged systems
Have you ever crashed and/or damaged a system?
Never
Sometimes
Often

If yes, was this:
Deliberate
Accidental
If deliberate, why did you do it?

Time spent hacking/phreaking

On average, how many hours do/did you spend hacking/phreaking?
1–3 hours
4–6 hours
7–10 hours
10–12 hours
More than 12 hours

Over the years, time spent in these activities is/was:
More
Less
Unchanged
If more or less, how much and why?

What is/was your favorite time and why?

Can/could you do without hacking/phreaking?
Yes
No
Sometimes (*please specify*)

If inactive for a lengthy period of time, have you ever felt "withdrawal symptoms"?
Yes, always
Yes, sometimes
No, never

Do/did you ever feel you were addicted to hacking/phreaking?
Yes
No

Awareness of illicitness of own activity

Are hacking and freaking considered an offense in your country?
Yes
No
If yes, when and how did you become aware of this fact?

In your view, are hacking and phreaking morally acceptable? Why?

In your view, should they also be legally acceptable? Why?

Do/did you feel you have/had damaged anyone and/or something with your activities?
Yes
No
If yes, who and/or what?

If no, why not?

Offenses committed with the use of a computer
What criminal offenses have you committed with a computer (*multiple answers*)?
Unauthorized access to systems and services
Unauthorized reproduction of copyrighted programs
Damage or modification of data or programs (*please specify*)
Computer fraud (*please specify*)
Computer forgery (*please specify*)
Other (*please specify*)

Have you ever been arrested and tried for hacking/phreaking?
Yes
No
If yes, how many times? Please indicate the sentence for each one, specifying the amount of the fine or term. If you were acquitted, explain reasons.

Have you ever been arrested and tried for other computer crimes?
Yes
No
If yes, how many times? Please indicate the type of crime(s) committed with sentence, specifying the amount of the fine or term. If you were acquitted explain reasons.

Crimes committed without the use of computers

Have you ever committed crimes unrelated to computers?

Yes

No

If yes, which ones and how many?

Have you ever been arrested and tried for them?

Yes

No

If yes, how many times? Please indicate the sentence for each one, specifying the amount of the fine or term. If you were acquitted, explain reasons.

Deterrent effect of the laws, sentences, penalties, and technical difficulties encountered during penetration of a system; causes for stopping hacking/phreaking activities

Are/were you afraid of discovery followed by arrest and sentencing for system violation?

Yes

No

No longer

If no or no longer, why (*multiple answers*)?

Precautions and technical devices adopted

Incompetence of investigators

Other (*please specify*)

Do/did laws against computer crimes have a deterrent effect on you?

Yes

No

No longer

If no or no longer, why? (*multiple answers*)

The penalties are not severe enough

It's difficult to be found out and incriminated for this kind of crime.

Other (*please specify*)

In your opinion, are most hacker/phreakers deterred by them?
Yes
No

If no, why (*multiple answers*)?
The penalties are not severe enough
It's difficult to be found out and incriminated for this kind of crime
Other (*please specify*)
Are/were you deterred by sentences inflicted on other hackers/phreakers?
Yes
No
No longer

If no or no longer, why (*multiple answers*)
Why should it happen to me?
Precautions and technical devices adopted
Because they are released immediately, or penalties are light
Other (*please specify*)

In your view, are most hackers/phreakers deterred by sentences inflicted on other hackers/phreakers?
Yes
No

If no, why (*multiple answers*)?
Excessive self-confidence
Superficiality
They think they have taken all possible precautions and technical devices
Lightness of sentences or because they are rarely imprisoned
Other (*please specify*)

Do/did technical difficulties encountered when penetrating a system act as a deterrent or as a challenge?
I felt challenged
I felt discouraged
Sometimes challenged, other times discouraged

In your view are most hackers/phreakers challenged or discouraged by this kind of difficulty?

If you no longer hack/phreak, when and why did you stop?

If you have stopped hacking/phreaking, did you continue to be involved in the subject (for example, working in computer security, etc.)?

Have you ever stopped hacking/phreaking and take it up again after a period of time?
Yes
No
If yes, why did you stop, and why did you start again?

Please add any comments you may have on this questionnaire.

Appendix B: Hacker Bios*

Throughout this volume we have often referred to hackers or groups of hackers. In the pages that follow, we have tried to collect biographical data on them.[†] Of course, we don't claim them to be exhaustive, and the more curious of you might find more information on the Net or by carefully going over the texts suggested in the bibliography. Our hope is quite simply that, after supplying the key to interpret the profiles that people this world, we can add some details, manage to draw an outline of the more distinctive characters, or at least the better-known ones, and maybe make another tool available to the readers to help them understand what we are claiming.

Captain Crunch

John T. Draper, a famous *phone phreaker* known under the nickname "Captain Crunch," "Crunch," or "Crunchman" (from Cap'n Crunch, the mascot of a brand of breakfast cereal), was born in 1944.

Thanks to a visually challenged friend called Joe Engressia (alias "Joybubbles"), Draper discovered how a toy whistle found in the Cap'n Crunch cereal boxes could be slightly modified to produce a 2600- Hz tone.

This was the same frequency used by AT&T's (American Telephone and Telegraph Companies, a U.S. phone company) international lines to indicate that a line is ready to address a new call (standard CCITT5). In this way, one end of the line could be disconnected, and the connected end would work in operator mode.

Basing himself on the way the whistle worked, Draper built some *blue boxes*—electronic devices capable of reproducing the tones used by telephone companies.

---

* The term "bio" is part of hacker slang. It comes from "biography," and is used to describe a short presentation about oneself. The plural, "bios," is also a pun on BIOS (acronym for basic input/output system), which is the first program the computer runs when it is switched on and is used to load the operating system.

† The list is in alphabetical order by nickname, with the exception of Kevin Mitnick and Kevin Lee Poulsen, who appear in the text with their names.

Draper, who was a member of the Homebrew Computer Club,* became notorious for being able to place free phone calls all over the world from a public telephone by using his discovery. One of the most frequently told anecdotes about him is the one that describes how he would place a call from a public telephone to the number of a phone next to the one he was using and hear his own voice—with long delays and echo effects—simply by redirecting the call through different *phone switches* in countries like Japan, Russia, and the United Kingdom.

The vulnerabilities Draper exploited can no longer be used today, thanks to the modernization of the telephone network (SS7 standard *out-of-band signaling*, while CCITT5 used so-called *in-band signaling*).

In the wake of this discovery, not only the "2600 groups" but also the quarterly magazine, *2600 The Hacker Quarterly*, took their names from the whistle's frequency.

Draper was accused of telephone fraud, arrested in 1972, and sentenced to 5 years' probation with social services.

Toward the mid 1970s, he passed his phone-phreaking know-how on to Steve Jobs and Steve Wozniak, the founders of Apple Computer, and he worked there for a while developing a telephone interface card for the Apple II personal computer. He was arrested again and in 1977 sentenced for wire fraud.[†] During his 4-months' detention, he served in the Lompoc, CA, federal prison and wrote EasyWriter, the first word processor for Apple II, which was later sold to IBM. At the moment, he writes *computer security software* and produces an Internet TV program called "Crunch TV."

Corrupt

Known under the nickname "Netw1z," and also by the name "John Farrington," his real name is John Lee Threat. He started hacking at age 16.

A Bed-Stuy, Brooklyn, NY, hacker, at first he belonged to a gang of common criminals, then during the 1980's he became a member of the largest hacker group in the world, the "Masters of Deception"

---

* This is a famous club of "computer hobbyists," founded in 1975 in Silicon Valley, California. Personages like Adam Osborne, Steve Jobs, and Steve Wozniak, who were destined to leave their mark on the computer world, took part in its meetings.

† For American law, any kind of fraud connected with electronic communications.

("MOD"), antagonists of the group called "Legion of Doom" ("LOD"). Incriminated by the FBI for illicit entry into an information system, Corrupt was sentenced to 6 months' detention.

Cult of the Dead Cow (cDc)

A hacker organization founded in June 1984 in Lubbock, TX, at the Slaughterhouse Farm, by "Grandmaster Ratte'" (also known as "Swamp Ratte'"), "Franken Gibe," and "Sid Vicious," three BBS *SysOps*,* The cDc group, with other two groups called "Ninja Strike Force" and "Hacktivismo," is part of a larger network known as "cDc communications." The group has its own Web site† and a blog of the same name, where it collects the thoughts and the opinions of its members. Their e-zine also has the same name, and it contributed to make the group famous on the BBS scene during the 1980s.

In order to pursue their objective of "global domination through media saturation," the cDc over the years collected the interviews they gave to the major newspapers (both printed and online versions), magazines, and newsreels.

In December 1990, cDc member "Drunkfux" started "HoHoCon," the first of five hacker conferences capable of brining together journalists and police agents.

In 1991, cDc was nominated the "Sassiest Underground Computer Group" by *Sassy* magazine.

In October 1994, the cDc Usenet newsgroup was created, the alt. fan.cult-dead-cow. In this way, they became the first hacker group to have their own Usenet newsgroup.

In February 2000, a documentary on cDc was filmed with the title "Disinformation." During the same month, "Mudge," who was also a member of the hacker group "L0pht" (today @stake, an Information Security multinational), met with then-U.S. President Bill Clinton, to discuss internet security problems.

The group became notorious for having developed one of the most famous hacker tools, the "Back Orifice Scanner," a *Trojan*

---

* "SysOp" identifies a BBS user with administrator privileges.
† http://www.cultdeadcow.com/.

horse program (backdoor) that was the first of its kind for Microsoft Windows environments.

Dispatchers (*The*)

A group dedicated to Web defacement as a defense against religious fanaticism. After the events of 9/11, its members attacked and disabled all Internet connections inside Afghanistan and Palestine and defaced the Web sites of religious organizations throughout the whole Middle East. They wanted to trace Internet use by Osama bin Laden's Al Qaeda network so as to launch attacks against the terrorist organization's communication system.

Eight-Legged Groove Machine (*The*)—*81gm*

A British hacker group set up by Pad and Gandalf. It owes its name to the debut recording of a famous British band of the 1980s and 1990s, the Wonder Stuff. The "81gm" (whose name according to some also stands for "8-Little Green Men") was one of the more notorious hacker groups between the 1980s and 1990s, boasting the highest number of violations and sensational actions with the German group "CCC" ("Chaos Computer Club"). Between 1990 and 1992, they carried out a series of scans on 22,000 addresses on the X.25 Datapack net, violating 380 information systems.

Electron

This is the nickname of Richard Jones, member of the hacker community "The Realm." Born in June 1969 in Melbourne, Australia, he was one of the members of the group arrested by the federal police on April 2, 1990. Toward the end of the 1980s and the beginning of 1990, Electron, Phoenix (whose real name is Nahshon Even-Chaim), and Nom (David John Woodcock) were convicted for illicit entry into the information systems of the Australian and American governments, the information systems of the American defense, and for the theft of an online newsletter on information security ("Zardoz"). Their intrusions provoked the reactions of the U.S., which brought pressure to bear on the Australian government, and in 1989 the first Australian federal law on computer crimes was passed.

Gandalf

A hacker from Liverpool, he can be considered one of the best hackers on the British hacker scene of the 1980s. With his friend Pad, he founded the 81gm group.

The name "Gandalf" was taken from that of a *terminal server* as well as being the name of the wizard in *The Lord of the Rings*. Gandalf became known for having violated NASA's information system.

With Pad, he pleaded guilty to two charges of computer conspiracy to obtain telecommunication services and conspiring to cause unauthorized changes to computerized material. For these crimes, he was sentenced to 3 months' detention. After serving his sentence, Pad and Gandalf started up a free information security consultancy online service, which became known under the name "81gm advisories," aimed at helping administrators to make their systems secure. Today, Pad and Gandalf work on commission as programming experts.

Genocide

Genocide, who grew up in Fairbanks, AK, in 1995 became one of the founding members of the "Genocide 2600" hacker group. Genocide was also a member of EHAP (Ethical Hackers Against Pedophilia). Today, he works as an information security expert for an important company that produces software and hardware components. In 1997, he wrote "The Hacker Manifesto,*" from which we quote:

> People generally believe that hackers have a malicious intent as a general rule. This, pardon my language is a crock of shit and obviously the idea/ ramblings of the most generally uninformed people on the Net, I do admit that "YES" there are those that are out to only destroy, and yes this group does occasionally add to that at a very small percentage (this will be explained later), but for the most part, we are in the pursuit of knowledge. I do not claim to be a 100% law abiding person, nor does the group, obviously if you have heard of us, or even after reading this you will be shaking your head at this point.

---

* You can easily find this document on the Net, for example, at http://www.genocide2600.com/history.html.

As a whole that we believe in a collective good, we believe that people who try to shut out other are people so others can't listen to them or people who try to censor our actions/language/activities are the people who deserve none of the above. We cling to our most basic civil rights. We also believe in retribution for what is lost.

Eye for an eye mentality is spoken here, take back what is yours.

Genocide 2600

A hacker group founded in 1995, originally consisting of Genocide, "WIZDom," "Alexu," "Astroboy," and "Malcolm." Today, it boasts over 100 members throughout the U.S. It is one of the many groups present on the U.S. territory, connected to the largest network, and headed by the hacker magazine *Phrack 2600*, from which it takes its name.

Hacking for Satan

American group headed by Pr0metheus and dedicated to the deface-ment of the Web sites of Christian churches and organizations. The defacement takes place by replacing their homepage with messages that hail Satanism, accompanied by an image representing a goat's face in a five-pointed star, known as "the sigil of Baphomet," and the words, "Owned by Hacking for Satan." The defaced pages also con-tain an e-mail address of the group.

For Pr0metheus, the group's leader, the defacement of Christian Web sites is not only part of a war against Christianity. The hate is directed against all organized religions, and the messages left serve also to recruit new adepts and disseminate the principles of Satanism and its symbols.

Kevin Mitnick

Kevin David Mitnick, alias "The Condor," was born in Van Nuys, CA, on August 6, 1963. He is possibly the most famous hacker and social engineer in history.

In 1980, at age 17, he got his first conviction for computer handbook theft. Other minor charges followed in 1983, 1987, and 1988. During the 1990s, he started to illegally enter the systems of progressively more important corporations, exploiting not only the vulnerabilities of the information systems but mainly using social engineering techniques.

The FBI got on his track, but Mitnick found out and started to intercept their communications. When they were about to catch up with him, he disappeared.

Mitnick was one of the first to use the IP spoofing technique, which makes one's computer untraceable. Confident in this technique, after declaring his intentions, he attacked the computer network belonging to Tsutomu Shimomura, a great computer security expert, with head-quarters at the San Diego Supercomputer Center (SDSC).

Shimomura accepted his challenge and cooperated with the FBI to hunt down the Condor. On February 14, 1995, Mitnick was arrested following a manhunt that had lasted 168 days.

Convicted, he was released in January 2002 with an injunction against using the Internet until January 21, 2003. At the moment, he is the CEO of Kevin Mitnick Consulting LLC, a consultancy company in the computer security sector.

Kevin Lee Poulsen

He was born in Pasadena, CA, in 1965. His hacking career lasted throughout the whole of the 1980s, and he became famous as a cracker and phreaker with the nickname "Dark Dante." By day, he worked for SRI International, while at night he kept on hacking. During that time, he reactivated disconnected telephone numbers, which were then used by an acquaintance of his to run a virtual escort agency. His most notorious hack is still the one that led him to win a series of Porche 944 S2s by taking control of all the telephone lines of the Los Angeles KIIS-FM radio station, so as to guarantee he would be the 102nd listener (i.e., the winner) to get his call answered and win the prizes.

He was arrested in April 1991 and in June 1994. Poulsen pleaded guilty to seven crimes, among them computer fraud, unauthorized access to computer systems, money laundering, and obstruction of justice. He was sentenced to 51 months' detention, and to pay $56,000 in damages. At the time, this was one of the stiffest sentences ever passed for hacking.

In 1997, Jonathan Littman wrote a book on Poulsen's computer adventures, entitled *The Watchman: The Twisted Life and Crimes of Serial Hacker Kevin Poulsen.*

Once released from federal prison, Poulsen abandoned entirely his criminal career and in 2000 started working as a journalist, initially writing articles on security and hacking for SecurityFocus.com, a California-based company (recently acquired by Symantec Corporation) that was active in the computer security sector. Later, in 2005, he turned free-lance. In June 2005, he became senior editor for *Wired News*, which publishes his blog "27BStroke6.*" Today he is married to a lawyer.

L0pht Heavy Industries

L0pht (pronounced *loft*) Heavy Industries was a famous hacker group based in Boston, MA, which operated from 1992 to 2000. It was founded in 1992 as a base from which its members could work on various projects and later became a company. It became known for giving various warnings on security holes in different systems and for creating many widely used types of software, the most famous of which is L0phtCrack, a password cracker for Windows NT.

In 1998, its members declared in front of the U.S. Congress that they had the know-how and the tools necessary to collapse the whole Internet network in 30 minutes.

In January 2000, L0pht Heavy Industries merged with @stake and became, to all intents and purposes, a computer security company. On October 9, 2004, @stake was bought by Symantec Corporation.

From the founding members, "Count Zero," "White Knight," "Brian Oblivion," and "Golgo 13," the group evolved, and today its members are Brian Oblivion, "Kingpin," Mudge, "Dildog," "Weld Pond," "Space Rogue," "Silicosis," and "John Tan." Mudge and Dildog, like Count Zero and White Knight, are also members of Cult of the Dead Cow.

LOD (Legion of Doom)

In 1984, the "Legion of Doom" ("LOD") group and BBS were founded, named after a superhero comic book. Founded by Lex Luthor when he

---

* http://blog.wired.com/27bstroke6/.

was 18, it arose from the ashes of the group "The Knight of Shadow" to later absorb the "Tribunal of Knowledge" group.

Inspired by LOD, groups like "Farmers of Doom" and "Justice League of America" later arose. LOD, in rivalry with MOD, was dedicated to help computer intrusion fans.

Its merging with the "Legion of Hackers" group gave birth to "Legion of Doom/Hackers," or "LOD/H." When "Compu-Phreak" and "Phucked Agent 04" left the group, the "/H" disappeared from the name.

The most active for number of intrusions were "Lex Luthor," "Blue Archer," "Gary Seven," "Kerrang Khan," "Master of Impact," "Silver Spy," "The Marauder," and "The Videosmith."

Mafiaboy

"Mafiaboy" was the nickname of a 15-year-old student from West Island, a neighborhood of Montreal, Canada. In 2000, he launched a DoS attack against various sites and Web portals and managed to bring to their knees giants of the Internet boom like Yahoo!, Amazon, eBay, and CNN.

The FBI and the Royal Canadian Mounted Police (RCMP) started getting interested in him when he claimed on IRC chat-rooms that he was responsible for these attacks. He became the prime suspect when he claimed to have put Dell's Web site out of service, an attack that hadn't been made public yet. To carry out those attacks, Mafiaboy used cracking tools supplied by other hackers. For this reason, it became clear to the FBI and the RCMP that they weren't dealing with a hacker with high technical skills, but rather with an unsophisticated script-kiddie.

He was charged, and at first Mafiaboy denied his responsibility, actually trying to justify himself by saying he had carried out tests to help the development of less vulnerable firewalls. Mafiaboy changed his defense on the first day of his trial (January 2001), pleaded guilty to 55 charges, and was sentenced to 8 months' detention in a juvenile detention center.

These attacks caused damages estimated at about US\$1.7 billion.

At the moment, he is working as an Internet security expert journalist for Montreal's *Le Journal*, the main French-language newspaper in the city.

Mentor (The)

Lloyd Blankenship (alias "The Mentor") is a well-known American hacker. In the 1980s, he was a member of LOD, but his celebrity is due to his authorship of "The Conscience of a Hacker," also known as "The Hacker Manifesto," which he wrote following his arrest. It was published on *Phrack* e-zine (1986). Lloyd read out and commended The Hacker Manifesto during the H2K2 hacker meeting in Las Vegas (2002).*

MOD (Masters of Deception)

A group based in New York, it was founded by "Acid Phreak" with "Scorpion" and "Hac." The name is a way of jeering at LOD, their rival group, and it reflects the ideology of its members who get what they want through lies and deception. The techniques they use are alternating nicknames, social engineering, and Trojan programs. MOD controlled the main RBOC's (telephone and call switching exchanges) of the American telephone system and X.25 networks, plus a large part of the Internet of the time.

Under investigation since 1990, following their part in the Great Hacker War,† five of its members were charged by a federal court in 1992. In 1993, all five pleaded guilty and were sentenced to detention and released on parole. Today, many of the former members work in the computer sector, mainly in security.

Among the members were: Mark Abene, alias "Phiber Optik"; Paul Stira, alias "Scorpion"; Eli Ladopoulos, alias "Acid Phreak"; John Lee, alias "Corrupt" (or "Netw1z"); and Julio Fernandez, alias "Outlaw." Other members whose real names are unknown were "Supernigger," Hac, "Wing," "Tumult," "Nynex Phreak," "Crazy Eddie," "The Plague," "ZOD," "Seeker," and "Red Knight" (who was also a member of Cult of the Dead Cow).

Otto Sync

On December 2, 1992, the 25-year-old "Otto Sync," obviously not his real name, was arrested and charged with unauthorized use of the Datapak computer network. The intrusions took place in November

---

* See also Chapter 3 and Appendix D.
† Around 1990, the "Great Hacker War" saw the rival groups MOD and LOD trying to violate each other's computer systems.

1992 at the expense of Televerket, at the time a Swedish state monopoly telephone company. The person who traced the hacker and ordered the arrest was Pege "White Knight" Gustafsson, at the time a keen 38-year-old security expert who wanted to have a brilliant career.

Today, Otto Sync is a well-known and highly regarded computer consultant, specialized in security issues in the field of telecommunications. He lives in Asia, and his real identity has never been revealed.

Pad

A hacker from Manchester, he can be considered one of the best hackers on the British scene in the 1980s. His name comes from X.25 PAD (packet assembler-disassembler). With his friend Gandalf, he founded the 81gm group, and with Gandalf he pleaded guilty to two conspiracies to commit computer crimes: conspiracy to obtain telecommunication services and conspiracy for causing unauthorized changes to computerized material. Pad also pleaded guilty to damages of £250,000 to a computer that belonged to the Central London Polytechnic.

Both were sentenced and released after 3 months in jail. Like Gandalf, today Pad is a highly esteemed programmer.

Par or Parmaster

His handle is a contraction of "Master of Parameters," which is what his friends called him because of his skill with parameters used to view correctly data delegated to PAD X.28.

His story is quite special and has romantic overtones, so it deserves a few lines more. Par was an American teenager who, during his adolescence, started to "penetrate" the telco systems with the MOD group, even though he never really belonged to the group. At age 17 (in early 1989), he violated the systems of Australian Citibank and managed to download a list of credit cards and make a total of US$500,000 worth of "authorized" purchases. On January 14, 1989, the first article* on the "Hacker case" appeared, a few months before the great operation *Crackdown* in the U.S.A.

> An elite group of Australian hackers has lifted more than $US500,000 ($580,000) out of America's Citibank in one of the more daring hacking

---

* Signed by Helen Meredith, copyright of News Ltd. Australia.

crimes in Australia's history. Australian federal authorities were reported late yesterday to be working with American authorities to pin down the Australian connection involving hackers in Melbourne and Sydney. These are the elite "freekers" of white collar crime...

As the article states, at the beginning the Melbourne and Sidney hackers were blamed, in other words the core team of "The Realm" BBS, founded by Electron. In reality, Par and Electron were the main ones responsible for this violation.

At the time, Electron was romantically involved with "Theorem," a 23-year-old European woman (a Swiss national) who had frequented Altos (a hacker chat on X.25 based in Hamburg, Germany) since 1986, and through which she had become a close friend of hackers like Pengo, Gandalf, and most of the elite European hacker scene of the times, when women online were a rarity.

In 1988, Par entered Altos, met Theorem, and fell in love with her. Suelette Dreyfus* explains in detail how this influenced the relations between the two, but at all events it did not stop their joint violation of Citibank in 1989.

The fact remains that Par and Theorem started having a relationship notwithstanding the geographic distance separating them.

She flew out to the U.S.A. and spent some time with Par. The months went by, and the FBI and the Australian secret service discovered the computer fraud. Par became a fugitive and hid with various hacker friends in the U.S.A., until he destroyed his whole hacker archive out of fear of being arrested, as he didn't want to have any evidence against him available. The archive consisted of 10MB of data, more than 4,000 credit cards, and 130,000 different electronic transactions—his trophy, destroyed, burned, was lost forever. He did this perhaps to save his life, and undoubtedly to save his future.

On December 23, 1991, Par pleaded guilty to two counts at the Monterey, CA Juvenile Court. He admitted everything: "Yes, I am The Parmaster. Yes, I violated computers. Yes, I stole thousands of credit cards, passwords, accounts. I am guilty as charged."

In the background of this sorry, commonplace story of hacking and arrest, there is a silver lining: Theorem did/didn't not leave Par, she

---

* Dreyfus S., *Underground: Tales of Hacking, Madness and Obsession on the Electronic Frontier*, Chapter 3, *The American Connection*, cit.

give up, nor did she run away. She sent him US$20,000 for his legal expenses and flew out to California twice in 1992 to be at the side of the man she loved.

Phiber Optik

Alias Mark Abilene, born in 1972, he started getting interested in computers when he was 10 or 11 years old. Around the end of the 1980s, he became a member of the LOD, and in 1989–1990, following a disagreement with one of the members of LOD, "Erik Bloodaxe," he moved to the rival group MOD.

Phiber's entry in MOD marked the beginning of the *Great Hacker War*, characterized by many years of rivalry between MOD and LOD.

On January 24, 1990, following the national collapse of the AT&T telephone system, the Secret Service searched Mark's home and seized all his electronic equipment. Phiber Optik and two other members of MOD, Acid Phreak and Scorpion, were interrogated, because they were suspected of having caused AT&T's collapse. However, at the end of the day, no formal charges were brought against them, and AT&T itself denied that the hackers had ever had anything to do with the incident, stating that it was all caused by an error in their software. For the first time, in February 1991, Phiber was arrested and charged, in accordance with the New York State consolidated laws, with first degree violation and tampering with an electronic system (*computer trespass and computer tampering in the first degree*).* He was also charged with a misdemeanor for *theft of*

---

* According to Section 156.10 of article 156 (offenses involving computers) title JA156 of the New York State consolidated laws, a person is guilty of computer trespass when he knowingly uses or causes to be used a computer or computer service without authorization and: 1. he/she does so with an intent to commit or attempt to commit or further the commission of any felony; or 2. he/she thereby knowingly gains access to computer material. Section 156.27 of the same article considers it first degree tampering of a computer when the person commits the crime of computer tampering in the fourth degree and he/she intentionally alters in any manner or destroys computer data or a computer program so as to cause damages in an aggregate amount exceeding $50,000. We must point out that, in accordance with section 156.20, a person is guilty of computer tampering in the fourth degree when he/she uses or causes to be used a computer or computer service and having no right to do so he/she intentionally alters in any manner or destroys computer data or a computer program of another person.

*Service** for a telephone call made free of charge from a 900 number (telephone number charged at a higher rate).

He pleaded not guilty on the first two charges and guilty of the misdemeanor. He was sentenced to 35 hours of community service.

In December 1991, with four other members of MOD, he was arrested again, and on July 8, 1995, all five were charged by the Manhattan federal grand jury on 11 counts. At first, Mark pleaded not guilty: later, he decided to plead guilty of two crimes: conspiracy, and unlawful access to a computer in the federal interest.

The first charge (conspiracy) was based on the fact that Phiber was held responsible for having received the login data to an information system and having given to another member information on how to call telephone numbers on a certain kind of phone-switching computer. All five of the accused were charged with damaging a system belonging to the Educational Broadcasting Company, where they had left the following message: "Happy Thanksgiving you turkeys from all of us at MOD."

The second charge (unlawful access to computers) was based on the fact that MOD was held responsible for having entered federal computers and in doing this had destroyed data. The charge was also based on the unlawful access to the Southwestern Bell systems causing damages of around US$370,000.

Phiber got the harsher sentence, 12 months detention, 3 months on parole with social services, and 600 hours of community service.

This sentence was quickly followed by another, a 1-year detention for conspiracy and unlawful access to telephone and information systems. He served his sentence at the Schuylkill, PA federal prison and was released in November 1994.

He later became system administrator at Radical Media Inc. and then was hired by Steve Lutz for Ernst & Young LLP as a computer security expert consultant, where he set up a special *tiger team*. After years as a consultant, he set up his own computer security company,

---

* Crime committed by whoever secures the performance of a service by deception or threat or any other illicit means, with the intent to avoid payment to the supplier of those services. This crime also covers unauthorized access to a computer or network or the use of computer software without paying for it, or the use of these instruments without respecting contractual restrictions.

Crossbar Security, with LOD former member Bill From RNOC (known also as Dave Buchwald) and Andrew Brown. The company went bankrupt in 2001.

Today, Mark works as an independent SysAdmin consultant and computer security expert.

Phoenix

Nahshon Even-Chiam is a hacker from Melbourne, Australia, who was a member of the group called "The Realm." He was arrested by the federal police on April 2, 1990, with Electron and "Nom" (David John Woodcock), who were also members of the group. They were charged with unlawful access to government and American defense information systems and, toward the end of the 1980s and the beginning of 1990, with theft of an online newsletter on information security ("Zardoz"). Their intrusions provoked the reaction of the U.S., which started to bring pressure to bear on the Australian government, leading to the passing of the first federal law on computer crimes in 1989.

RaFa

Rafael Nuñez, a Venezuelan former hacker member of the group "World of Hell," became famous for establishing a record of 679 simultaneous Web defacements (July 2001). "RaFa" was arrested on April 2, 2005, by U.S., immigration agents for having defaced, in June 2001, a Web site managed by the Defense Information Systems Agency (DISA) for the United States Air Force (USAF).

Today, he works as a computer security expert and is deputy director of the Counter Pedophilia Investigative Unit (CPIU), an independent organization that gives support to investigators in pedo-pornography crimes.

Rockstar

A hacker from Sidney, Australia, and a UNIX expert, he is recognized as the creator of *login-sniffer*, a program capable of recording the first 128 characters of all connections, including usernames and passwords used at login. In this way, it records the access credentials of anyone connecting to or disconnecting from the system.

Scorpion

His name is Paul Stira, and he was one of the founding members of the MOD (Masters of Deception) group. An expert in programming and in cracking the anti-copy protection codes for computer games, in 1992 he was sentenced to 6 months' parole and community service. In 1990, with Phiber Optik and Acid Phreak, he was involved in the investigation on the collapse of AT&T's telephone network. However, he wasn't charged.

Starla Pureheart

Alias "Anna Moore," from Norman, OK, she belongs to one of the many "2600" hacker clubs. At age 15, she won the *Ethical Hacking Contest* organized during the 2001 edition of the Las Vega hacker meeting DefCon. She was the first female hacker to win the competition. She is an icon for all women interested in hacking and the IT world.

Trax

Trax was the father of Australian phreaking and is particularly known for having managed to carry out untraceable calls by inventing *Multi-Frequency Code Phreaking*. He also wrote three handbooks on the subject: the *Trax Toolbox* (a sort of guide to phreaking), *The Australian Phreaker's Manual, Volumes 1–7* (wherein he explained how to make untraceable free telephone calls without the cost being debited to anyone), and *The Advanced Phreaker's Manual 2*.

World of Hell (WoH)

Hacker group founded by "Cowhead2000," which numbered RaFa and "FonE-TonE" among its members. Dedicated to Web defacement, it concentrated its massive attacks on the Web pages of private companies, American and foreign government agencies, and various military organizations. For WoH, violating Web sites was a trademark. The Web sites targeted by these attacks number in the thousands.

The objective, though, was never that of destroying information or contents but only to prove that the Web servers were not secure. This was the openly proclaimed philosophy of the group, which became known for an action that simultaneously defaced many Web sites (around 120 Mexican and Russian sites) during the course of 2001.

Appendix C: The Nine Hacker Categories

Throughout this book, we have tried to show how often there is only a very thin line between one category of hacker and another. Technical skills, relationships, background, and motives are only a few of the variables involved in a "hacker profile."

At the same time, we have also referred repeatedly to nine categories of hackers, the ones we feel we can confirm on the basis of the data available to the HPP WG.

Today, these different types of hackers people the Net and the underground, and for us they are a reference point for our future investigation. For this reason, we think it only fair to produce a table to outline their basic traits.

Table C.1 Description, Hacking Preferences (Alone/Group), Targets, and Motivations

CATEGORY	DESCRIPTION	ACTS ALONE/ IN GROUP	TARGET	MOTIVATIONS
Wannabe lamer	9–8 years old "I wanna be a hacker but I can't 'hack' it"	Group	Final users	It's the "in" thing to do
Script-kiddie	10–18 years old The script kid	Group	PMI with known vulnerabilities	To vent anger and grab media attention
Cracker	17–35 years old The destroyer	Alone	Private companies	To prove their power and get media attention
Ethical hacker	15–50 years old The Hacker "par excellence"	Alone (rarely in a group, for fun or research)	Large corporations and complex systems, wherever there is a challenge or a vulnerability worth investigating	Out of curiosity, to learn, for unselfish reasons, to improve working skills

(*continued*)

Table C.1   (*continued*)

CATEGORY	DESCRIPTION	ACTS ALONE/ IN GROUP	TARGET	MOTIVATIONS
Quiet, paranoid, skilled hacker	16–50 years old Highly specialized hacker, uncommunicative, extremely paranoid	Alone	Nonspecific	Out of curiosity, to learn, but also out of pure selfishness
Cyber warrior	18–50 years old The mercenary	Alone	Companies and "emblematic" bodies, final users	For financial gain
Industrial spy	22–50 years old The industrial spy	Alone	Business companies, corporations, multinationals	For financial gain
Government agent	25–45 years old The government agent (CIA, Mossad, FBI, etc.)	Alone or in a group	Governments, suspected terrorists, strategic industries, individuals	Professionally (espionage/ counter-espionage, vulnerability test, activity monitoring)
Military hacker	25–45 years old Recruited to fight "with a computer"	Alone or in a group	Governments, strategic industries	Professionally and for a cause (controlling and damaging systems)

Table C.2   Respect for the Hacker Ethics, Damage Caused, and Awareness of Illegality of Actions

CATEGORY	RESPECT FOR *HACKER ETHICS*	DAMAGING OR CRASHING VIOLATED SYSTEMS	AWARENESS OF ILLEGALITY OF OWN ACTIONS
Wannabe lamer	No, they aren't familiar with the principles of the *hacker ethics*	Yes, both deliberately or inadvertently (lack of experience, of technical skills)	Yes, but they think they won't get caught
Script-kiddies	No, they make up their own ethics	No, but (sometimes) they modify/delete data	Yes, but they find justifications for their actions
Cracker	No, there is no *hacker ethics*	Yes, always deliberately	Yes, but blame their actions on the distributors of unsafe software or systems

(*continued*)

Table C.2   (*continued*)

CATEGORY	RESPECT FOR *HACKER ETHICS*	DAMAGING OR CRASHING VIOLATED SYSTEMS	AWARENESS OF ILLEGALITY OF OWN ACTIONS
Ethical hacker	Yes, they uphold it	No, it can happen only by accident	Yes, but they consider their activities morally acceptable
Quiet, paranoid, skilled hacker	No, they have their own personal ethics, often very close to the *hacker ethics*	No	Yes, they feel guilty about problems caused to SysAdmin and other victims
Cyber warrior	No	Yes; furthermore, they modify/delete/steal data and sell them	Yes, but they have no scruples about it
Industrial spy	No, but they follow some sort of "unwritten rules"	No, they steal and sell information	Yes, but they have no scruples about it
Government agent	No, they betray the *hacker ethics*	Yes (including deleting/editing/ stealing the data) / no (during "stealth" attacks)	N/A
Military hacker	No, they betray the *hacker ethics*	Yes, (including deleting/editing/ stealing the data) / no (during "stealth" attacks)	N/A

Table C.3   Deterrent Effect of Laws, Sentences, and Technical Difficulties

CATEGORY	LAWS	SENTENCES PASSED ON OTHER HACKERS	OWN CONVICTIONS	TECHNICAL DIFFICULTIES
Wannabe lamer	None	None	Practically none	High
Script-kiddie	None	None	High: they stop at the first conviction	High
Cracker	None	None	None	Moderate
Ethical hacker	None	None	High: they stop at the first conviction	None
Quiet, paranoid, skilled hacker	None	None	None	None
Cyber warrior	None	None	None	None; it's their profession
Industrial spy	None	None	None	None; it's their profession
Government agent	N/A	N/A	N/A	N/A
Military hacker	N/A	N/A	N/A	N/A

Appendix D: The Hacker Manifesto (Conscience of a Hacker)

I'm sure many of you would love to get inside a hacker's head. For this reason, we thought we'd put in this appendix a brief unabridged statement by The Mentor, dated 1986.

Short, yes, but still one of the main building blocks of the hacker spirit and movement of the 1980s and 1990s, so much so that the original title, "Conscience of a Hacker," later became "The Hacker Manifesto."

The Mentor wrote this text following his arrest. His crime? He had penetrated the computer of a public library. We have quoted from this document at the beginning of each chapter, etc., of this book, but we also decided to put the whole text down here so the reader can understand and appreciate these words, written over 20 years ago and yet still relevant today.

> Another one got caught today, it's all over the papers. "Teenager Arrested in Computer Crime Scandal," "Hacker Arrested after Bank Tampering..."
>
> Damn kids. They're all alike.
>
> But did you, in your three-piece psychology and 1950s technobrain, ever take a look behind the eyes of the hacker? Did you ever wonder what made him tick, what forces shaped him, what may have molded him?
>
> I am a hacker, enter my world...
>
> Mine is a world that begins with school... I'm smarter than most of the other kids, this crap they teach us bores me...
>
> Damn underachiever. They're all alike.
>
> I'm in junior high or high school. I've listened to teachers explain for the 15th time how to reduce a fraction. I understand it. "No, Ms. Smith, I didn't show my work. I did it in my head..."
>
> Damn kid. Probably copied it. They're all alike.
>
> I made a discovery today. I found a computer. Wait a second, this is cool. It does what I want it to. If it makes a mistake, it's because I screwed it up. Not because it doesn't like me... or feels threatened by me... or thinks I'm a smart-ass... or doesn't like teaching and shouldn't be here...

Damn kid. All he does is play games. They're all alike.

And then it happened... a door opened to a world... rushing through the phone line like heroin through an addict's veins, an electronic pulse is sent out, a refuge from the day-to-day incompetencies is sought... a board is found.

"This is it... this is where I belong..." I know everyone here... even if I've never met them, never talked to them, may never hear from them again... I know you all...

Damn kid. Tying up the phone line again. They're all alike...

You bet your ass we're all alike.... we've been spoon-fed baby food at school when we hungered for steak... the bits of meat that you did let slip through were prechewed and tasteless. We've been dominated by sadists, or ignored by the apathetic.

The few that had something to teach found us willing pupils, but those few are like drops of water in the desert.

This is our world now... the world of the electron and the switch, the beauty of the baud. We make use of a service already existing without paying for what could be dirt-cheap if it wasn't run by profiteering gluttons, and you callus criminals. We explore... and you call us criminals. We seek after knowledge... and you call us criminals. We exist without skin color, without nationality, without religious bias... and you call us criminals. You build atomic bombs, you wage wars, you murder, cheat, and lie to us and try to make us believe it's for our own good, yet we're the criminals.

Yes, I am a criminal. My crime is that of curiosity. My crime is that of judging people by what they say and think, not what they look like. My crime is that of outsmarting you, something that you will never forgive me for.

I am a hacker, and this is my manifesto.

You may stop this individual, but you can't stop us all... after all, we're all alike.

The Mentor, 08/01/1986

Bibliography and Online References

Hacking and Hackers

Books

Amanda Chandler, *The Changing Definition and Image of Hackers in Popular Discourse*, in *International Journal of the Sociology of Law*, Academic Press, 1996.

Nicolas Chantler, *Profile of a Computer Hacker*, Infowar, Florida 1997.

Raoul Chiesa, *La Storia di Otto Sync e White Knight*, Apogeo, Milano, 2003, http://www.apogeonline.com/libri/88-503-1079-X/ebook/libro.

Raoul Chiesa, *Vola Condor, Vola*, Apogeo, Milano, 1999, http://www.apogeon line.com/libri/88-503-1056-0/ebook/libro.

Dorothy E. Denning, *Information Warfare and Security*, Addison-Wesley, 1998.

Suelette Dreyfus, *Underground: Tales of Hacking, Madness and Obsession on the Electronic Frontier*, Random House, Australia, 1997.

Roy D. Dutta, *Individual Characteristics for the Success in Computer Programming*, in *Journal of Personality and Clinical Studies*, 19, 1, 2003.

Gennaro Francione, *Hacker. I Robin Hood del Cyberspazio*, Lupetti—Editori di Comunicazione, Milano, 2004.

Katie Hafner and John Markoff, *Cyberpunks: Outlaws and Hackers on the Computer Frontier*, Simon & Schuster, 1995.

Tim Jordan and Paul Taylor, *A Sociology of Hackers*, The Editorial Board of The Sociological Review, 1998, http://www.dvara.net/HK/1244356.pdf.

Steven Levy, *Hackers: Heroes of the Computer Revolution*, Shake Edizioni, 2002.

Jonathan Littman, *The Fugitive Game: Online with Kevin Mitnick*, Little, Brown & Company, United Kingdom, 1997.

Jonathan Littman, *The Watchman: The Twisted Life and Crimes of Serial Hacker Kevin Poulsen*, Little, Brown & Company, United Kingdom, February 1997.

Johnny Long, Tim Mullen, Ryan Russell, *Stealing the Network—How to Own a Shadow*, Syngress Publishing, Rockland, MA, 2007.

Johnny Long, Tim Mullen, Ryan Russell, *Stealing the Network—How to Own an Identity*, Syngress Publishing, Rockland, MA, 2005.

Johnny Long, Tim Mullen, Ryan Russell, *Stealing the Network—How to Own a Continent*, Syngress Publishing, Rockland, MA, 2004.

Johnny Long, Tim Mullen, Ryan Russell, *Stealing the Network—How to Own the Box*, Syngress Publishing, Rockland, MA, 2003.

Charles C. Mann, David H. Freedman, *@ Large: the Strange Case of the World's Biggest Internet Invasion*, Simon & Schuster, New York, 1997.

John Markoff, Tsutomu Shimomura, *Takedown: The Pursuit and Capture of Kevin Mitnick*, Martin Secker & Warburg Limited, 1996.

Kevin D. Mitnick and William L. Simon, *The Art of Intrusion*, Wiley Publishing, Inc., Indianapolis, IN, 2005.

Kevin D. Mitnick, William L. Simon, *The Art of Deception*, Wiley Publishing, Inc., Indianapolis, IN, 2002.

Marc Rogers, *Modern-Day Robin Hood or Moral Disengagement. Understanding the Justification for Criminal Computer Activity*, 1999, http://www.infowar.com.

Marc Rogers, *The Psychology of Hackers: The Need for a New Taxonomy*, 1999, http://www.infowar.com.

Michelle Slatalla, Joshua Quittner, *Masters of Deception: The Gang that Ruled Cyberspace*, HarperCollins, New York, 1995.

Bruce Sterling, *The Hacker Crackdown. Law and Disorder on the Electronic Frontier*, Penguin Books Ltd., New York, 1994.

Clifford Stoll, *The Cuckoo's Egg—Tracking a Spy Through the Maze of Computer Espionage*, Doubleday, New York, 1989.

Paul Taylor, *Hackers—Cyberpunks or Microserfs?*, in *Information, Communication and Society*, Taylor & Francis, Boca Raton, FL, 1999.

Paul Taylor, *Hackers: A Case-Study of the Social Shaping of Computing*, doctoral thesis, University of Edinburgh, 1993.

Dan Verton, *The Hacker Diaries: Confessions of Teenage Hackers*, McGraw-Hill, Osborne Media, 2002.

Alexander E. Voiskounsky, Olga V. Smyslova, *Flow-Based Model of Computer Hackers' Motivation*, in *Cyber-Psychology & Behavior*, 6, 2003.

Sam Williams, *Free as in Freedom*, O'Reilly Media, Inc., California, March 1, 2002.

H. J. Woo, *The Hacker Mentality: Exploring the Relationship Between Psychological Variables and Hacking Activities*, doctoral thesis, University of Georgia, 2003.

Michal Zalewski, *Silence on the Wire*, No Starch Press, California, April 15, 2005.

Articl es

Fabio Brivio, "Hacker's Profiling Project: Intervista a Raoul Chiesa e Stefania Ducci," September 2006, http://www.apogeonline.com/webzine/2006/09/07/19/2006090719789.

Raoul Chiesa, "Così Attaccano gli Ingegneri Sociali," in *Internet News*, Edizioni Tecniche, Nuove, April 2003.

Raoul Chiesa, *Social Engineering Arte Sconosciuta*, in *Internet News*, Edizioni Tecniche Nuove, March, 2003.

Raoul Chiesa, "Le 10 Regole dell'Hacking," in *Internos*, August 1999.

Raoul Chiesa, "Who is Who: Hackers, chi sono?," in *Internos*, June 1999.

Raoul Chiesa, "Io ero Nobody e Tutte le Notti me ne Volavo in Francia, via Qatar," in *Hacker Culture*, 2001, http://www.dvara.net/HK/nobo-dy.asp.

Carlotta Managnini, *Grande Muraglia Hacker*. "Un Esercito di Cyber-Pirati che Infestano la Rete in Cerca di Segreti Industriali. È il Volto Nascosto del Boom Cinese," in *L'Espresso*, 10 November 2005.

Steven Mizrach, "Is there a Hacker Ethics for 90s Hackers?," http://www.fiu.edu/~mizrachs/hackethic.html.

Debasis Mohanty, "Demystifying Google Hacks," November 2005, http://www.securitydocs.com/library/3098.

Fredi Ricchioni, Raoul Chiesa, "Hacking e Criminalità," in *ICT*, 2002, No. 2, http://www.apogeonline.com/webzine/2002/05/24/01/200205240101.

Reports

Yvette Agostini, Raoul Chiesa, *Storia ed Etica Hacker*, 2nd Ethical Hackers' Speech @ SMAU2002, Milano, 26 ottobre 2002, Blackhats Italia, http://www.clusit.it/smau_milano_2002/itbh_storia_ed_etica_hacker.pdf.

Avantgarde, *Time to Live on the Network*, Avantgarde, San Francisco, 2004, http://www.avantgarde.com/.

CORECOM (Comitato Regionale per le Comunicazioni), *Pirata Sarai Tu! Atti del Convegno*. Primo Convegno Nazionale sulla Pirateria, Torino, 31 marzo 2004, http://www.obiettivominori.it/be/public/view/Pirata%20sari%20tu.pdf.

Kfir Damari, Ami Chayun, Gadi Evron, *Case-study: a Cyber-terrorism Attack. Analysis and Response*, beSIRT, 12 July 2006, http://www.beyondsecurity.com/.

EURISPES, *Rapporto Eurispes 2006—Seconda Parte, Scheda 27—In Questo Mondo di Ladri: Hacker, Cracker e Truffe Telematiche*, EURISPES, 2006, http://download.repubblica.it/pdf/2006/secondaparte_sintesi_RI2006.pdf.

Andrea Ghirardini, *Social Engineering, Una Guida Introduttiva*, ITBH Italian Black Hats Association, 2002, http://www.blackhats.it/it/papers/social_engineering.pdf.

Eric S. Raymond, *How to Become a Hacker*, 2001, http://www.catb.org/~esr/faqs/hacker-howto.html.

Marcus K. Rogers, *Basic Computer Forensics: The Mind of the Computer Criminal, Week 13 Lecture Notes*, Purdue University, 2006.

Symantec, *Client-Side Exploits: Forensic Analysis of a Compromised Laptop*, Incident Analysis, 17 June 2004, http://www.batori.com.br/downloads/040617-Analysis-FinancialInstitutionCompromise.pdf.

Web Application Security Consortium, *Threat Classification*, Version: 1.00, Web Application Security Consortium, 2004, http://www.we-bappsec.org.

Stefano Zanero for the Italian Blackhats Association, *Ethical Hacking, Unethical Laws*, SMAU, Milan, 28 October 2002, http://www.clusit.it/smau_milano_2002/itbh_ethica_hacking_unethical_laws.pdf.

Zone-H, *2005 Web Server Intrusion Statistics*, Zone-H, 2006, http://www.zone-h.org/files/60/2005stats.pdf.

Zone-H, *2004 Web Server Intrusion Statistics*, Zone-H, 2005, http://www.securitymanagement.com/library/ZoneHorg0705.pdf.

Web Sites

Associazione Italiana Blackhats, http://www.blackhats.it.

CLUSIB (Club de la Sécurité Informatique Belge—Belgium), https://www.belcliv.be/clusib/.

CLUSIF (Club de la Sécurité de l'Information Français—France), https://www.clusif.asso.fr/index.asp.

CLUSIS (Association Suisse de la Sécurité des Systèmes d'Information—Switzerland), http://www.clusis.ch.

CLUSIT (Associazione Italiana per la Sicurezza Informatica—Italy), http://www.clusit.it./.

CLUSSIL (Club de la Sécurité des Systèmes d'Information—Luxemburg), http://www.clussil.lu/tiki-view_articles.php.

ISECOM (Institute for Security and Open Methodologies), http://www.isecom.org./.

Jargon File, http://www.catb.org/jargon/.

Mitre, http://www.mitre.org/.

Security Focus, http://www.securityfocus.com/.

Criminology and Criminal Profiling

Books

Albert Bandura, "Mechanism of Moral Disengagement in Terrorism," in *The Psycology of Terrorism: Behaviors, World Views, States of Mind*, Cambridge University Press, New York, 1990.

Renato Borruso, Giovanni Buonomo, Giuseppe Corasanti, Gianfranco D'Aietti, *Profili penali dell'informatica*, Giuffrè, Milano, 1994.

Elisa Bortolani. *Esperti e Utenti a Confronto: Significati Psico-Sociali e Aspetti Organizzativi Dell'Interazione Uomo-Tecnologia*, Ph.D., 2005.

Paoul J. Brantingham, Patricia L. Brantingham, *Patterns in Crime*, MacMillan, New York, 1984.

David Canter, *Criminal Shadows*, HarperCollins, London, 1994.

Silvio Ciappi, *Serial Killer. Metodi di Identificazione E Procedure Giudiziarie*, Franco Angeli, Milano, 1998.

Mihaly Csikszentmihalyi, *Beyond Boredom and Anxiety*, Jossey-Bass, San Francisco, 1975.

John E. Douglas, Ann W. Burgess, Allen G. Burgess, Robert Ressler, *Crime Classification Manual*, Jossey-Bass, San Francisco, 1997.

John E. Douglas, Mark Olshaker, *Journey into Darkness*, Simon & Schuster, New York, 1997.

John E. Douglas, Mark Olshaker, *Mindhunter*, Plenum, New York, 1995.

Ugo Fornari, *Trattato di psichiatria forense*, UTET, Torino, 1997.

Guglielmo Gulotta, *Elementi di psicologia giuridica e di diritto psicologico: civile, penale, minorile*, Giuffrè, Milano, 2000.

Pekka Himanem, *The Hacker Ethic*, Random House, 2001.

Pierpaolo Martucci, *La criminalità economica*, Laterza, Roma-Bari, 2006.

Massimo Picozzi, Angelo Zappalà, *Criminal Profiling. Dall'Analisi della Scena del Delitto al Profilo Psicologico del Criminale*, McGraw-Hill, Milano, 2002.

Gianluigi Ponti, *Compendio di Criminologia*, IV edizione, Raffaello Cortina Editore, Milano, 1999.

Ernesto U. Savona, *Crime and Technology. New Frontiers for Regulation, Law Enforcement and Research*, Springer, Dordrecht, The Netherlands, 2004.

Klaus Tiedemann, "Criminalità da Computer" in Franco Ferracuti (a cura di) *Trattato di criminologia, medicina criminologica e psichiatria forense*, volume X, Giuffrè Editore, 1990.

Klaus Tiedemann, "Il Cambiamento delle Forme di Criminalità e Devianza," in Franco Ferracuti (a cura di) *Trattato di criminologia, medicina criminologica e psichiatria forense*, volume X, Giuffrè Editore, 1990.

Brent E. Turvey, *Criminal Profiling*, Academic Press, San Diego, CA, 1999.

Brent E. Turvey, *Criminal Profiling: An Introduction to Behavioral Evidence analysis*, Academic Press, San Diego, CA, 1997.

Articles

Craig Bennell, Natalie J. Jones, Paul J. Taylor, Brent Snook, "Validities and Abilities in Criminal Profiling: A Critique of the Studies Conducted by Richard Kocsis and His Colleagues," in *International Journal of Offender Therapy and Comparative Criminology*, vol. 50, no. 3, Sage Publications, June 2006.

Richard N. Kocsis, "Validities and Abilities in Criminal Profiling. The Dilemma for David Canter's Investigative Psychology," in *International Journal of Offender Therapy and Comparative Criminology*, vol. 50, no. 4, Sage Publications, August 2006.

Richard N. Kocsis, Jenny Middledorp, Andrew C. Try, "Cognitive Processes in Criminal Profiling Construction: a Preliminary Study," in *International Journal of Offender Therapy and Comparative Criminology*, 49(6), Sage Publications, 2005.

Cesare Lombroso, "Sui Recenti Processi Bancari di Roma e Parigi," Archivio di Psichiatria, Scienze Penali ed Antropologia Criminale, XIV, 1893.

Mara Mignone, "I "Cybercriminali": Rischi e Limiti dei Profili Criminologici," in *Ciberspazio e Diritto*, vol. I, no. II, Mucchi editore, Modena, 2000, http://www.ciberspazioediritto.org/articoli/mignone.pdf.

Enzo Scannella, "Banca Osama. Le Finanze del Terrore," in *Rivista di Intelligence*, 2/2006, CESINT, 2006, pp. 62–71.

Brent E. Turvey, "Deductive Criminal Profiling: Comparing Applied Methodologies Between Inductive and Deductive Criminal Profiling Techniques," *Knowledge Solutions Library*, January 1998.

United Nations, "United Nations Manual on the Prevention and Control of Computer-Related Crime," in *International Review of Criminal Policy*, no. 43 and 44, 1990, http://www.uncjin.org/Documents/EighthCongress.html.

Reports

Roderic G. Broadhurst, *International Cooperation in Cybercrime Research*, in *Proceedings 11th UN Congress on Crime Prevention and Criminal Justice, Workshop 6: "Measures to Combat Computer Related Crime,"* Bangkok, 18–25 April 2005, http://eprints.qut.edu.au/archive/00004448/.

Scott Charney, *Combating Cybercrime: A Public-Private Strategy in the Digital Environment*, 31 March 2005, http://www.nwacc.org/programs/conf05/UNCrimeCongressPaper.doc.

CLUSIF, *An Overview of Cybercrime*, 2004, 2005, http://www.clusif.asso.fr/.

Council of Europe, *Octopus Programme, Organised Crime in Europe: The Threat of Cybercrime. Situation Report 2004*, Council of Europe Publishing, Strasbourg, March 2005.

Guy De Vel, *International cooperation to Prevent and Combat Cybercrime*, in *Proceedings 11th UN Congress on Crime Prevention and Criminal Justice, Workshop 6: "Measures to Combat Computer Related Crime,"* Bangkok, 18–25 April 2005, http://www.kicjp.re.kr/.

Ehab Maher Elsonbaty, *Cyber Crime, New Suit or Different Cut? Harmonization is the Way!*, in *Proceedings 11th UN Congress on Crime Prevention and Criminal Justice, Workshop 6: "Measures to Combat Computer Related Crime,"* Bangkok, 18–25 April 2005, http://www.kicjp.re.kr/.

EURIM-IPPR, *Partnership Policing for the Information Society—Fifth Discussion Paper: The Reporting of Cybercrime*, 2004, http://www.eurim.org.uk/activities/ecrime/reporting.doc.

EURIM-IPPR, *Partnership Policing for the Information Society—Fourth discussion paper: Reducing Opportunities for E-crime*, 2004, http://www.eurim.org.uk/activities/ecrime/reducingops.doc.

Peter Grabosky, *Recent Trends in Cybercrime*, in *Proceedings 11th UN Congress on Crime Prevention and Criminal Justice, Workshop 6: "Measures to Combat Computer Related Crime,"* Bangkok, 18–25 April, 2005, http://www.kicjp.re.kr/.

D.K. Matai, *Cyberland Security: Organised Crime, Terrorism and the Internet*, Oxford Internet Institute, University of Oxford, mi2g, 10 February 2005.

Ernesto U. Savona, Mara Mignone, *The Impact of Technology on Crime*, International Conference on Crime and Technology: New Frontiers for Legislation, Law Enforcement and Research, Courmayeur Monte Bianco, Italy, 28–30 November 2003.

United Nations, *Workshop 6: Measures to Combat Computer Related Crime. Background Paper*, in *11th United Nations Congress on Crime Prevention and Criminal Justice*, Bangkok, 18–25 April 2005, A/CONF.203/14, United Nations, New York, 14 March 2005, http://www.unodc.org/unodc/en/commissions/crime-congresses-11-documents.html.

United States—White House, *The National Strategy to Secure Cyberspace*, February 2003, http://www.whitehouse.gov/pcipb/.

Web Sites

Academy of Behavioral Profiling, http://www.profiling.org/.
Centre for Investigative Psychology, http://www.i-psy.com/.
Criminal Profiling, http://www.criminalprofiling.com/.
Criminal Profiling Research Site (CH), http://www.criminalprofiling.ch./.
LARC—Laboratorio di Analisi e Ricerca sul Crimine—Università Carlo Cattaneo LIUC, http://www.i-psy.net/.

Index